PARADISE
ROAD

PARADISE ROAD

Jack Kerouac's Lost Highway and My Search for America

JAY ATKINSON

John Wiley & Sons, Inc.

Published by John Wiley & Sons, Inc., Hoboken, New Jersey
Published simultaneously in Canada

For general information about our other products and services, please contact our Customer Care Department within the United States at (800) 762-2974, outside the United States at (317) 572-3993 or fax (317) 572-4002.

Wiley also publishes its books in a variety of electronic formats. Some content that appears in print may not be available in electronic books. For more information about Wiley products, visit our web site at www.wiley.com.

Library of Congress Cataloging-in-Publication Data:

Atkinson, Jay, date.
    Paradise road : Jack Kerouac's lost highway and my search for America / Jay Atkinson.
        p.   cm.
    Includes index.
    "A fascinating journey recreating Jack Kerouac's travels in contemporary America."
    ISBN 978-0-470-23769-4 (cloth); ISBN 978-0-470-59427-8 (ebk);
    ISBN 978-0-470-59428-5 (ebk); ISBN 978-0-470-59429-2 (ebk)
        1. Kerouac, Jack, 1922–1969—Criticism and interpretation.   2. Kerouac, Jack, 1922–1969. On the road.   3. Beat generation—Literary collections.   4. Beat generation—Biography.   I. Title.
    PS3521.E735Z558 2010
    813'.54—dc22   2009037621

Printed in the United States of America
10 9 8 7 6 5 4 3 2 1

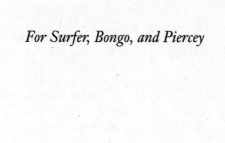
For Surfer, Bongo, and Piercey

When you've understood this scripture, throw it away. If you can't understand this scripture, throw it away. I insist on your freedom.

—Jack Kerouac, *The Scripture of the Golden Eternity*

CONTENTS

PREFACE

"The Big, Rushing Tremendousness"

In the spring of 1947, a young unknown writer rode the 7th Avenue subway to the end of the line at 242nd Street and then took a trolley to Yonkers, New York, stuck out his thumb, and began hitchhiking. His trip, and the novel that grew out of it, would change the course of American literature. For that athletic, dark-haired young man rushing off the platform at Yonkers was Jack Kerouac, and his wanderings over the next three years, from New York to Chicago to Denver and back again, in freight trains, travel bureau cars, and buses; San Francisco to Fresno; North Carolina to New Orleans; through Colorado, across the arid plains of Texas, and down to Mexico City, would be immortalized in his 1957 masterpiece, *On the Road*.

By traditional standards, the Kerouac of those early years was a failure. A Columbia University dropout and washed-up football star, discharged from World War II military service for having an "indifferent character," the Lowell, Massachusetts, native was, at age twenty-five, living with his widowed mother, Gabrielle, in a tiny apartment in Ozone Park, New York. But Kerouac, nicknamed "Memory Babe" by his old school chums for his prodigious recall, was determined to become a published writer, sleeping all day, waking after dark to take long walks through Brooklyn and Queens, and churning out what he hoped would be the Great American Novel. His first book, which grew into more than a thousand pages of raw manuscript and owed a great debt to Thomas Wolfe, would be published in 1950 as *The Town and the City*. It could be said, however, that Kerouac's tale of a war-torn New England family was in black and white, and soon he would be writing in color.

Later on, he would name his new method "spontaneous prose," an intoxicating mix of sharp, clear observations and descriptions, made-up words, popular and obscure references, poetic insights, and spiritual longing, all strung together with long dashes, ampersands, and ellipses. Of his stylistic breakthrough, Kerouac wrote in his journal, "Here, I think, is one of the secrets that will lead to the miraculous novel of the future, and when I'm finished with T & C in all its aspects, I'm going to discover a way of preserving the big rushing tremendousness in me and in all poets." At age thirty-five, ten years after he set out from Yonkers with his old sea bag, Jack Kerouac would become famous (he called it "fame mouse")—a condition he was particularly unsuited for—and his "miraculous novel,"*On the Road*, would be recognized as the hallmark of his contribution to American letters.

Of course, Kerouac didn't know any of this back then. Fascinated by letters written by a young, Denver-based car thief named Neal Cassady—called Dean Moriarty in *On the Road*—Kerouac longed to see the West. The fog of war had lifted, and like many other young Americans, at least those who had rejected the suburbs, a steady job, and a two-car garage, Kerouac was seeking "girls, visions, everything." Many of the future Beats appear in *On the Road*—Allen Ginsberg, Herbert Huncke, William Burroughs—but none so dramatically and explosively as Cassady, the "Adonis of Denver," Kerouac's chauffeur, comic foil, and amorous rival, popping up at irregular intervals to shock the young writer—here called Sal Paradise—from his solitary pursuits.

It's believed that Kerouac first used the written word "beat" as an adjective in his 1948 journal, referring to Huncke. But he never embraced the definition of beat or the "Beat Generation," such as it was, as "defeated" or 'beaten," preferring the Catholic notion of "beatific vision," or the immediate knowledge of God that the angels enjoy in heaven. It's also important to note that the Beat writers and wannabes were no more a literary or social movement than a group of anarchists could be called a political party. In fact, as early as 1958 the literary critic John Sisk called the Beats "an ephemeral oddity," claiming that they and their unruly works would soon fade from the public memory. Obviously, that has not been the case. In recent years, Kerouac's image has been used to sell name-brand khakis and running shoes, and his book sales have risen steadily. Still, in the minds of many hoary-handed academics, Kerouac and his iconoclastic friends, particularly Cassady, remain the louts of American Lit.

A legendary con artist and ladies' man, Cassady, so they say, had literally been born on the road, in a moving car outside of Salt Lake City, and grew up in the sporadic company of his father, Neal Sr., a onetime tinsmith turned wino and bum. They spent most of their time in Denver, with young Neal hustling pool on Larimer Street and appearing in court on behalf of his ne'er-do-well dad when Neal Sr. was picked up for vagrancy and other two-bit crimes. Left mostly to his own devices, Neal was sent to reform school at age sixteen for stealing a car, then drifted in and out of various institutions over the next few years. By the age of twenty-one, when he made the acquaintance of Kerouac, Cassady was an impressive figure: lean, bony-faced, and muscular, with wavy brown hair and blue eyes. Possessed of native-born intelligence and a keen sense of other peoples' vulnerability, Cassady expended most of his energy in pursuit of "kicks," most notably girls, jazz music, and lengthy, Benzedrine-fueled conversations aimed at teasing out the meaning of life.

In Cassady, the so-called Holy Goof, Kerouac found a charismatic replacement for his brother, Gerard, who died when he was only nine years old and Jack was four. Shy by nature and uncomfortable speaking English—the Kerouacs spoke mostly French at home—Jack was emboldened by the power and presence of Neal Cassady, somehow licensed to engage in wild flights of his own. Certainly, there would be no *On the Road* without this gasoline-fueled muse, driving them across country like the Angel of Terror himself and exhorting Sal/Jack to "eschew geometry and geometrical systems of thinking," whatever that meant.

Kerouac made most of his cross-country jaunts on a shoestring. His mother gave him some money, and occasionally he'd buy a train or bus ticket with his GI education bill checks. He picked cotton for a spell in Selma, California, and he and his old friend from prep school Henry Cru, called Remi Boncoeur in the novel, had a short but hilarious stint as armed security guards in Marin City, California. Believing that apple pie and ice cream were highly nutritious, Kerouac often subsisted on this confection when he was traveling and took occasional respites in small town parks, doing headstands to relieve his phlebitis, a painful and debilitating circulatory disease. He met a legion of interesting folks on the road, farmers and hill-billies and salesmen, ordinary Americans possessed of quirks and tics that never escaped Kerouac's eye or his ear. Montana Slim and Mississippi Gene and Denver D. Doll and Big Ed Dunkel have therefore taken their rightful place in the pantheon of unforgettable literary characters. Sal Paradise himself is one of the most unlikely heroes in all of literature, and his eccentric and existential journey forms an American Odyssey of the twentieth century.

Critics have mentioned that *On the Road* has no beginning, middle, and end. Certainly, there is a plotless and improvisational aspect to Kerouac's narrative, just as there was an unscripted and plotless aspect to his road-going experience. For that reason alone, the enduring popularity of *On the Road*, which continues to sell a hundred thou-sand copies a year in English, reveals the boldness and originality of Kerouac's artistic vision. He believed in a simple "me-to-you and you-to-me" brand of storytelling and not the "grammatically inhib-ited and unenlightened debris" favored by the literati. However, during Kerouac's short life, the stuffy New York suits were never able to grasp the ineffable, indescribable "IT" of his testimony. Attempts by celebrated editors like Malcolm Cowley of Viking Press and Grove Press's Don Allen to neuter his prose style "were a typically American business idea," Kerouac once wrote, "like removing the vitamins out of rice to make it white (popular)." Due to the tastes and standards of the day, Kerouac would look on with frustration as his original drafts were cut down and sanitized, and the kinetic pro-gression of encapsulated *nows* he was trying to recreate on the page were broken up into more digestible pieces.

It has never been easy to separate the riot of Jack Kerouac's life from the tumult of his art. For instance, the king of road books usually lacked a driver's license and often hated to travel. Nicknamed "Ti Jean" as a child, Kerouac revered family life, yet avoided paying child support for his daughter, Jan (by Joan Haverty, the second of his three wives). Like the comedian Groucho Marx, who insisted he would never join a club that would have him as a member, Kerouac swore off the Beat movement, declaring in a 1958 letter to the poet Gary Snyder, "No wonder Hemingway went to Cuba and [James] Joyce to France." He also noted throughout his voluminous correspondence with a number of old friends that he was going to build a log cabin in the woods and pursue the solitary existence of a "Zen lunatic saint," yet he lived mostly with his mother. And the granddaddy of free-swinging prose stylists admitted in a letter to his editor Don Allen that even "Hemingway has nothing over me when it comes to persnickitiness about craft."

First among the Kerouac myths is that he never revised his stories. But the writer in his prime—a long, prolific stretch of twenty years, from 1941 to 1961—was an indefatigable worker and reworker of great chunks of material. It's a misunderstanding of Kerouac's writing process and his status as a literary craftsman to believe that everything he did was spontaneous—that he simply "blew" like an inspired jazz musician. After his first novel, *The Town and the City*, was published, Kerouac may have abandoned traditional line editing, but his letters and journals illustrate that he never resorted to single draft composition.

Even the most famous version of the *On the Road* manuscript, a 120-foot scroll that Kerouac typed in just three weeks in the spring of 1951, contains numerous written corrections, crossed-out lines, and inserted passages. Assembled by Scotch-taping eight irregular-size pieces of tracing paper together, this particular draft came out of Kerouac in a caffeine-induced fury. He created what amounts to a dense, single-spaced paragraph forty yards long, complete with the real names and detailed exploits of his friends and acquaintances. Now frayed, yellowed, and nearly translucent, it looks like something dug out of a cave by a team of drunken archaeologists. The conclusion of the scroll is ripped and ragged; it is believed that a friend of Kerouac's named Lucien Carr owned a cocker spaniel that bit off the end of the manuscript. Purchased for $2.4 million by Indianapolis Colts owner Jim Irsay Jr., the raggedy manuscript was published in 2007 as *On the Road: The Original Scroll* and has been rightly celebrated as Kerouac's unexpurgated and righteous vision for the book.

Jack Kerouac died in St. Petersburg, Florida, in 1969, his dark good looks and athlete's physique ravaged by alcohol. He was forty-seven years old. What happened to the young, eager, productive scribbler, who, fueled by old radio serials, pulp fiction, and his own early adventures, claimed to have written a million words before age twenty-one? Dig it, man, whither has he gone, in that shiny car in the night?

I believe the answer is out there. On the road.

• • •

My grandfather, the critic Brooks Atkinson, once wrote, "Ever since I was a boy, I have been indebted to librarians." I'm just kidding; the estimable Mr. Atkinson was no relation. My paternal grandfather, Wray, a baker from Methuen, Massachusetts, was too busy making pies to study literature. Therefore, what I know about books I gained merely by reading them and from feeling a certain way when I read certain passages. No less an authority than the Roman poet Horace said in 14 BC that narrative art should "blend in one the delightful and the useful"; in other words, it must entertain before it can educate. And there are particular stories that kept me riveted to the page, firing my determination to become a writer. If you believe, as I do, that writing is a kind of geology, and that stories are acquired through the pipeline of your subconscious like oil—created by the accumulated detritus of your reading and pressed under the weight of years—then you believe that the quality and depth of that reading will determine the "grade" of your work. Throughout my experience, I've searched for high-octane stories—tales of vigor, with a steep and vivid narrative line. In the sort of yarn that appeals to me, you can feel the ground shake from momentous events, hear the call of bugles, and smell fires burning. This kind of writing prompts a physical response—knuckles get white, hearts palpitate—that doesn't typically occur as a result of most "serious" literature these days. For my money, if a story doesn't take place in a real landscape populated by flesh-and-blood characters, it isn't worth reading.

Despite growing up less than ten miles from Jack Kerouac, I never heard of him until I went away to Acadia University in Wolfville, Nova Scotia. One day on Main Street a classmate named Keith Bowden, whom we called Bongo, gave me a dog-eared copy of *On the Road*, and as I looked it over, he let out an abrupt giggle and walked away. I called after him, asking what sort of novel it was, and Bongo laughed again and said I'd find out soon enough. Since it was published, Kerouac's masterpiece has been a watershed for restless young Americans, and that's exactly what we were.

On the Road was one of those rare books that I didn't want to end, yet I zoomed through like it was a comic book. Sometime after dark I heard the wail of a freight train charging along the Bay of Fundy and had the most acute sensation of homesickness I'd ever felt. Later that night, when I finished reading, I listened to Bruce Springsteen's "Thunder Road" and Kerouac's blue-collar voice was reinforced: hip, iconoclastic, with a brashness that contained notes of joy underscored by a lament. Because for all its exuberance, *On the Road* was a sad story and Kerouac a guy like me, a watcher, born in Lowell, two towns over from mine: "And in his excited way of speaking I heard again the voices of old companions and brothers under the bridge, among the motorcycles, along the wash-lined neighborhood and drowsy doorsteps of afternoon."

This book went beyond something I wished I'd written—a common enough occurrence—but was a story that I *knew*, for each page came spooling out like a precious red thread unwound from the interstices of my heart. Just as Kerouac had done, I'd traded my small town in Massachusetts for someplace else, held great philosophical debates in moving automobiles, and stood on lonely roadways with my thumb out and four dollars in my pocket. Kerouac's subject, of course, is more than just bop parties and boxcars, or drinking wine and chasing women. Like a Brueghel painting, *On the Road* teems with life, celebrating our moments on earth even as it mourns them. As Sal Paradise says, "The only people for me are the mad ones."

A few weeks later, I hitchhiked home for Christmas, and one night Bongo turned up with another friend named Geoff Pitcher, and the three of us drove over to Lowell. At Edson Cemetery, I parked my dad's station wagon beside an oak tree, and we scrambled onto the roof, grabbed the lowest branches, and swung ourselves over the fence. After a short hike, we arrived at Kerouac's grave, a small granite tablet sunk into the ground and dusted with snow.

"Ti Jean"
John L. Kerouac
Mar. 12, 1922 — Oct. 21, 1969
—He Honored Life—

Bongo and Pitch and I stood around in our old varsity jackets sipping cans of beer, not saying very much. The ground over Kerouac's tomb was littered with whiskey bottles, poems, dead flowers, and unjacketed copies of his books. (Bongo said that caretakers would gather up this tribute every few days and then return to the grave and find all new stuff.) In the darkness of the cemetery I realized that Kerouac's triumph was the intimacy he shared with millions of readers. Once asked by Steve Allen on the *Tonight Show* to define his work, Ti Jean merely shrugged and replied, "Sympathetic." Kerouac never felt superior to his audience and therefore never tried to put anything over on them—he believed in simply telling his story and letting it stand on the merits.

After I read Kerouac's novel and became enamored of its "innumerable riotous angelic particulars," I said to hell with law school and tax shelters and prudent real estate investments. I had no *time* for any of that, and a preoccupation with time and how to best make use of it runs straight through *On the Road*. Oddly enough, Kerouac has been accused of squandering his life on drugs and booze and loose women. In many ways he was the prototypical slacker, dressed in khakis and a flannel shirt, his arm dangling from the window of a Hudson. But Jack Kerouac cared little for the conventions of society, and dared to write in his own voice. All told, I see his signature work as a precious American deposit that deepens the well of my experience, fuels my own writing, and reminds me what it means to be alive.

It's been thirty years since I walked out of that darkened cemetery with Bongo and Pitch. Since then, I've reread *On the Road* several times, pontificated on it in front of audiences, and written about it for magazines; I've also absorbed many other literary influences besides Kerouac and published four books of my own. But *On the Road* has persisted in my imagination across that span of years, and lately I've come to realize that I've thought about Kerouac's saintly vision of America long enough. It's time to go experience it for myself.

PROLOGUE

Ghosts of the Pawtucketville Night

Night descends on the crumbling storefronts and tenements of downtown Lowell, falling in the spaces between buildings and shedding gloom over the rooftops. Beside the whirring traffic, my volunteer tour guide Roger Brunelle stands on the corner, holding a laminated file card with a passage from one of Jack Kerouac's books typed on it. In a loud voice, Brunelle reads, "The other night I had a dream that I was sitting on the sidewalk on Moody Street, Pawtucketville, Lowell, Mass., with a pencil and paper in my hand saying to myself 'Describe the wrinkly tar of this sidewalk.'. . ."

With his wispy gray hair and neatly trimmed beard, Roger Brunelle looks like a courtier in a Rembrandt painting. Coming toward us are a pair of glowering young men in large, puffy black coats, black do-rags, and black baseball caps pulled down low, but the seventy-two-year-old Brunelle is undaunted, holding his ground as the youths approach. "Some authors write about the River Seine," says Brunelle, gesturing operatically at the surrounding neighborhood, a grim collection of dingy businesses and triple-deckers. "But *Jack*, Jack wrote about Lowell, in glowing terms."

One of the youths smiles with his gold tooth at Brunelle, and they dismount the sidewalk and cross over to the other side of the

1

street. "I used to dig and dig at this stuff, sweating over the books with a pencil, underlining everything," says Brunelle, holding the tiny rectangle up to the streetlight. "But now, you know, I got it all on cards."

Brunelle has given this nocturnal walking tour, which he calls "Ghosts of the Pawtucketville Night" after the opening section of Kerouac's *Dr. Sax*, intermittently for more than twenty years, most nights, including this one, leading pilgrims around Kerouac's old haunts for the sheer fun of it. Although celebrated for *On the Road*, Kerouac published five books set here in his native Lowell, a small, postindustrial city twenty-five miles north of Boston on the Merrimack River. Taken together with his entire body of work, these "true-story novels" form a single epic known as "the Duluoz Legend," chronicling Kerouac's physical, emotional, and spiritual journey across the American landscape.

Brunelle is a high school Latin teacher, not a trained literary scholar, but he knows what he's talking about. He grew up in this once French Canadian section of Lowell and still resides on Campaw Street, where he lived as a boy. Brunelle attended the St. Louis de France grammar school a few blocks away, same as Kerouac, and spoke the same patois at home, fielding questions in French from his parents and replying to them in English. "Kerouac never moved out, really," says Brunelle. "He was hooked on the umbilical cord. Kerouac's heart was always here, in Lowell."

It's growing cold as the sun disappears for good behind the wall of tenements. Brunelle is dressed in a shiny black leather coat, a gray-green herringbone scarf, and khaki pants; he limps slightly on an arthritic knee but hops about and shakes his fist with enthusiasm as we move along. The atmosphere is thin, and every sound—cornering automobiles, the knock of our boots against the pavement—is sharpened and amplified, full of portent. "Kerouac delineated *everything* for Lowell, just like James Joyce did for Dublin," says Brunelle, waving his arms. "The guy's on fire, and he's putting it down on paper."

A couple of blocks east, we ascend a narrow paved road, and Brunelle mentions that two of Kerouac's childhood friends are still around and living in Lowell. Not long ago, he ran into one of the old gents, who gave Brunelle a ride in his battered Chevrolet and instructed him to open the glove compartment. Inside was a pocket first edition of *On the Road* in mint condition, inscribed to the author's boyhood chum and autographed.

"Did you read it?" Brunelle asked, turning the book over in his hands.

"No," the fellow said. "I just bought it, and put it 'dere."

When I ask Brunelle why so many old Lowell types have never read Kerouac's books, his laughter rings out against the house fronts. "They aren't readers, most of them," he says. "They just bought Jack's book because they loved him."

At the apex of Phoebe Avenue, we halt in front of No. 17, a small white cottage illuminated by a glass globe affixed to the porch. Kerouac lived here when he was ten years old. Above is the high, cold winter sky, dark blue now, punctured with holes we call stars and gleaming with the heavenly fire beyond. Referring to *On the Road*, Brunelle says, "I don't read it before I go to bed anymore. It's like—*wooo*. Dynamite. I like to read it in the morning so I can forget about it."

Earlier, we visited Kerouac and Brunelle's old stomping ground, Ecole de St. Louis, a four-story brick building on Boisvert Street. Despite all the French street names, and the St. Jeanne D'Arc church and Peter J. Dechene fire house, Kerouac's schoolboy neighborhood is a polyglot mishmash of Lebanese, Dominicans, Puerto Ricans, East Africans, and Haitians. Kids on bicycles were calling to one another in Creole, and from over the housetops a church bell tolled the noon hour.

After walking past the little house on Beaulieu Street where Jack's brother Gerard had died, Brunelle and I went around the block, the low winter sun slanting between the buildings and throwing shafts of gold on the sidewalk. It's Saturday, and the school is closed. Resting his back against the locked door of Ecole de St. Louis, Roger mopped his brow with a handkerchief and said, "In the morning, everything here was in French. In the afternoon, it was English." Brunelle also noted that the diverse student body still receives an hour of instruction in French each day, taught by the school's principal. "St. Louis hasn't changed—"

Just then, someone inside the school opened the door, and Brunelle nearly tumbled into the lobby. "St. Louis hasn't changed in a hundred years," said a nun who was standing there. The school's principal, Sister Irene Martineau, sixty-nine, is a short, bespectacled woman with gray hair, dressed in a neat gray skirt, gray jacket, and white blouse, with a crucifix dangling around her neck.

We were welcomed into the empty school for a tour. Sister Irene, who belongs to an order of French Canadian nuns with headquarters in Quebec, Canada, has been an educator for fifty years, the last twenty-eight as principal of Ecole de St. Louis. She was born in Salem, Mass. "I tell the children I was one of the witches who escaped, and they believe me," she said with a small, prim smile. When Sister Irene was a young woman, the nun's habit included a thick rubberized cowl that hid everything but the oval of her face. She told us that the order eventually got rid of the headpiece because it was so hot and uncomfortable and caused the nuns' hair to fall out.

"It was a cross we had to bear for Christ," she said, with a wistful expression. "I miss it."

Outside a third-grade classroom is a framed passage from Kerouac that reads, in part, "Parochial schools gave me a good early education. They made it possible for me to begin writing stories and even one novel at the age of eleven. These schools, in Lowell, Mass. were called St. Louis de France and St. Joseph. . . ."

Brunelle recalled that when he was at St. Louis, the nuns employed a small wooden device called a *claquet*, which produced a sharp clicking sound when squeezed between thumb and forefinger. "One click meant to stand, two meant 'sit,' and three 'kneel,'" he said, as Sister Irene nodded her approval. We entered the classroom, which was redolent of chalk dust and oil soap. Its tiny wooden desks were lined up in rows, and a construction paper frieze ran around the upper edge of the room, explaining the vowels and their sounds.

Going slowly, Brunelle walked up one row and down the other and then stopped, gazing out the window at an azure sky. "When we heard three clicks, we knew we had to turn around"—he squeezed into one of the desks, grunting over his arthritic knees as he held out his arms in supplication—"kneel like this, and pray."

• • •

Back on Phoebe Avenue, Brunelle and I scurry along the pavement, blowing on our hands and swinging our arms. It's been a long day of walking and reflecting, and we agree that we must pause to lubricate our senses. Around the corner at 123 University Avenue is the Social Club de Pawtucketville, the oldest French club in the city, founded in 1897. It's a low brick building sandwiched between an insurance agent and the Chung Hair & Nail Salon. Inside the tiny glass foyer is a security door that requires a pass card; the Pawtucketville Social Club is a private organization. A sign on the wall announces that dues are $30 a year, and "Smokers are welcome."

Brunelle raps on the interior door. Through a small, wire grille portal we can see nearly a dozen patrons ranged along the bar, drinking long-neck bottles of beer and watching the evening news on a television in the corner. Kerouac's father, Leo, once managed the club, and the young Jack worked as a pinsetter in the bowling alley in the cellar.

The drinkers are ignoring us. Brunelle knocks more insistently this time, and, without turning around, a very large man in a navy windbreaker yells out, "Try turning the knob," and the other patrons laugh.

The door isn't even locked. We enter the dense, smoky interior of the club, and Brunelle goes over to the man in the windbreaker. He's wide through the shoulders and balding, so large that flesh hangs over the barstool on either side like bags of suet. Above the man's head is a little orange sign that reads: "No fucking profanity will be fucking tolerated." There's a jukebox on the opposite wall playing an old Bob Seger tune and I'm reminded of Kerouac's adage that men love good bars, and good bars should be loved.

It turns out that the big man knows Roger's uncle, and we're invited in for a drink. The room is long and dark, with the only light coming from over the cash register, which is decorated with a placard that says, "Mind Your Own Business." Beers are $2 a bottle, and we take ours to a little round table in the shadows beyond the bar.

Brunelle has talked us into every place we've been, and I soon discover the source of his affability. "My grandfather was a stand-up comedian," he says. "He'd get up at places like this and tell stories in French, about the priest sleeping with the cook and things like that." The Pawtucketville Social Club is the perfect place to drink beer, eat peanuts, and talk about Kerouac because "Jack wasn't a snob," Brunelle says. "He was part of the working class. Look at the pictures of him. Always wearing boots and a lumberjack shirt and carrying a book."

In fact, not long after *On the Road* was published, Kerouac was asked to participate in a Brandeis University forum titled "Is There a Beat Generation?" In a subsequent letter to Berkeley librarian John Montgomery, Kerouac described his argument with the other panelists: "I tangled with James Wechsler and wore his hat and went off stage and played the piano in the back and insulted photographers and generally acted like a mad drunken fool just off a freight train, which is precisely the way I am and precisely what I think of universities. I even pushed the Dean aside to yell shit over the mike."

It's therefore no small irony that nearly four decades after Kerouac's death, academics are showering his books with the sort of canonical praise denied in his short lifetime. But the Lowell native's view of his own writing was that of "swimming in seas of English with no discipline other than the story line."

The local university has capitalized on Kerouac's popularity in recent years, offering courses in Beat literature, a biannual academic conference on Kerouac's work and its deeper meanings, and other events. (The University of Massachusetts Lowell, as it's called, recently awarded Kerouac, a 1939 Lowell High graduate and Columbia University dropout, an honorary doctor of letters degree.) Here in Lowell and across the country, there's a burgeoning cottage industry in all things Kerouac. "Ten, fifteen years ago, nobody wanted anything to do with him, now he's the king," I say. "It's kinda scary."

"It is, but I'm not afraid of it," says Brunelle.

Inside the smoke-filled club, Brunelle reminds me that the French didn't want to discuss their great poet Rimbaud for fifty years after he died. "It's just starting here in the U.S. for Kerouac," Roger says. "It's all disjointed, this spontaneous prose. There's no subject-verb-object. Some teachers still won't touch him."

The big man in the windbreaker has overheard us. "Kerouac left, and I took over," he says, to the laughter of his drinking companions. But there's tolerance for Kerouac here, maybe even a tinge of affection among the roofers and Sheetrockers and Vietnam vets collected along the bar. Kerouac never considered himself anything more than one of them and by portraying his own life in his work became "vox populi," the voice of the people.

Tattooed on Roger Brunelle's right forearm are the letters "SPQR"—*Senatus Populusque Romanus*—the Senate and the People of Rome. "The *idea* of Kerouac," says Brunelle, "is that anyone can become a writer, because everyone has a story to tell. The ones who are remembered are the ones who did it best."

As we pay up our $4.93 tab, the man in the windbreaker says, "See you in a couple years," and I reply, "See you in a couple days. I love it here."

Outside the club, Roger turns up the collar of his leather jacket as we head for his car. "I'd like to go across the river now, to a holy place, the holiest place in Lowell," he says.

Traffic is nonexistent as we cross the span of the old Moody Street Bridge, the corrugated road singing beneath the tires. The river is black and sinuous in the dim light of the stars, curling over the semi-submerged rocks and breaking into three distinct streams to avoid the pilings of the bridge. The river is omnipresent in Kerouac's work, as it was in his life, gushing from his heart onto the page in *The Town and the City*, *Dr. Sax*, *Visions of Gerard*, *Maggie Cassidy*, *Vanity of Duluoz*, and even *On the Road*. "What is Kerouac if not the Merrimack?" Roger asks.

Our final destination this evening is Notre Dame de Lourdes Grotto, a spectral place where the mysterious caped figure of Dr. Sax was said to reside. Situated behind the Franco-American School on Pawtucketville Street, which functioned as an orphanage in Kerouac's youth, the grotto is wreathed in shadows and deserted at this hour. It consists of the Fourteen Stations of the Cross depicting Christ's Passion, each set on a concrete pillar, boxed in Plexiglas, and lighted from above in eerie pastels. At the conclusion of the sloped drive is a great shrine of poured concrete, fifty feet high, covered in dormant ivy and topped with an outsize crucifix.

When Kerouac was a boy, he visited the grotto with his mother and his aunts; in his later writings, he referred to Lowell as a "vast collection of Christians."

"When we were little, we were afraid of this place," says Brunelle, wrapping his scarf about his neck. "No kid wants to end up in an orphanage." He halts in front of the first Plexiglas box, where the two-foot ceramic Jesus is bathed in a weird greenish-blue light. Of course, the inscription is in French: *Jésus Est Condamné à Mort*.

Beyond the row of statues, on the other side of an empty parking lot, is the Archambault Funeral Home, where Kerouac's wake was held in 1969. Brunelle reads from one of his file cards, something that Kerouac had written about the grotto and "the undertaker in his house of death," noting that Kerouac's mother had his body brought here from Florida, in part, because Archambault was the premier French Canadian funeral director in Lowell.

"I see the great-grandson of Dewey Archambault in the spring, tending to the place," says Roger, gazing at the darkened windows. "That's where Jack was laid out."

We descend the paved way, the gabled brick orphanage looming beneath the trees like a medieval fortress. Behind the huge cement outcropping of the memorial is a set of stone steps, leading up to the crucified Christ. The steps are numerous and shallow, and Roger says that pilgrims were meant to climb them on their knees, lingering on each one to say a decade of the rosary. "When I was little, I had nightmares that took place here," he says.

At the top of the stairs, Christ rises into the night on his concrete cross, his muscles tightened into wires and the sacrificial blood painted over his wounds in a bright, surreal crimson. Kerouac once wrote that "hysterical critics," obsessed with the bohemian tone of his work, failed to notice his ardent Catholic faith. In fact, he saw the tormented pageant of his life as a mere prelude to the world that came after, when he would be "safe in heaven, dead."

Coming down the other side of the manmade hill, the stairs are set at a normal height. At the base of the shrine, there's a bank of votive candles glowing red in their netted glass sconces. Halfway up the vine-covered mount, a larger-than-life statue of the Virgin is beveled into a niche, wearing a double-ringed neon halo of blue light, her hands clasped in prayer.

It was on this patch of wrinkly tar that the poet Allen Ginsberg told Roger Brunelle a story about the visit he paid to the grotto in 1975, accompanied by Bob Dylan. The famous troubadour was in the midst of his "Rolling Thunder Revue" and had detoured to Lowell for the express purpose of seeing Kerouac's hometown. The two men were alone at the grotto on the night in question, and Dylan, who had not yet converted to Christianity, asked the bearded and bespectacled poet, who was also Jewish, about the purpose of the candles.

Ginsberg replied that Catholics would put money in the poor box, then light a candle while praying for some intention. They believed that the flame of the candle carried their prayers to heaven and perpetuated them there.

Dylan walked over, put $2 into the poor box, solemnly lit a candle, and then started walking up the driveway with the candle in his hand. "That's not how it works," said Ginsberg. "You're not supposed to keep the candle."

"Why not?" asked Dylan. "I paid for it."

Suddenly, the moon appears in the sky above Archambault Funeral Home, like a lost coin or a key, shedding its bluish tint over the stunted pine trees and shrubs bordering the orphanage. As Roger and I head for the car, scraping the hard soles of our shoes on the pavement, I realize I don't want to go home.

I just want to *go*.

PART ONE

NEW YORK

1

Riding a mountain bike over the crest of Metropolitan Avenue, I'm reminded of Thomas Wolfe's declaration that "only the dead know Brooklyn." Linden Hill Jewish Cemetery takes up the entire landscape to my right, with vast neighborhoods consisting of mausoleums bigger than the house I live in, and an incongruous mattress and box spring piled up on the sidewalk outside the gates. On the other side is All Faiths Cemetery and for what seems like an eternity I'm traveling through an urban netherworld, with monuments and spires and ten-foot granite angels occupying the landscape to the horizon.

I'm launching my literary and spiritual investigations here, in Brooklyn and Queens, where Kerouac was living when he wrote *The Town and the City* and started his first big road trip back in 1947. But I smashed up my ankle in a mountain climbing accident last summer, and can't walk very far without keeling over. So my rugby pal Chris Pierce suggested I rent a good bicycle in New York and cruise around to Kerouac's old hangouts in style. Piercey is a "can-do" guy, a former Ithaca College wrestler and soccer player and crackerjack physical therapist. Rolling past all these dead people, I make a note to listen to Piercey more often.

Sixty years after the kid from Lowell set out on a journey that would reshape the American novel, I intend to see Kerouac's road for myself. Starting right now, I plan to hitchhike out of Manhattan to visit Kerouac's old friend, the musician and composer David Amram; drive from New York City to New Orleans with "Surfer" John Hearin, the Neal Cassady of the New Millenium; bomb down from Denver to Mexico City with Keith "Bongo" Bowden; hang around the bars and bike shops of San Francisco before making a mad dash to LA in the company of Chris Pierce; and then ride the bus from New York to Chicago and follow Kerouac's route back to Larimer Street in Denver. My "scope and purpose" here, just as Kerouac characterized his own, is to see the countryside and its inhabitants, to examine the cloudy vistas of the past through the lens of the present, and to try my hand at writing "simply poetry, or, natural description."

When Kerouac took these trips, he was a young man with little money and few responsibilities. Today, I'm as old as his book, fraught with the demands of teaching and coaching and parenting, but I'm going anyway. For the one thing I've gained from reading Kerouac is the belief that, every so often, you have to put all your chips down on a single number and let the wheel go around. Sure, I could get murdered while hitchhiking (a scenario my rugby friends think is so likely they've created a pool), kidnapped by a roving pervert, thrown in a Mexican prison, or otherwise fucked up. But it's a chance I'm willing to take—here, now, and perhaps for the last time—just to see America from the window of a speeding car.

I'll be traveling down an actual road and, simultaneously, deep into the pages of a book, into a treasured story that has become so familiar that it seems like my own. In so doing, I'll pass into that murky realm where the conscious and the subconscious meet, where the indelible figures of *On the Road* and the most charismatic people in my own life merge into a single cast of characters: idiosyncratic, inimitable, beloved.

Pedaling between the cemeteries, it occurs to me that *On the Road* has something in common with another one of my favorite books, *Memoirs of a Fox Hunting Man*, by Siegfried Sassoon. In their fictionalized autobiographies, each of these authors claimed that he lived with his aunt, not his mother, erasing his dead father and siblings from the story. In fact, Kerouac and Sassoon share a number of striking characteristics. Both were loners, introverts, and poets, both endured a world war, and each was an accomplished athlete and sportsman in his youth. In a way, manipulating the basic facts of their experience allowed each of these writers to focus more clearly on who they really were, and what they felt about what was happening to them. Right at the outset of his tale, Sassoon writes something that very much reminds me of Kerouac: "Sitting here, alone with my slowly moving thoughts, I rediscover many little details, known only to myself, details otherwise dead and forgotten with all who shared that time; and I am inclined to loiter among them as long as possible."

Flying down the other side of the hill, I pass several enormous junkyards, their ten-foot cement walls strung with concertina wire and splattered with gang graffiti. Past the Lin Ching Trading Company at 46-55 Metropolitan Avenue in Ridgewood, its sign made of Chinese characters advertising some item that's only 99 cents, though I can't read Chinese and don't know what it is. At the corner of Woodward and Metropolitan avenues is Western Beef, a gigantic orange-brick building that takes up an entire city block: "The Meat Supermarket: We Know the Neighborhood." It has a Texas-style gate across the entrance to the lot, and printed in huge letters along the upper edge of the building is a run-on sentence that looks like it could've been written by Kerouac: "We got Eggs Pancakes Bagels Cigarettes Gyro Hamburgers Phili Steaks Sandwiches" and so on, around the corner and out of sight.

Kerouac once wrote in a letter to John Clellon Holmes that there was "something rotten in America and I'm gonna find out what it is on my next trip to New York." All around me, there's urban sprawl that extends to the horizon. Signs hanging from the façade of nondescript cinder-block buildings advertise "$59 mattresses" and "$99 dinettes." A pretty girl behind the smoked-glass wall of a bank smiles at me: black pants, black sweater, white blouse. She's in a strip mall that forms a sliding montage as I zoom past: Rose's Pizza Mattress Furniture Car Wash Chinese Restaurant. She's gone before I can wave to her, yet there's an image of the girl's face imprinted on my mind.

Above the corrugated iron fence of A&G Auto Salvage are what looks like a million used engine blocks displayed like sides of beef wrapped in plastic, for your individuated perusal and pleasure. There's a big hand-painted sign with a giant arrow on the rusted iron facade saying "A&G Office" with the arrow pointing down at a gaping doorway. It looks like the inner circle of automotive hell, and just as I ride past, a thousand-year-old, impossibly muscular black man wanders out of the steamy interior with a devilish wrench in his hand. There are entire cars and parts of cars and neatly dissected cars and hideously smashed up cars displayed on racks towering high above the twenty-foot level of the fence, and I pedal furiously by, shivering.

It's a cloudy, breezy day, threatening showers, and when I reach Ozone Park, where Kerouac lived for more than six years, I'm already soaked through with perspiration and then it begins to rain. Stopping beneath a railroad overpass, I fish around in my backpack and pull out my cell phone. I'm traveling light and realize I don't have an address in Ozone Park for either of the two places where Kerouac lived with Mémère, his widowed mother. But I have the greatest Jack Kerouac resource in the world on speed dial: the poet and community organizer Paul Marion, who lives in Lowell.

Paul and I have been friends for fifteen years or so, but we knew of each other long before that, like two up-and-coming prizefighters working the local undercards. Now in his early fifties, Paul is a youthful, curly-haired fellow, with a smart and beautiful wife and an adoring son. We consider ourselves blue-collar guys like our own dads, out plying the scribbler's trade alongside the plumbers and Teamsters and firemen we grew up with.

I reach the Marion household on the second ring, and Paul's wife, Rosemary Noon, greets me with delight and calls her husband from the other room. It's late Sunday morning, and I imagine my buddy clearing away the sports section of the *Boston Globe*, mussing young Joe's hair, and advancing toward the hall extension with an old Dalton Jones coffee mug in his hand.

"Is this the Jack Kerouac Information Bureau?" I ask when he greets me. "For I'm a charter member in good standing, despite my delinquent dues and the fact that I have not attended a meeting in . . . well, decades."

Paul's enthusiasm for my quixotic endeavor crackles from cell tower to cell tower across the breadth of Brooklyn and Queens, and within a minute of our initial contact, I can hear him barging around in the far reaches of his living room, searching for that missing cog that will make my engine go. With the rain now falling in sheets, I have complete confidence that the former domicile of "the Wizard of Ozone Park" will not escape Paul Marion's detective skills.

Arguably, there would be no Kerouac revival or trumpeted entrance into the literary canon, in Lowell or anywhere else, if not for Paul Marion. The author of several volumes of poetry, including his most recent book, *What Is the City?* as well as the editor of *Atop an*

Underwood: Early Stories and Other Writings by Jack Kerouac, Paul has been a key literary adviser to John Sampas, Kerouac's brother-in-law and the principal executor of the Kerouac estate. Paul is also an inde-fatigable personal champion of the man who, at times, appeared to be Lowell's least favorite son. It was Paul Marion's doggedness, poetic erudition, and intimate knowledge of Lowell politics that eventually led to the creation of the Jack Kerouac Commemorative at the corner of French and Bridge streets. Today, if you visit the commemorative, you'll see local teenagers and elderly folks and shopkeepers reading what looks like giant pages from the great stone book of the world, and you'll realize that Paul was right.

Just a few weeks ago, I was visiting the Boott Museum in Lowell for the opening of an exhibit featuring the original "scroll" version of *On the Road*. It was laid out in a glass case like a miniature road, and people were milling around, nibbling on hors d'oeuvres and drinking long-stemmed glasses of wine. Soon after the crowd was called to attention, a local politician got up there and took credit for it all, mangling Kerouac's name so that it sounded like "Jerk Carraway." A few minutes later, another dignitary introduced Paul Marion, call-ing him "a hero of Lowell." I was standing off to the side with Joe Marion and my own son, and young Joe called out, "Hooray! My dad's the hero of Lowell."

In a moment, Paul returns to the line and rattles off the two addresses in New York where the Kerouacs lived in the 1940s. The rain has stopped now, and a short distance along the sidewalk a man has emerged from one of the neat little row houses and is tuning up a massive leaf-blowing device. My time to talk is growing short.

"My ear is tuned to the street," I say.

"Report thee well, and truly," says Paul, and then the leaf blower makes a roar like a jet engine.

2

At the terminus of Metropolitan Avenue, I confer with a trio of power company employees who are waist deep in the middle of the road, and one of the hard hats climbs out of the trench to assist me. He has a reddened face and beefy forearms, and after wiping his neck with a bandana and scrutinizing my map for a few seconds, he provides me with directions to both of the houses I'm looking for.

"Eleven blocks that way," he says, raising his arm. "It's about a mile. You'll see the Indians. Then come back this way, to Cross Bay Boulevard, and the second place you want to go is about two miles that way."

9421 134th Street is a two-story, beige vinyl–sided cape with ornate iron bars on the lower windows and a six-foot wrought iron fence out front. It's divided into two units, and there's a small front lawn with a hydrangea bush to the right of the house and a cement urn beside the walkway that's empty at the moment. Two lanes of concrete sidewalk with a grassy strip down the middle form the driveway. There's an unregistered car beside the house, and a small garage out back. It very much reminds me of Kerouac's old childhood residence on Beaulieu Street in Lowell, which is no surprise because the writer's father, Leo-Alcide Kerouac, often rented the same type of modest home, always with an eye toward something bigger and better.

Although his remark puzzled me at first, the hard hat was right: there are a lot of ethnic Indians around here. Across the street three Indian men are up on a scaffold painting the trim of a yellow-brick building. They're dressed in white coveralls and talking in spirited voices. One is wearing a dazzlingly white turban, another is in a dark blue turban, and the third man is sporting a maroon turban. They're dabbing paint on the trim, with a beautiful brand new Cadillac glistening in the driveway. One of the men spatters the Caddy with paint drops and is berated by the fellow in the white turban, who shouts and waves his arms, dropping more paint onto the Cadillac. They're the Three Stooges of Ozone Park, and my head swivels back to the house where Kerouac lived, and I imagine old Zagg himself peeking out from under the shade, drinking Tokay wine and laughing at this neighborhood scene.

Rain is falling harder now. On Cross Bay Boulevard, there's an eight-foot plaster statue of what looks like a 1950s hoodlum chained to a second-floor balcony. He's perched above the lintel of a building that houses the offices of "Fertig and Fertig, Attorneys at Law," wearing blue jeans, a leather jacket, slicked-back hair, and black motorcycle boots. It's a weird-looking sight, particularly for this modest residential area, almost as if some pranksters had erected a surreptitious "Monument to Herbert Huncke" when the Fertig brothers were away on vacation. Somehow, no one's ever noticed this forty-year-old plaster beatnik shackled to the roof.

Just down the street, 133-01 Cross Bay Boulevard is a two-story place at the end of a row of attached buildings. The lower half is made of brick and occupied by the Little Shoppe of Flowers; the upper floor is pink stucco with a trio of small windows across the front. It shares a façade with a tax preparation company, insurance broker, Chinese restaurant, and Laundromat. Across the rainy street are Glenn Patrick's Pub and a couple of small, well-kept houses.

A young blond woman comes gliding outside to tend the hanging plants under the canopy of the shop. Her hair is dampened by previous trips and she resembles Sandro Botticelli's *Birth of Venus*, with her ruminative eyes and dainty manner. When she sees me scribbling in a notebook, the girl approaches and tells me that Kerouac did, in fact, live here and "wrote part of that book, *On the Road*, upstairs."

A customer emerges from the shop with a question, and I wheel my bicycle to the side of the building, where a small round wooden plaque says:

> Jack Kerouac 1922–1969. The poet and novelist lived here from 1943–1949. During those years he wrote his first novel *The Town and the City* 1950 and planned *On the Road*, 1957, his seminal novel that defined the Beat Generation. Historical St. Marks Preservation Center.

It was in this "ambiguous house of [his] dreams" that Kerouac, before he had even finished his first book, started writing *On the Road* in bursts of somnambulistic insight, what he referred to in his journal as mysterious thousand-word trances, occasionally taking time-outs to drink beer and watch football at the bar across the street. In a moment, the shop girl, whose name is Anna, returns to the sidewalk and our conversation. She says that her boss's husband knows a lot more about Kerouac than she does, but "it's a fact" the

writer used to go across to Glenn Patrick's Pub with his mother's
teapot and have it filled up with beer and then bring it back home.

"It was called the Linden back then. There was another Linden
three blocks down and three blocks over, but he never went there,"
says Anna, gesturing toward the green-and-white tavern on the
other side of the boulevard. "That's definitely the place."

Inside my backpack are a handful of energy bars, a black Mead
composition book with a stiff marbled cover, four #2 pencils, a street
map of Brooklyn, and a copy of *On the Road*. Anna takes the novel
from my hand and looks it over. "I want to read this book," she says,
turning it over. "It's not too long. I thought it would be thicker."

Anna raises her eyes, which are framed by tendrils of her dampened yellow hair, and the earnestness of her gaze passes right through
me. I want to say something about the book, about what it means to
me and how it might free her somehow from the narrow universe
of the flower shop, but I can't express it and the two of us remain in
tableau, staring dumbly at the cover. A moment later we exchange
our farewells, and as I mount the bicycle I spot a single dirty canvas
work glove on the street outside Kerouac's old house with the ini-
tials "N.Y.C.I.A." printed on it.

Glenn Patrick's Pub is beige stucco with dark green trim, green
awnings, a green door kitty-corner to the street, and a leprechaun with
a foaming mug of beer in his hand that decorates the awning. Little
white bulbs on a green cord are hanging from the awning, and their
weak light is visible on this gloomy afternoon. Back in 1947, not long
after the two men struck up their acquaintance, Kerouac and Neal
Cassady greased the wheels of their friendship by getting drunk here.

Since I have no lock for the bike, with the spokes clicking I wheel
it inside, my pants crusted with mud at the cuffs and rain dripping
from my visor. Inside the bar there's a Guinness clock on the wall
indicating that it's always time for a pint of stout. The barmaid, a
smiling buxom girl with dark hair, immediately picks up an empty
glass from the rack at her elbow and positions it beneath the tap and
asks me if I want a pint.

Declining the beer, I ask if it's all right to bring the bike inside,
and a portly fellow laughs and says, "Sure, there have been many
bicycles at the bar and quite a few other things." When I ask him

about Jack Kerouac, he points to the other end of the room and follows after me, beer in hand, noting that others have come through looking for the place where Kerouac purchased his teapots of beer.

On the rear wall next to the exit there's a framed photograph and clipping from *Newsday* magazine titled "Kerouac in Queens: Is the Wizard of Ozone Park forgotten in the bar where he first went 'On the Road'?" A second article from the local paper is hanging beside it: "The Jack I Knew: My Prom Date," reported by a local elderly woman.

My guide to these wonders is Bill Davis, a retired cop from Queens wearing a red sweatshirt and a black baseball cap with "117" on the front. He leaves me alone at the shrine for a few moments, and when I turn away, he rumbles along the carpet toward me. "I been coming here for twenty years," he says, explaining that the joint used to be called McNulty's. As I wave to the barmaid and exit the pub, struggling with the inert bicycle, Bill Davis pushes open the heavy wooden door for me and then, still holding his glass of beer, comes outside, the rain dappling his shoulders.

Pointing along Cross Bay Boulevard, Davis indicates the fastest way back to Manhattan and then the easiest way—a route where I can't get lost—counting the major intersections in his head and then bestowing that number on me. "I hope you find everything all right," he says, wishing me luck. Then Bill Davis shakes my hand, returning to the warmth of the bar with what's left of his beer.

Kerouac often had his nose in a book and his ass on a barstool, in New York and elsewhere. My experience at Glenn Patrick's Pub in Queens is testimony to the fact that, as in yesteryear, the blue-collar joints of America are filled with men of goodwill. These dank, dark roosting places are havens for the Bill Davises of the world, with no axes to grind and no enemies to speak of.

3

Riding back toward the city on Metropolitan, I encounter an old nearsighted locksmith with straggly white hair peering through the bars of his shop; he's locked himself out. A Guatemalan woman is walking past the Brushless Car Wash on Grant Street with her teenage son, and gives him a good whack across the shoulder and neck when he says something she doesn't like. He's nearly a foot taller than his mother, and the boy shoots me a look of embarrassment as I pass. A guy who resembles a shopworn version of baseball manager Felipe Alou is walking down Grant Street in uniform pants and a New York Mets warm-up jacket of dark blue silk with orange-and-white trim. Alou shuffles along with his hands in his pockets, looking at the sidewalk like the Mets have been beaten in the bottom of the thirteenth inning and he's out of a job.

It's time to eat, and within a minute of that decision I'm sitting in Najeeb's Falafel and More in the Williamsburg section of Brooklyn. The smell of cooking lentils has drawn me into this tiny, yellow-walled place, with its mismatched glass tables and wrought iron chairs. Behind the cash register is a poster titled "First Aid for Choking," with a 1970s schematic describing the Heimlich maneuver. There are three large decorative ouds, the stringed instrument peculiar to the Middle East, hanging on the wall opposite my chair, and the proprietor is behind the counter on a stool, tuning a handcrafted oud that looks like half of a pinstriped black melon.

Najeeb Shaheen is a tall, saturnine gent in his fifties, wearing a faded baseball cap that barely contains his gray hair. When I state that I live in northern Massachusetts and love Lebanese food, he begins playing the oud and, over his strumming, tells me to forget about my desire for the chicken platter.

"You must have mujaddara," he says.

Putting aside his instrument, Najeeb comes around the gleaming display case and points at a serving dish filled with what looks like hash. "I just cooked it," he says. "With fresh salad and yogurt—that's what you'll have."

The plate comes out, garnished with dabs of plain yogurt and hummus, the lentils cooked soft and spicy and mixed with bulgur wheat. As a kid, I was tormented by a vicious punk named Shaheen and dreaded the smell of kibbee that emanated from the tenement where he lived, but I like this Najeeb Shaheen and even forgive the old one-eyebrow bully from Saratoga Street.

I order a Styrofoam cup of his rosewater lemonade and sit eating in the delicious cold of the air conditioner. It's been quiet since Najeeb laid aside his oud, but now the sound system clicks on and the tiny restaurant echoes with the wails of a harmonica and then Bob Dylan begins singing "You're Gonna Make Me Lonesome When You Go."

It occurs to me that there'd be no Dylan without Kerouac. I can hear the "road" in his raspy Hibbing voice, and the rolling bluesy Americana of his songs. What contemporary American artist—musical, visual, literary—has not been influenced by Kerouac's saintly vision or consciously sought to avoid that influence and was smitten by it nonetheless? When Ken Kesey, driven across country in a bus named "Further" by Kerouac's old buddy Neal Cassady, came to New York to see Timothy Leary and party with Kerouac, it was like kissing the slipper of the king. Of course, the Jack of those days, hounded by his admirers and battered by whiskey and wine, was more fool than king and suffered from bad feet. But the trip to see him meant the same thing, anyway.

Several years ago, I attended a Bob Dylan concert at a minor league baseball stadium in Nashua, New Hampshire. A good buddy of mine, Jeff Ness, was a rabid fan of Dylan's and his old back-up group, the Band, and procured tickets for both of our girlfriends and us. It was a muggy summer evening and, since the concert was general admission, the girls spread out a blanket on the infield grass while roadies put the finishing touches on the stage in center field.

Jeff was a tall, dark-haired, handsome fellow, with a gap between his front teeth and an easygoing manner. A Lawrence, Mass., firefighter with a remarkable fondness for Harley Davidson motorcycles and stray dogs, Jeff stayed on the blanket drinking Buds during the recorded music that preceded Dylan's set, but he eventually grew itchy and wanted to move. The girls remained in place with the cooler and picnic basket, and Jeff, taking me along with him, began working his way through the crowd down the first base line. He was six feet tall and handy with his fists, but it was Jeff's smile and his banter that kept us moving inexorably toward the lip of the stage.

The mosquitoes came out in force when the sun went down behind the stadium. Dylan looked his gray-haired frazzled best, wearing a black frock coat that hung to his knees, snakeskin boots, and a black, flat-brimmed hat girdled by a strand of figured silver. His four-piece band was tight, and when he kicked off the show with one of his new songs, Dylan stood with his back to the crowd, enjoying the company of his sidemen and inserting expressive little guitar phrases between what they were doing.

Jeff and I finagled our way to the space right at Dylan's feet. He is an economical and laconic performer, and he ran through a medley of his old hits and his newer songs with an acute sense of professional dispatch. The only words that Dylan uttered were one or two nodding remarks to his band mates, uttered sotto voce during the songs. Then the band moved into the introduction to "Idiot Wind," and Dylan stepped away from the microphone, turning to the segment of the crowd within natural earshot and working his lips.

We waited for the message. Certainly, all and sundry contained within the boundaries of that grassy diamond knew that Dylan was there to deliver the Word; that he had traveled to the hinterlands of New Hampshire as every good bard should, to plant, raise, harvest, and reveal a kernel of the Truth. Along with six or seven of our fellow acolytes in that little corner of the throng, we swayed and held our collective breath and waited for enlightenment.

Swatting at a mosquito, Dylan looked down past the toes of his boots at Jeff and me and said, "Pretty buggy up here."

We roared with delight. Pretty buggy up here. Of course, that was it. Dylan was right. The element that distinguished our experience in Holman stadium that night was the proliferation of Anopheles Quadrimaculatus—the four-spotted mosquito—and would always be so. Once again, the great troubadour had captured the zeitgeist. He had summarized and capitalized the spirit of the age.

From that night forward Jeff and I would repeat Dylan's remark to each other many times, always delivered in the singer's nasal twang. It was a moment that we shared that popped up here and there like a snapshot of our long friendship, which had begun when Jeff and I were just fourteen years old.

Jeff was killed on his motorcycle three years ago. And here at the table in Najeeb's shop, as Dylan sings from the restaurant speakers, that image appears from the recesses of my memory and, in it, Jeff is laughing.

. . .

Najeeb emerges from behind the counter once more and picks up a book I have with Kerouac's photograph from 1950 on the cover. "Do you know him?" I ask, as Najeeb stares at the image. "He's a great American writer."

Najeeb shakes his head. "No," he says. But when I mention *On the Road*, he turns a brilliant smile on me and says, "Of course. Everyone knows that book."

"When did he pass away?" asks Najeeb, as he cashes me out.

"Nineteen sixty-nine."

In the background, Dylan is singing about far flung places on the American map.

"Here in New York?"

I shake my head. "St. Petersburg, Florida. He was only forty-seven years old." I make a drinking motion with my hand.

Najeeb swats the air in front of his face. "Fuck him. Amazing."

The cash register emits a musical tone, and he hands over two wrinkled bank notes and a few coins. "Come back," he says. "We will talk."

4

Occasionally, I glimpse the massive arch of the Williamsburg Bridge between the gaunt edifices of Brooklyn. After a few twists in the road, with steam rising from the grates and a cacophony of horns everywhere, I round the final turn and there's the bridge right in front of me, a great hoop of green steel arching over to Manhattan. There's a bike and foot path to one side, and switching gears, I start climbing toward the highest point in the span. I've been riding for more than six hours, and it's heavy going.

Batches of Orthodox Jews are making a pilgrimage over to the city and back, wearing long black trench coats, black yarmulkes, and high white socks. One passes by who appears to be praying, making his intentions for all of humanity: every nearsighted locksmith and faux Felipe Alou; every Guatemalan woman and her misbehaving son; all the blond shop clerks and oud players; the Bill Davises of this world and the next; and every last bodhisattva as far as the eye can see. Beside the rabbi is his gigantic teenage son. A hulking lad with long curls hanging from either side of his forehead, the boy looks at me as I grind ever upward. He smiles, and in his eyes I see the message: *let us pray.*

At the apex of the bridge, cars are roaring by on either side, and the dizzying girders rise above me toward the inverted bowl of the sky. I can make out a baseball field on the far shore of the East River where a game is going on under the lights, although it is barely three in the afternoon. An old wizened Jewish fellow with a long white beard approaches just as I reach the top—my lungs heaving, quads burning from my all-day ride. He looks just like the "old bearded realizer" that Kerouac was always searching for, and I wait for him to bestow some piece of ancient wisdom upon me, but the man simply gazes ahead and begins his descent into Brooklyn.

I pause there for a moment, my breath coming in gasps as I drink from the water bottle and survey the gigantic horizon. There's a bit of Quixote in every domestic traveler, because you have to delude yourself into thinking that your journey is important; otherwise, you're just an ant crawling along the maze of America. Right in front of me in a long pendulum that comes down from New York State is gray, shrouded Manhattan, and I push off and ride down the slope, faster and faster, to the beginning of my journey—the beginning of the road.

5

After returning my bike to the rental shop, I descend underground to wait for the A train with some New York hipsters, young and not-so-young men and women in sunglasses and pointy black boots and fluorescent jackets. Trains are arriving at the station with a great roar, like subterranean prehistoric insects devouring the hipsters and belching steam. As I mount the train, glancing back I see my friend Paul Marion, or at least some cool Gramercy Park version of him: wearing a World War I ambulance driver's tunic, a pork-pie hat with a turned-up brim, and a soul patch under his lower lip.

He walks by with his hands in his pockets, whistling a tune of blue skies and the open road, then winks at me as the doors close on him with a whoosh.

The A train is only running as far as 168th Street today, so I climb back out of the tunnel and board a bus that will take me another four stops. It's an unseasonably cool 60 degrees and overcast as I disembark at Broadway and 181st, looking for the Henry Hudson Highway. Crossing over Broadway with my knapsack, I climb the hill going west and stop at a little health food store at 181st and Cabrini Boulevard for a pick-me-up. The place smells of gingerroot and cloves, and the neatly arranged shelves are lined with little brown jars of whey powder and brewer's yeast and omega-3 fish oil. Posters for various social justice organizations and offbeat artistic endeavors decorate the walls, and a young rosy-cheeked woman in black tights and a zip-up fleece jacket peruses bunches of radishes and celery that have been trucked in from an organic farm upstate.

There's funky R&B music playing, and the clerk, a small, wiry dude named Juan, comes down the aisle to the juice bar against the rear wall and explains the various ingredients that he can blend into an invigorating tonic.

"I need some energy for hitchhiking," I tell him. "Something to get me going."

Juan laughs. "You probably need a shot of bourbon for that."

He whirls me up $8.79 worth of apples, ginger, beets, celery, and wheat grass in the blender, while talking nonstop about President Bush and the war. Like many people I'll meet on the road, Juan is fixated on what he perceives as the peccadilloes of the Bush administration, the vice president in particular. Across Middle America, Dick Cheney has come to symbolize the smugness and cynicism of the empowered class, and many a streetcar philosopher and soapbox orator I'll encounter in my travels will rain vitriol on the Man from Lincoln, Nebraska. It's Cheney's sense of entitlement, of his own self-declared greatness, that irks people the most.

"If I'm at home battering my wife, I can't send people to arrest you for wife battering," Juan says. I sip on my green drink and mull over this riddle, wandering among the jars of bee pollen and flaxseed and piles of forked gingerroot, which look like little brown homunculi.

In a moment, Juan magically reappears behind the cash register at the front of the store, and I pay for the drink and some energy bars with my one and only banknote, a fifty-dollar bill.

"Keep the faith," Juan says, handing me the change.

"Right on, brother," I say, going with the vibe of the place.

The bicycle overpass spanning the Henry Hudson Highway is less than a hundred yards from the store. I cinch the straps on my backpack and tramp over this light, flexible arch, my boots chiming against the metal as I reach the zenith and go booming down the other side. My spirits have been galvanized for the task at hand, with the ginger burning at my throat and my sinuses filled with the tang of wheat grass.

Cars are hurtling below me at deadly speeds. Traversing the footbridge, I'm mindful of a rambling man named Jack, not Kerouac, or even Elliott, but Jack London. Kerouac devoured London's books as a young man and set out to be an adventurer and sojourner himself. What intrigued me about the unnamed prospector in London's "To Build a Fire" was his absolute belief in his own abilities. And although his hubris resulted in his demise, it was thrilling to see him travel over the inhospitable white expanse of the Yukon. Exposed to 107 degrees of frost, the man's only disconcerting thought was "that he had not devised a nose strap of the sort that Bud wore in cold snaps." The story glowed as I read along, like an old movie where light accents the pages of a book, and I was left to ponder London's maxim: *Any man who was a man could travel alone.*

In the shadow of the George Washington Bridge, I lean over the Jersey barrier and survey the cars whizzing toward me. On the other side of the road is the breakdown lane, separated from Upper Manhattan by a fifty-foot wall made of granite blocks. I need to cross three lanes of fast-moving traffic on a bad leg so I can start hitchhiking. For this, I need a break of fifteen or twenty seconds between cars, and for what seems like a half-hour, there isn't one and I have time to reconsider my plans.

Kerouac was lucky; he left New York with fifty dollars in his pocket. I only have thirty-six. And the last time I hitchhiked with any regularity, back and forth between Lake Winnipesaukee in Meredith, New Hampshire, and my home in Methuen, Massachusetts, was almost thirty years ago. It was the summer I graduated from college, and, tanned very dark from working on Bear Island, I made it home once a week to play for my soccer team, the Wanderers FC, in the old city league. We appeared in the finals that year, and on my last long hitch, a pretty blonde in a VW convertible picked me up and we raced down I-93 with the Allman Brothers wailing over the radio and long, streaming tendrils of her hair whipping my face.

Now, I'm a fledging geriatric in orthopedic shoes, and my old soccer cleats are in a trunk, gathering dust somewhere. Inside my backpack are my dirty cycling togs, a road map, two pints of water, half a dozen energy bars, a couple of paperbacks, my cell phone, a composition book, and a phalanx of undersharpened pencils. It occurs to me that I've been trying, over these action-packed years, to preserve my life, through rest and reading, proper nutrition, abstinence, persistence, and Zenlike stillness, to extend the foreground of the great narrative epic I'm engaged in. Now, I should be trying to throw it away; at age fifty, surviving mostly intact, I have to crank up the intensity of what I'm doing, bringing a more reckless edge to the force I'm applying to the world and its obstacles. Otherwise, there's no point in making it this far with so much gas in the tank—so much energy waiting to be burned up in pursuit of what's left. *That's* Kerouac's message, as I read it and hear it.

Finally, there's a lull in the traffic, and I galumph across the wide stretch of pavement and throw myself over the barrier on the other side. Letting out a long "Yee-haw," after a moment I collect myself, lift my shoulders and take a long deep breath, and exhale it sharply. My heart is beating fast as I straighten out my pack straps, swing one leg and then the other over the Jersey barrier, and stick out my thumb.

It's almost noon, the sun's out for the time being, and I'm standing almost flush with a gabled stone wall, more than five stories high and covered with graffiti, that keeps the bulge of Upper Manhattan

from spilling into the Hudson. The voice inside my head says, *Fuck it.*
I'm taking a shot.

In front of me is a small opening between the Jersey barriers that
affords a little bit of protection from the oncoming cars. As they go
rushing past, the faces of the occupants are frozen for a moment
like Instamatic pictures: very clear and yet somehow indistinct at
the same time, like police mug shots, or the photographs of Civil
War dead. As my upraised arm begins to tire, these images take on a
sinister quality, and irrational fears invade my thoughts. I have been
warned of kidnappings and murders, of the terrible, nameless psy-
chopaths and sociopaths that wander the highways and byways of
today's America. Nobody hitchhikes anymore, my friends and family
members said, and with good reason.

One of my friends who is a Massachusetts state trooper said that
I would be crazy to hitchhike without a weapon and suggested I get
a license to carry, and then buy, a small handgun. When I replied that
even with a permit, I wouldn't be allowed to carry a firearm across state
lines, the trooper shrugged and said I could carry it in a little fanny
pack and dump it if the heat was on. "Everything is fluid," he said.

Additionally, it soon becomes clear that the motoring public is
divided into two categories: drivers who'll never give me a ride, and
those whom I would never ride with:

"Get a car, you fucking loser!"
"Get a job. Fuck you!"

These are some of the tamer exhortations coming my way. But I
take heart when a young black guy on a bicycle going the other way
gives me a thumbs-up and flashes a smile. He can't believe I'm doing it.

Neither can I. After twenty minutes, I haven't had any luck
and am supporting my hitchhiking arm by propping my left hand
beneath my right elbow. I keep my back straight and attempt to
make eye contact with the drivers. In 1947, Kerouac got as far
as Bear Mountain on a rainy day and then had to turn back. So
far, I haven't gotten a single friendly nod, and the sun is shining
brightly.

A lot of nice cars are going by, Mercedes and Porsches and Peugeots and Fiats. There's no "Maxwells and Saxons and Dorts" from the days of William Saroyan. A man drives by in a Lexus with his passenger's bare feet up on the dashboard, illuminated by a shaft of sunlight like something in a painting by René Magritte.

Clouds converge overhead and it begins raining, just a light patter of drops. Suddenly, a white late-model Buick pulls over and I run up to the passenger door, wondering if I should call the license plate in to my buddy John Goodwin's voice mail. He's a police lieutenant in Revere, Mass., and when I told him I was going to hitchhike in New York, Goody assured me that he wouldn't rest until they found my killer.

But it's too late. Although I don't have much to base it on, I'm riding on faith. I'm going to trust the road-going public of America.

Inside the car is a young Moroccan fellow, perched sideways on the seat and smoking a cigarette pinched between his thumb and forefinger like a character in a French movie.

"Are you broken down?" asks the man, expelling a stream of smoke. "I can take you to the next exit."

When I tell the guy, no, I'm not a stranded motorist and I'm going all the way through, into New York State proper, he says, "I used to hitchhike all the time when I was in Morocco, so good luck."

We bid each other farewell, and, buoyed by this experience, I jut my hip out a little farther and raise my thumb high. Less than two minutes later, a brand-new, jet-black Humvee stops a short distance up the highway. Inside is a slender, clean-shaven guy in his late twenties wearing khaki pants, a cream-colored polo shirt, and a dark green baseball hat.

"Where you heading?" the guy asks, and when I tell him, he offers to give me a lift about halfway. There's a baby seat in the back, and he's listening to National Public Radio, so I figure it's safe to get in.

Soon I learn that my benefactor is a successful real estate developer working on mixed-use projects up to $30 million, and that he's on his way to Riverdale to meet with one of his design team. It turns out that the man's father is an accomplished businessman who has published two books, which were actually ghostwritten by his mother. One of the books is titled *I'm Not the Boss, I Just Work Here*, which the guy describes as "a book on faith, more than anything."

"It was published in America and then translated into Hebrew," says the young real estate tycoon. "It sold well in Israel, though my father doesn't speak any Hebrew at all."

It strikes me funny that the son of a devout Jewish guy who doesn't speak Hebrew is the only man brave enough to give me a ride. Like the Moroccan fellow who stopped for me, the young developer says that he hitchhikes all the time when he's visiting Israel with his family. I'm jacked up about getting such a great ride and go yammering on about my project: ". . . one of Kerouac's great preoccupations was God, and man's role on earth as a representative of God. He was Roman Catholic by birth and formal training, and then when he met all these people in New York in the 1940s he became a Buddhist. But it's interesting to me that your father, an important businessman, chose to write about his faith in God because that's one of the things that runs through all of Kerouac's work. . . ."

He's a gentle, soft-spoken kid, and he listens to my crazy story with a great biblical patience reflected in his eyes. The signs for Riverdale go floating past my window, and I'm getting ever closer to my destination and just go with the flow. Soon the kid has driven me ten miles out of his way and drops me right at the bottom of the entrance ramp to the Taconic Parkway.

After we yell pleasantries at each other over the roar of the engine and shake hands, I climb down from the cab, and he zooms off to the next exit and over the crossing bridge and back on the highway going in the other direction. His diligent and loving father ran a successful business, and his doting and industrious mother wrote books, and all the while they taught him to do unto others as he would have them do unto him.

6

I'm loitering on a grassy embankment, right next to a sign for Sleepy Hollow and Pleasantville. I dig an energy bar out of my backpack, peel it open, and sling the pack over one shoulder. An afternoon breeze has wafted in, and I'm enchanted by the twitter of birds and the green thrashing of the trees beyond the parkway. I haven't felt this unburdened by the encumbrances of middle age in quite some time; the sun is shining, my thumb is out, and I don't have a care in the world.

From a distance I can see the Westchester County police car aimed toward me and then its purposeful detour to the shoulder of the road. The young patrolman looks over and smiles like we're parties to the same joke. Turning on his revolving blue lights, the cop beckons to me, and I walk over to the car and lean into the passenger side window. We exchange greetings and then the officer asks me for identification, and I hand over my driver's license.

"Is there a problem?" I ask.

Keying his radio handset, the patrolman calls in my name and date of birth. "Yeah, there is," he says pleasantly. "You can't hitchhike in the state of New York. It's a two-hundred-dollar summons and fine."

Officer Greer is a compact, sturdily built fellow with short dark hair and a wry manner. While he's getting out of his car, a second cruiser arrives, and we're joined on the side of the highway by the patrol supervisor, an older, heavier man, wearing his sergeant's stripes and a pair of wraparound sunglasses with a rainbow tint. He hitches up his gun belt and puts on his hat just as a New York State trooper pulls up. I can feel lines of sweat beginning to creep down my back; on such a beautiful day in Sleepy Hollow, I'm Public Enemy #1.

The jowly sergeant waves the trooper off, and he and Officer Greer stand a few feet away, conferring for a moment, and then turn to behold what they've found. Wetting his lips, the sergeant angles his head to one side and then pivots his skull toward the other cop and grins. Officer Greer looks off at the horizon, barely managing to keep a straight face.

Then, drawing himself into a command posture, the sergeant clears his throat, settles his gaze on me and says, "What the hell are you doing?"

I explain that I'm researching a book about Jack Kerouac, and that I'm on my way to David Amram's farm up the road in Peekskill. While the two cops are mulling this over, Officer Greer's radio squawks and he goes over to hear the upshot of my background check—I have a clean record.

"Obviously, you're not a menace to society. You're involved in a noble pursuit: a journalist trying to get his story," says the sergeant, who's yanking my chain just a little. "But I don't want you getting killed out here."

Back in the old days, cops, reporters, teachers, and firemen were all considered equal in that blue collar/no collar sort of way, and for an instant I can make out a glimmer of that behind the sergeant's dark glasses. "Now, I could simply remove you from the highway without a summons," he says, trying not to smile. "And there's nothing saying you couldn't wait a while and then come back down and start hitch-hiking again."

Standing in a column of light beside Officer Greer and me, the sergeant appears peaceful and beneficent. But all of a sudden, the planes of his face harden like cement and he looks upon me as just another Steinbeckian vagabond he has to get rid of. "The only difference between you and Jack Kerouac is, back in those days, every nitwit with a cell phone wasn't calling 911, saying 'There's a deranged man walking around on the Taconic Parkway,'" the sergeant says. "If you get hit by a car, you'll end up looking like a mangled deer wearing a fleece sweatshirt."

A cloud passes overhead, and the sergeant digs in his pocket for a handkerchief and mops his face with it. "Bottom line, I gotta get you off my highway," he says.

It's a cordial encounter, three solid citizens reflecting on the prospects of the day. The sergeant decides that Officer Greer will transport me to the next exit, where I can perhaps walk the bike path the twenty or so miles to Amram's farm. I point to the brace on my ankle, saying that normally I wouldn't mind such a trek but under the present circumstances I can't walk twenty yards without breaking into a cold sweat.

Finally, the sergeant bids me adieu, and Officer Greer and I amble over to his patrol car. By rule, my personal belongings go into the front seat and I'm ushered into the back. At this moment I realize that carrying a gun would've been a big mistake, permit or not.

There's a sheet of heavy-duty Plexiglas dividing the two compartments of the police car, and I wedge my way into the tight confines of the back seat. "I'm only a hundred-seventy pounds," I say, turning sideways to get in. "How do you fit big guys back here?"

Officer Greer smiles and says, "Oh, we fit 'em in there, all right," and closes the door.

Westchester County police cars are white with orange-and-blue trim, and this one's equipped with a powerful engine that sends us rocketing up the parkway. There's no seat belt back here, and I'm flung sideways as a result of the quick acceleration, terrified by the other cars that loom up in front of us, then dart to the inner lanes. The other drivers are equally spooked by the encounter, their moon faces peering at me like I'm some killer on my way to the chair. The funny thing is, under my fleece I'm wearing a Massachusetts State Police T-shirt my pal Gene Kee gave to me.

Soon we're going nearly a hundred miles per hour, and it's the heart-pumping ride of a lifetime. Amid the crackle of radio static, I hear a dispatch that the suspected vagrant is actually "a journalist in the midst of a journalistic pursuit. He's going to avail himself of private transportation." I laugh when I realize that Officer Greer and his sergeant are personally seeing to it that I get to Amram in one piece.

Within a few minutes, we arrive at my exit, and Officer Greer pulls into a tiny parking lot used by cyclists to unload their gear. He's a nice fellow and waits patiently while I call David Amram on my cell phone and ask him to pick me up. Officer Greer takes the phone to give Amram precise directions, and they soon realize there's no southbound exit ramp to where we are, and the amiable policeman decides he'll give me another short ride, to a more accessible location. He confirms the exit number with Amram, and we jump back in the cruiser and take another brief, hair-raising trip on the parkway.

On reaching our destination, Officer Greer departs with a firm handshake, and I'm left on a small, triangular island to lounge beneath a weeping willow tree. While I'm waiting for Amram, I take out my notebook and begin writing: *So far I got picked up by a Muslim, a Jew, and the cops. That's hitchhiking in America these days and you can bet your Saudi Arabian oil futures that . . .*

My phone rings and it's "Surfer" John Hearin, my old college roommate and frequent road buddy. Back in the day, he and I played on a championship rugby team at the University of Florida and over the years have traveled to four continents together. Surfer's an aerospace engineer at NASA, and his schedule is so tight he's calling to confirm details of our upcoming sojourn from New York City to New Orleans by car.

"I've done enough hitchhiking that I didn't put myself in a bad spot," I tell him. "I was ten feet off the road, but the cop said, 'You could get killed out here.' I said, 'Ehh, everything's a risk in life,' but I'm already rethinking the Chicago to Denver thing because hitchhiking is just an enormous fucking hassle, at least in this part of the country."

In anticipation of our trip, Surfer has been reading *On the Road* for the first time in many years. Like many of Kerouac's admirers, my old teammate was introduced to the novel in the bloom of his youth and thought that Dean Moriarty would have been an ideal traveling companion: the king of all lady killers, indefatigable, charismatic, and consistent in his maddening inconsistency. But Surfer John, an ex-Marine, lives by the phrase "Semper Fidelis." Like me, he prizes his own loyalty and that of his friends above all else. Therefore, with millions of road miles having passed beneath his own feet, these days, my old roommate has a markedly different opinion of the "Adonis of Denver." Neal Cassady leeched money from his friends, stole their girlfriends, and abandoned them in times of need, all of which contradicts Surfer's personal code of conduct. "Moriarty was a dick," he says. "Leaving Sal in Mexico like that was a bullshit move. He used everybody and was just out for himself."

I point out that Sal was no dummy and that he, in turn, used Dean to generate momentum, both on the road and in his work. It was a symbiotic relationship. And besides, at the end of *On the Road*, Moriarty got his comeuppance when Paradise and Remi Boncoeur left him on a New York street corner in his ratty old coat.

"Symbiosis, my ass," Surfer says. "Good riddance."

I laugh and hang up, laying back to chew on a spear of grass while the good citizens of Pleasantville drive by in their suburban assault vehicles, gawking at me. Judgments are being made in the blink of an eye. Situated on a sliver of public land, I'm educated, clean-shaven, and fairly well dressed, but America has become the land of surveillance and suspicion.

7

In just under half an hour, David Amram rolls down the ramp in his little black Nissan, waving at me through the driver's side window.

Amram is a walking American treasure, a celebrated and well-traveled composer, musician, author, and recording artist who befriended Jack Kerouac in New York in the 1950s and collaborated with him on the infamous Beat movie *Pull My Daisy*.

I met "Uncle Dave," as I call him, a few years ago when he was in town for a Lowell Celebrates Kerouac! event. We hit it off, just a couple of guys who came from nowhere, and have been friends ever since. He's even the subject of a couplet from Raffi, the children's music man, and for decades has kept up a frenetic schedule of writing and performing that would put a hyperactive teenager to shame.

I climb in the car with Uncle Dave, and immediately we jump back into the conversation we were having when we last saw each other several months ago. Amram is describing Kerouac's initial hitchhiking trip out of New York in 1947 and how it was raining on top of Bear Mountain: "He got stuck up there and had to take the bus all the way out to Chicago, but it turned out all right because he eventually made it to Denver and had a funkitissimo time with all those cats out there."

The soft green hills of New York State are passing by the windows, and I'm nodding in agreement with everything that Uncle Dave is saying. "So today, instead of going to Bear Mountain and being in the middle of nowhere and hitching back, I changed the itinerary slightly to be that I'm going to your house," I say. "And I will put everything in my story about your peregrinations and perambulations, and we will no doubt have a bang-up time when all our works come to fruition."

Amram makes a gesture with his hands like he's quieting an orchestra. "Then, without further delay, I will deliver my four-hour commercial lecture," he says.

Now seventy-seven years old but appearing much younger, Amram is a lanky, handsome fellow, with a magician's bearing and tousled salt-and-pepper hair. He's wearing a blue satin Peekskill Hollow Farm jacket with "David" embroidered in white on the chest, beat-up jeans, a dark shirt, and an old pair of boots. As we drive along through the rolling farmlands of the Hudson River Valley, I ask Uncle Dave a question that has plagued me since I've known him.

"Every time I've seen you in public, you've had strings and strings of Native American beads and charms and amulets around your neck," I say. "Do you shower with those on?"

Amram laughs. "When I was in Africa in 1975, people had all kinds of stuff around their necks to ward off the deleterious forces of the adult world," he says, explaining that he wears charms that have been given to him over the years. He even dons the jewelry when he's in white tux and tails, directing a symphony orchestra.

Long before the term "world music" came into vogue, Amram had been everywhere and played with everybody, from Leonard Bernstein, Charles Mingus, and Thelonius Monk, to Neil Young and Sonic Youth. He has written more than a hundred symphonies, as well as the scores for a number of Hollywood films, including *The Manchurian Candidate* and *Splendor in the Grass*. When Amram was still in his twenties but had enjoyed a fair amount of musical success, Dizzy Gillespie told him that it "was time to put something back into the pot"—advice that Amram has taken to heart. For the last twenty years, he has donated his musical talents to Farm Aid, playing with Willie Nelson, John Mellencamp, and others, to help out American farmers. And well into his eighth decade, having earned the rank of *eminence gris*, he's still down-home enough to play church socials for free and go off jamming with street musicians.

Amram has finely chiseled features, his pink-cheeked complexion weathered by being outside and decorated with a little Sunday morning stubble. His love for his old buddy is plain as he describes what the corporate publishers and promoters have done to Kerouac's legacy by insisting he was the head writer for the Beat Generation, like it was some kind of TV show. "The other Beat writers' books, some of them anyway, sell because they were Jack's friends," says Amram. "But stereotyping is a full-time occupation. What happened to Jack never happened to Hemingway. When they study Hemingway and Fitzgerald in school, they don't call them the 'Lost Generation' writers. They don't lump them together. Since we live in a business culture and [Kerouac's] books keep selling more and more, he'll be less identified with the Beat movement, which never existed as far as I knew, except later on, and I was there."

He describes the Manhattan scene in the late fifties and early sixties, jam-packed with "beat wannabes: stockbrokers and lawyers dressed up like plumbers and carpenters, crowding into the Cedar Tavern with their fake Dutch accents, telling us all how beautiful it all was. Well, guess what?" Uncle Dave shakes his finger at me. "Jack Kerouac would've been just as great a writer if he'd never come to New York, and a *lot* of people don't like to hear that."

Amram jabs his hands out from the steering wheel, his memories and opinions flying thick and fast in the summer air. "Jack wrote so much before he got anything out there that he realized you had to be true to yourself and make something beautiful, or you become part of industrialized society. You become the enemy. Or you become so victimized by it that it destroys the only thing you got, which is your creativity. Listen, man. The perception that a dumb football player from Lowell and a car thief from Denver met in New York with these two intellectual geniuses—Allen Ginsberg and William Burroughs—and kinda learned how to articulate a sentence, finish it, and write it down, is not the truth," Amram says. "Check out what Jack wrote *when he was seventeen*. It was a précis to everything he ever wrote. It was beautiful. All of us were lucky to know him. Case dismissed."

American flags are hanging from the front porches of the houses rushing past our windows. "Jack was so patriotic that in the sixties, he warned that the excesses of the antiwar movement were going to hand the country over to the right wing," says Amram, "which they did. In a TV interview with William F. Buckley, which never gets quoted, Kerouac said that the Vietnam War was about selling Jeeps, and that the North and South Vietnamese were cousins and we just didn't get it. They didn't really want to fight each other. It's like what we're doing in Iraq, now."

Uncle Dave is in the groove, like a saxophonist blowing a mad solo, and I know enough to just keep a soft beat on the dashboard with my hand and let him go: "I tried to get this one guy who's writing a biography of Jack to talk to Billy Koumantzelis. He's the one that accompanied Jack to the Buckley show and held Jack in a headlock in the elevator afterwards so Jack wouldn't attack the poet Ed Sanders. Jack was mad because Sanders had tried to hog the show. The guy writing the biography asked Koumantzelis if he really thought that *Maggie Cassidy* and *The Town and the City* and *Visions of Gerard* were basically 'Lowell' books and if Lowell really was the heart and soul of what Jack was about, and Koumantzelis said, 'Once Jack gave all that stuff to me and I read about three pages and handed them back. Frankly, it wasn't my cup of tea.' Then he said the best line: 'But Jack didn't care, 'cause we were buddies.' The [biographer] was so horrified, he didn't want to interview him.

"These old Lowell buddies, these were guys Jack didn't have much intellectual congress with but were there to look after him when he went on a television show, stuff like that," says Uncle Dave. He goes on to say that he and Kerouac became good friends because neither suffered from any pretensions, and both had humble origins. Dave's great-great-grandfather, Moses Amram, emigrated from Echte-bei Nordheim in Germany in the 1850s and was living in Savannah, Georgia, during the Civil War. But old Moses never owned slaves "because he wasn't much better off himself," David says.

Peekskill Hollow Farm is situated along a shady country lane. You descend the driveway into a little hollow, naturally, then cross a wooden bridge over a fast-moving stream and climb up the other side to the house, which is a white frame building with a small barn adjacent to it. The sloping front lawn is dotted with fruit trees, and there's a small dump truck parked at the top of the drive. A big white dog named Tony rushes out to greet any visitors, and birds are calling out a medley of cheerful notes from nearby treetops.

Amram explains that he had to sell his beloved farm when he got divorced a few years ago, and now he's renting it back from the new owners. "It ain't mine anymore," he says, rubbing Tony behind the ears.

Amram has just returned from back-to-back musical residencies in Ohio and upstate New York, with three more scheduled for out of state in the coming weeks. Lately, he's been working sixteen-hour days, writing a new book and slaving away at *Symphonic Variations on a Song by Woody Guthrie*, which will receive its world premiere in San Jose, California, with maestro Paul Polivnick conducting the Symphony Silicone Valley. The usual breakneck pace of Amram's schedule has worn out and driven away his most recent girlfriend, an attractive, energetic woman more than thirty years his junior. We sit at Amram's kitchen table in the afternoon light, drinking from huge ceramic mugs filled with chai tea. Uncle Dave has got to be the most approachable celebrity in the known universe, a guy who'd sit and talk with the janitor at the White House for hours on his way to play at a state dinner. When Jack Kerouac went to a party, Amram says, "He'd hang out with the most insecure person there. And that really used to create some bad vibes after he became famous because he was supposed to be the number-one cat; he was supposed to be casing the room to see who he was supposed to talk to. Find the most important person, and snub everyone else."

Amram recalls sitting with John Houseman's wife when the accomplished stage actor and director performed Shakespeare in the park in Avon, Connecticut. The woman sniffed at the makeshift stage and rickety chairs and whispered, "Isn't this embarrassing?"

"Check that out," says David, shaking his head. "As if I'd feel the same way about any kind of art. Kerouac believed in something much deeper and that had more profound value than that shit. He didn't have to join the low life, proletariat, unwashed subhumans in order to feel politically correct or something. Jack desperately wanted to be recognized as a writer and an artist, but he was humble as a person."

In 1959, at the height of their friendship, Amram and Kerouac would walk for hours all over New York City, and one time, after a reading at Brooklyn College, they were riding the subway "and these Puerto Rican guys said, 'Hey *cono mulatto*,' which means 'Hey, a woman's organ, and a person of mixed race,' an affectionate term that people used in the street, and then Jack went over with a bottle and they said, 'Hey, you're all right, baby,' and they hung out with us on the subway. They didn't know that Jack had written *On the Road* or anything. He looked like he'd just gotten off work from cleaning the sewers. But he always knew that everyday people *were* the people, that scientists hadn't discovered the 'über mensch,' and that superman hadn't shown up yet."

That makes me laugh, and I tell Uncle Dave about having lunch with my agent when I arrived in New York a few days earlier. The Union Square Café is long and deep, with a high, shiny wooden bar at the entrance, followed by the narrow dining room, its right-hand wall adorned with the grandiose mural of a one-breasted dame surrounded by baskets filled with ghostly impressionistic apples. The tables are dressed in stiff white linen, each one accented with a tall green bottle of Acqua di Nepi and a spray of flowers. Just as we were being seated, the owner walked by in a pinstriped suit and silk tie, looking like Claude Rains in an old black-and-white movie. In the late fifties, Kerouac used to come to places like the Union Square Café with his editors Malcolm Cowley and Robert Giroux, sip Merlot, and spoon up consommé, thinking it was always going to be like this and that he was on his way to the big time. I have had no such delusions.

Channeling Thoreau, I leaned over and said, "What does one want to dwell near to? Not to many editors and publishers, surely."

After lunch, I sat in an empty office in my agent's building, high above Fifth Avenue, with a slender glass vase filled with pink carnations at my elbow. Below were the granite and sandstone facades of the city, many of the lower rooftops equipped with squat, World War II–era water tanks and potted geraniums; in between the giant city blocks were small green trees running along the avenues.

Jackhammering rose from somewhere on the streets below, and in the distance was the caterwauling of sirens. Far off beyond Third Avenue, at the top of a tower, I could barely make out an American flag streaming in the wind. It looked tiny, a flag for tin soldiers a half mile off. A toy helicopter flew past it, bound for uptown, and in the space of the Hudson River visible to my eye, a slow-moving passenger ferry was chewing its way up the edge of New Jersey. In a letter to his friend Hal Chase, "Prince Hal," that Kerouac wrote from Brooklyn fifty years ago, the boy from Lowell, Mass., gazing upon a similar landscape, said, "My subject as a writer is of course America, and simply, I must know everything about it."

David Amram used to receive letters just like that one, and in the afternoon stillness of his kitchen says, "Kerouac loved America but felt more at home somewhere else. The small and the personal just felt increasingly worthless in America. Jack's stuff is so full of yea-saying and so positive and so human that people get energy from the spirit of it. That's the big part of the equation that intellectuals don't get. It's been beaten out of them, and it's now considered a gauche way of behaving, to be enthusiastic."

Back in his early New York days, Amram was the "party piano player" for the writer George Plimpton and his highbrow friends, a calculated move, "so I could raise my IQ being around all those smart people," he says. (Someone asked me if I was "doing the Plimpton thing," by participating in the action of these books I'm writing, and I said, "If I wanted to do the 'Plimpton thing,' I'd move to Paris, start a snooty literary magazine, and look down my aristocratic nose at everyone.") Just a few years ago, not long before Plimpton died, David was attending the famous writer's birthday party. His own new book, *Offbeat*, was about to be reviewed in the *New York Times*, and when he expressed his enthusiasm for that milestone, one of the snobs in attendance remarked, "You mean you're still excited about something like *that*, at this stage of your career?"

The review was a big thrill for Amram and when he declared that fact, the man walked away in disgust. "What really upset him was that I was grateful," says David.

Tony wanders over to the table as his master is speaking, and the great white bulk of the dog comes to rest against my leg. "Jack understood all that, and his Catholic upbringing made him compassionate toward others. We'd go to these New York literary parties and he'd wear a big silver cross around his neck and back then, as they do now, the Eastern Seaboard intellectuals thought that Roman Catholicism was some kind of funky, low-class thing. That big cross used to spook everybody. William F. Buckley was the only other guy who could be Catholic and get away with it, but he had the fake English accent to excuse that flaw." Amram points out that contrary to popular belief, Kerouac never denounced his Catholicism—rather, he was "preaching religious tolerance by embracing Buddhism."

To Kerouac, contemporary Buddhism was the path to the most Christlike behavior in today's world, according to Amram. "He saw Buddhism as an everyday way to be like Christ, or at least, as close as you could get. If you say that to people, they say, 'Oh, he had a mental problem' or he was trying to start a sect. You know, Jack was the first guy ever to take me to Mass," says Amram, who grew up Jewish on a 160-acre farm in Featerville, Pennsylvania. "One day he just said, 'C'mon, man,' and I went up there and was about to take the wafer, and the other guys with us, the poets Phillip Lamantia and Howard Hart, shook their heads and said 'No.' Jack turned and said, 'That's okay, man, you're with me.' He didn't mean it disrespectfully—he just meant that since we were such good friends, it was okay for me to do that."

For most of the afternoon, dappled sunlight has been filtering through the trees outside, and now the failure of that light has advanced in an even gray tone that eclipses the table. I have to return to the city so I can catch the train back to Boston, and after Uncle Dave clears the table, he bestows several gifts on me: a rare photograph of him, Kerouac, and the artist Dodi Mueller, taken by Robert Frank in 1960, and several music CDs spanning Amram's career.

We bustle outside, throw my loaded backpack in the car, and David guns it over the little bridge and out to the county road. On the way to the Croton-Harmon train station, Amram tells stories of talking baseball with Peewee Reese and painting with Franz Kline. But in the midst of all that glamorous talk, he decides to call our mutual friend, Roger Brunelle, and fishes between the seats for his cell phone.

"*Rogier*," says Amram, reaching Roger's voice mail. He leaves a lengthy message in French, even switching to a different register as he improvises a little dialogue that includes a second character.

Roger Brunelle admires Kerouac in an almost counterintellectual, inarticulate, French Canadian way. Don't get me wrong. Roger is an erudite fellow, speaks Latin and French beautifully, always quoting the poets, and it's only when he talks about Kerouac that he gets tongue-tied. His love for "Ti Jean" is so wild and uncouth, when he gets on the subject he's reduced to making boplike sounds. For that reason alone, he stands in contradistinction to all the Jack Kerouac opportunists who are popping up like fungi out there.

At the train station, we hurry through the ticket line as a few late-arriving passengers wave good-bye to their relatives and two young lovers share a final embrace. The dwindling light gleams on the shiny corrugated side of the train, and it gives out a loud chuff of impending movement just as the conductor pops his head out and yells, "'Board." Standing on the platform with my bag slung over one shoulder, I feel like Humphrey Bogart.

As the train is about to depart, some of the mirth fades out of Uncle Dave, and he turns to rest a hand on my shoulder. "Remember, son, you're not a Civil War reenactor," he says with a little smile. "Just *go*, and have a funkitissimo time of your own."

PART TWO

NEW ORLEANS

1

Eight a.m., and I'm riding in an Amtrak train from South Boston down along the coast to Penn Station in New York. Surfer John Hearin is flying into JFK from Orlando, and I've arranged to meet him in Brooklyn at noon. In the slanted morning light, America is every little estuary and inlet, every isthmus, a million primordial pools along the rail side and one baby deer, in Rhode Island somewhere, alarmed by the passing train.

"Good morning," says a businessman a few rows ahead of me, talking into his cell phone. "I'm on the road."

Junkyards become more numerous, and the streams along the Maine to Pennsylvania line turn brown and murky as the train draws closer to New York. By eleven a.m. we're pulling into the quaint stone station in New Rochelle, NY, looking just as it never did in the old *Dick van Dyke Show*. I half expect Laura Petrie to be waiting there on the platform for me, in her black stretch pants and bumblebee hairdo, the first lady of my wet dreams. When Kerouac was a boy, he loved radio serials like *The Shadow* and *Dark Venture*, and in his adulthood watched television shows and laughed at the antics of comedians like Laurel & Hardy and Sid Caesar and Jerry Lewis; pop culture was part of the culture, and Kerouac wasn't afraid to include those references in his work. (*On the Road* includes cameo appearances by Groucho Marx, Burgess Meredith, Charlie Parker, Slim Gaillard, Jerry Colonna, Veronica Lake, Joel McCrea, W. C. Fields, and many other celebrities of that era.)

Twenty minutes later, I'm inside the buzzing, blooming confusion of Penn Station, where I catch the subway to the bottom of Manhattan and then beneath the East River to Brooklyn. Soon I'm walking up Graham Avenue with my bag, reading the numbers on the storefronts until I find the one I'm looking for and go inside. The bell rings over the entrance to "Najeeb's Falafel and More," and, precisely at noon, Surfer John walks in right behind me and throws his backpack onto one of the plastic chairs.

"Hey, bitch," he says. Surfer is wearing sunglasses, a Michigan Rugby T-shirt, hiking shorts, and sneakers. His blond hair is cut short, and he's tanned from competing on Florida's triathlon circuit. We shake hands and then regard each other, laughing at the inside joke of our friendship.

Najeeb looks up from behind the counter, where he's tuning an oud. "Hello, my friend," he says.

"Told you I'd be back."

"Of course," says the mustachioed proprietor. "Lots of pretty girls in here today."

Surfer picks up a menu, but Najeeb decides we will have mujadd-ara, grape leaves, hummus with onions and pickles, and giant Styrofoam cups of rosewater lemonade. "I don't want American women," he says. "Did you see Sheera? She just left. A beautiful black woman. Think *yeeoww*. I love blacks and Latinas. They are real women, my friends. They don't want to be men, like American chicks. Wearing pants and making money, having 'a career.' I don't under-stand any of that."

He brings out the hot steaming plates of lentils with bulgur wheat and slings them onto the table. Surfer is watching and listen-ing with a huge grin on his face. He has heard my stories about the philosopher king of Graham Avenue and is taking it all in. Najeeb continues his rap: "The bees are disappearing. They say they leave a trail in the air from their—what do you call it?—their beehives. They can go up to a mile away. But they can't find their way back home anymore. So they die. They think it's the"—Najeeb waves his hand in the air—"static from all the cell phones. Do you know that Einstein said if the bees disappeared from the planet, humans would be gone in five years?"

"Big pollinators, the bees," Surfer says, devouring the grape leaves.

Najeeb refills our glasses of lemonade. "We don't deserve the planet, anyway," he says, cocking an eyebrow. "We are aliens here."

My Lebanese friend is a devotee of a late-night radio program dedicated to conspiracy theories, talk of the end times, graven stones pointing to other civilizations far away in the cosmos, and government duplicity over the endless poisoning of our habitat, as well as the ticking atom bomb at the heart of the world that will blow us all to kingdom come, along with our carefully devised tax and bomb shelters. The funny thing is, our complete destruction is imminent, and we're powerless to stop it. But Najeeb Shaheen has a simple strategy for dealing with all this doom-clock and gloom-talk.

"I chase black pussy," he says. "But I only have sex every two months. I have so much reading to do, not to mention performing, teaching, making instruments, and this"—Najeeb gestures toward the small, tidy dining area of his restaurant—"that I cannot possibly find time for more pussy than that."

He's half sitting on the edge of the next table, his hands in his lap, and he looks at us and shakes his head at the indubitable conclusion he has arrived at. "After one hundred and sixty-three women in my life, I am too busy for them now."

2

On our way to pick up the rental car, Surfer and I stop in Lower Manhattan to visit Ground Zero. Neither of us has ever been here before, but I can sense the great profane hole in the city from several blocks away. Gusts of wind carry scraps of paper in little tornadoes across the boulevard, and the cacophony of horns and sirens is like a melancholy echo from the past.

There's this profound moment in *On the Road*, when Kerouac and Cassady are driving through New Jersey toward Manhattan in the wintertime. The car heater is broken, and Cassady is wearing a sweater wrapped around his head to keep warm, and he announces that they are "a band of Arabs coming to blow up New York," proving once more that Kerouac's masterpiece is a treatise of prophetic dimensions.

As we approach the tall chain-link fence that rings the site, Surfer John begins muttering about the blue T-shirted protesters handing out flyers detailing their cockeyed version of what "really happened" on 9/11. A guy tries to hand over one of the pamphlets, and Surfer pulls away like it's a leaf of poison ivy.

"Get lost," he says.

My old roommate is a card-carrying member of the military-industrial complex: he works as a "rocket scientist" at NASA and served as a second lieutenant in the Marines. Finally, cursing under his breath, he picks up one of the flyers that's tumbling along the sidewalk and reads from it. All of 9/11 was a government plot, the Bush administration knew about it ahead of time, and so on. There's a list of "coincidences" that supports the theory that the murder of three thousand Americans was part of a White House conspiracy to wage war on Iraq. With a quick, angry movement, Surfer balls up the flyer and tosses it into a wastebasket before he can get halfway through this litany of bullshit.

"These guys are desecrating a national memorial," says Surfer, who looks like he's going to have a stroke. "It's like marching up and down in front of the Tomb of the Unknown Soldier saying, 'It's all a scam.' What a bunch of fucking idiots."

A majority of the protesters are near the front gate, and Surfer leads me around the side and down a narrow street that parallels the construction site. Most of the work is still being done underground. Gazing through the apertures in the fence, I can see dozens of hard hats on foot and riding on trucks as they journey into the concrete-and-steel underbelly of the next World Trade Center. There's a military precision to what they're doing, and it strikes me that here in Lower Manhattan, America is literally girding itself for another attack.

Beside this underground city is a tiny brick firehouse adorned with a simple plaque. The bronze etching depicts the faces of the half-dozen firefighters from "Ten House" who lost their lives that day. Since we arrived, John has been asking me if I want any pictures of the site. It's here that I ask him to take out his camera.

A lot of my friends back home, including Billy Giarusso and Original Sully and the late Jeff Ness and Glenn Gallant and his brother Cliff, are firefighters. For years, a large group of us would sneak away from our families early on Thanksgiving morning and meet at the Bavarian Club for beers and coffee laced with Bailey's

Irish Cream. We'd shoot pool and listen to high school football games playing on the radio from behind the old wood-paneled bar. One year, just before nine o'clock in the morning, a Vietnam vet and firefighter named Steve Battles came in, surveyed the room, and asked, "How many said they were just running out to Store 24 for bread stuffing?" and everyone laughed.

Seeing the little plaque with the firefighters engraved on it brings that all back for me, and then I'm reminded of something else. Several years ago, I visited one of the death camps in Germany. When I came back, a newspaper editor named Dan Warner, who hired me to write about the trip, said I should tell his readers exactly what I was feeling when I walked out of Dachau. Today, as I stand beside the plaque, my face getting tight around my eyes, I realize that I feel the same way now as I did then: shame mingled with rage. I'm ashamed that human beings would torment other human beings like this, and I'm pissed off that the planners who engineered this act of terrorism seem to have gotten away with it.

3

I'm waiting at the Hertz counter with Surfer over near Battery Park, when some dickweed from New Jersey becomes exasperated over the car he requested not being available. When he finally accepts something else and pulls out and then gets stuck at the automated gate, Surfer and I and the Jamaican woman behind the rental desk all look out through the glass while the guy beeps his horn and pounds on the steering wheel.

"I could write a book about what goes on here," says the Jamaican woman in her musical voice. "I swear, I could write a big, fat book."

Surfer is wrangling all the credit card subterfuge, the maps and insurance waivers, and double indemnities of this fragile planet, as he has always been a Holy Goof for the New Millennium, albeit with a U.S. government security clearance, a PhD in engineering, and a can-do attitude hearkening back to his years in the military. It's the same type of detail management handled by Neal Cassady when he and Kerouac took their trips out of New York, except that Surfer is a version of Cassady with government credentials and a conscience.

Just when it appears we're destined for a minivan, Surfer flashes his Daytona Beach smile, and the Jamaican woman upgrades us to a fancy new Volvo with GPS and a sunroof. Surfer's girlfriend, Ghazala, a brainy Indian American beauty, has put together a varied collection of music for our trip. Blasting Springsteen from the CD player, we pull out of the garage with Surfer at the wheel and go booming over the West Side Highway, past the site of Ground Zero with the cranes soaring high into the clear summer sky. A fifty-foot billboard of Paul Simon's face is staring out at the water pollution control site across the highway. He reigns supreme over Manhattan, the King Kong of singer-songwriters.

To our left, the Hudson River is a choppy blue-gray and dotted with sailboats. Just ahead, the span of the George Washington Bridge is shining like gold in the sun, the tiny cars rolling over it like toys. A month ago, I began hitchhiking from this spot, and gazing out the window I can see an image of my lonesome self beneath the graffiti-strewn wall. The great center tower of the GW Bridge is ominous and thrilling, like some engineering feat of ancient Egypt transplanted into the green-draped walls of the Hudson Valley.

Springsteen is wailing from the speakers and my heart is thumping wildly as Surfer guns the Volvo up and around the ascending ramp and onto the span. There's a giant sign that says Wow! arched over the highway; beyond it, the sky opens up to heavenly golden vistas. We are enjoying a royal entrance into Jersey, with the Bard of Asbury Park blasting his harmonica into the open sky.

Immediately, Surfer and I agree in principle and reality that there should be no agenda and no schedule and that we'll head for New Orleans with no preconceived notions in our minds. Johnny Cash is singing over the radio about balling the jack, and that's what Surfer is doing as we cruise down I-78, zipping along beside a phalanx of fifteen or twenty huge roaring motorcycles ridden by long-haired, tattooed men in cut-off leather vests and denim jackets.

All of a sudden, we have a police escort. Although they appear out of the dust like some kind of Mongol horde, wearing fucked-up-looking German helmets and goggles and knee-high leather boots, they're actually a group of motorcycle-riding cops known as the Renegade Pigs. Shouting over the music, I explain to Surfer how they're constantly getting hassled by the Hell's Angels for wearing their name rocker-style across the backs of their vests. But as one of them said to an Angel up in Laconia, New Hampshire, a couple of years ago, "Fuck you. We're the biggest gang in the country. We're the police."

In a short time, we're riding through the big open valleys of eastern Pennsylvania with giant cloud phalanxes overhead and lush green hills on either side. Back in the late 1930s, Adolf Hitler invited the road commissioners from Pennsylvania up in a dirigible to see the Autobahn. When they returned home, they built the first divided highway in the U.S., 160 miles of four-lane concrete from just west of Harrisburg to twenty miles east of Pittsburgh. The Pennsylvania Turnpike opened in 1940, making it a weird historical fact that our system of roads is based on the Nazis'.

Surfer turns onto a county two-lane, and we pass beneath a long, leafy canopy of trees, with farmland spreading out on both sides. Beneath the shade of a giant oak is a little white clapboard building that serves as headquarters for Seitz Brothers Pest Control. On the brown patch of lawn out front is a portable marquee with "Pest of the Month: Earwigs" written in red plastic letters. Going past, I mention that the clever Seitz brothers are the masters of subliminal advertising. "They got these farmers convinced their places are crawling with earwigs," I say. "You watch. Next month it'll be boll weevils."

Soon there are dozens of cardboard signs at intervals along the roadway announcing the "Kutztown German Festival," which lies somewhere up ahead. Cassady was forever dragging Kerouac to the midget auto races, and I have to laugh when Surfer says, "We gotta go there. Dig the scene. Get our kicks."

"Somewhere along the line the bratwurst will be handed to me," I say, paraphrasing Kerouac's line.

A half-hour later we enter the tree-lined streets of Kutztown, among the neat, well-maintained brick homes and tidy little businesses. Following the signs, we're directed onto a large, grassy hill where we park the car overlooking the fairgrounds. Approaching the gates, we're hailed by a straw-hatted fellow who's about to charge us $12 apiece to gain admission when a man in a yellow T-shirt whispers, "Pssst," from the other side of the fence.

"Sir," he says, reaching through to hand us each something. I look down at a little strip of cardboard with *Admit One Adult* printed on each side. "Somewhere along the line the free ticket will be handed to me," I tell Surfer.

Once we're inside, a guy named Dave in an alpine hat says that we've just entered the 58th Annual Kutztown German Festival, the oldest folk life festival in the U.S. The fairgrounds consist of several large open-air pavilions; a bandstand with a theater of seats rising from it; wooden pens and corrals; a dozen iron-barred paddocks stocked with award-winning cattle and sheep and pigs; and a long, double row of concession stands. One of them offers an "All-You-Can-Eat Wiener Schnitzel Buffet" for $9.99, and a nearby booth operated by the Virginville Grange Club sells red creams and sarsaparilla handed out by plump, blushing women in lace caps.

Surfer and I wander up and down the aisles, looking through the slanted glass cases at the smoked pork jowls and "extra meaty ham shanks"; past the shoo fly pie and funnel cake stands, the leather tooling exhibits and face painting booths and 4-H displays, encompassed by a throng of happy, bovine folks wearing belts and suspenders, Pennsylvania T-shirts, and flowered sun dresses with wide-brimmed summer hats. A lad with red hair plays the banjo under a canopy, singing in a voice that sounds like a gargling cat. Beneath the tin awning of the beer stand a gargantuan fellow is perched on a tiny stool with his yard of ale, the crisscross of his leather suspenders making a large fleshy X in his back.

"You don't see many skinny guys eating wiener schnitzel," I say.

While Surfer goes in search of the mystical bratwurst, I purchase a turkey sandwich and a glass of lemonade and sit in the last row of the theater. On stage, a troupe of amateur thespians in period costume are carrying out some kind of sad farm drama that very few people under the shade of the roof are paying much attention to.

"What's this?" asks Surfer, walking up with his sausage and birch beer.

"The kind of thing that Thornton Wilder would've written if he was Pennsylvania Dutch and suicidal," I say.

We drift toward the western exit of the fairgrounds. A man in lederhosen is playing an accordion under the tin roof where the banjo player had been. He's bawling out a patriotic song—*this is my country*—and a quartet of old men in VFW caps, a woman in a little motorized cart, and several chubby preadolescent girls with ribbons in their hair are nearby, listening to the music with reverential looks on their faces. It occurs to me, as I watch the picnickers on the adjoining hillside tearing into their kielbasa and deep-fried chocolate cheesecake, that I haven't seen a single police officer or even a security guard at the fairgrounds, despite the fact that there are thousands of people here—and they're serving liquor.

Just last week I was walking around a tiny carnival in Lynn, Massachusetts, with Bob Hogan, a Lynn police detective, alongside dozens of other uniformed and plainclothes cops who were in attendance. Gang kids were flashing signs and threatening one another, and the pathetic little midway had an undercurrent of dread running through it. Apparently, the Pennsylvania Germans are a God-fearing, law-abiding bunch of folks, and that's nothing to sneeze at.

4

Leaving the fairgrounds, Surfer decides not to backtrack to the two-lane highway, and we end up on a sun-dappled country lane. With a light afternoon breeze coming in the windows, we roll along through rural farm country accompanied by a live recording of Stan Getz tootling on his saxophone. The woman's voice built into the GPS keeps telling us to take a U-turn, that we've gone the wrong way.

"I'm going with my instincts on this one," says Surfer.

"Fuck technology," I say, cracking open a bottle of green tea from our supply bag. "America was built on instinct. On improvisation. Would Stan Getz color inside the lines just because this pushy, so-called expert of a GPS woman told him to? I think not."

The next several minutes are lost in profane discussion of the various imaginary qualities possessed by the woman buried within the guts of the Volvo. Despite the repressed sexuality in her tone of voice, Surfer and I speculate that she does indeed have an immense libido and must therefore maintain a businesslike demeanor or risk being fired by the German auto manufacturer that has employed her. We also determine that if global positioning systems had been available in 1947, the woman's precise directions and tacit unavailability probably would have driven Neal Cassady insane. Out on some Pennsylvania road in the middle of the night, old Neal would have torn that Hudson apart, trying to get at her.

Just then the GPS woman intones, "When possible, make a legal U-turn."

"Don't listen to her, Surf. She doesn't know what she's talking about. If Najeeb was here, and I have no idea why he isn't, he would say she's a white woman trying to assert her power over us. I say: dump her."

Surfer nods his head, smiling broadly with his perfect teeth. "We don't need no stinkin' GPS," he says.

But with her next command, the disembodied woman guides us back onto Route 30. "We're getting back together with her," I say.

The afternoon has entered its decline. On the outskirts of Paradise Township, an Amish family passes in the other direction, a husband and his young wife with their two young daughters, seated primly on the benches of a horse-drawn cart. Beyond them, cemeteries and well-groomed farms fill the landscape, marked by an occasional riderless tractor. The corn is already as high as a mule's eye and spread as far as the horizon in every direction. Shafts of light fall between the oak trees that line Route 30, teeming with motes of pollen rising from the fields.

We pass a sign for "Malleable Road" and then cross a long low bridge over the mighty Susquehanna. The drone of insects reigns, overcome by the sound of a motorcycle ascending through its gears. Suddenly, a kid riding a low-slung Japanese bike passes us and zooms ahead. Approximately seventy-five yards out, he lifts the bike into a long wheel stand, showing off for us, the noise of his engine cleaving the silence. When he comes out of the wheelie, the front tire lands wrong, and suddenly the bike swerves back and forth, the kid swinging like a rag doll, trying to hang on. Everything goes into slow motion, and the motorcyclist is contorted into various spastic tableaus against the roseate sky of an impending sunset. Death looms by the side of the road, and at the last possible instant somehow the kid rights the bike, gears down, and then roars into the distance.

"Man, I thought he was going to bite it," says Surfer, and we drive on, supercharged with adrenaline.

5

Just after sunrise, I'm sitting on a wall outside the gates of the Gettysburg National Cemetery, writing in my notebook. In his 1948 journal, Kerouac made note of the mathematical formula aimed at calculating his "batting average," which was founded on how many words he got down on paper each day. Right now I'm batting about .280, and as soon as I finish writing I'll go looking for a workout; with my leg so banged up, I have to get creative. This morning, Surfer and I are about to enter the land of the honored dead, where we will tour the park on mountain bikes.

After consulting our map, Surfer and I mount the rented bikes and head off down the road, skirting the cemetery and riding through town and then twice crossing a main thoroughfare before entering the park. On this very ground, the Union and Confederate armies fought a bloody set piece that resulted in more than fifty thousand casualties. Reynolds Avenue is a broad, paved street lined with eerie-looking monuments, obelisks and tablets, and figured bronze statues put up at strategic points along the way to commemorate individual units or momentous occurrences in the battle. Each monument is bigger and more elaborate than the next. It plays out like an obscene competition between the states; a grudge that as everyone knows will last forever, between those who want to forget what happened here and those who never will.

On Cemetery Ridge, we park the bicycles and climb to the top of a four-story viewing platform overlooking the town of Gettysburg and the treed hills, ridges, plains, grassy fields, and stone walls that formed the stage for the bloody deeds of July 1, 1863, exactly 144 years ago. This is where Americans turned killing other Americans into a brutal and efficient mechanized activity.

Standing in the midst of a group of tourists from Indiana, a park guide is describing Confederate general Alfred Iverson's charge at the stone wall, where concealed Union infantry, the dreaded "black hats," fired a curtain of lead "from eighty yards, dropping the Confederates in perfectly even rows."

The heels of the dead formed a straight line, and Iverson had what amounted to a nervous breakdown when he visited the field later that day. Shortly thereafter, he was relieved of his command, "which was good for his men," says the guide.

As usual, Surfer is equipped with a guidebook, a map, and his solid-gold sense of direction, and we diverge from the Indiana tourists as quickly as possible and make our own way among the battle sites. It's early morning, and the mist is rising from the lowlands, and not many visitors are about. On Seminary Ridge, where Pickett's ill-fated assault began, you can hear the conversations between the proud, stubborn, and doomed General Pickett and his equally brave but more circumspect commander, General James E. Longstreet. "*May I make the assault, sir?*" asked Pickett. Longstreet couldn't bring himself to reply and only nodded.

The Confederate States Army concentrated their attention on a copse of trees that's only three-quarters of a mile away from where we're standing, under a vaulted blue sky that's striated with clouds. The Confederates had won two years' worth of battles and felt the end was in sight. "Home's on the other side of those trees, boys," said one of the regulars.

Leaning beside our mountain bikes in the early morning sunshine, I tell Surfer that I once dated General Longstreet's great-great-great-great-granddaughter, a lissome blond girl I met in my twenties while vacationing in the White Mountains. Surfer is intrigued by my brush with history until I admit that on our first date, I took the beautiful young Longstreet girl to a Three Stooges festival at an outdoor bar in North Conway, New Hampshire, and that, in the wake of this decision, she never returned any of my calls.

"That was a strategic blunder of historic proportions," says Surfer, pushing his bicycle over the grassy hummocks of the battlefield.

This end of the park is deserted at such an early hour, the ground mist heavy over the roadway and the hum of insects rising from the meadows surrounding us on all sides. Turning the corner of West Confederate Avenue, we come upon a stout, bespectacled gent in an open gray tunic and black kepi. With the stub of a cigar in his teeth, he's walking along the side of the road carrying an Enfield rifle, occasionally pausing to consult his map. There's no one else around.

Captain Steve of the First Maryland Battalion, Company A, greets us without comment and stands in the knee-high weeds studying the tree line to the north, where the Union infantry was hidden. Expressing regret at the weather, which is overcast and humid, he notes that on July 2, 1863, these same conditions formed a "sound inversion," silencing General Longstreet's artillery barrage to the ears of the one-legged General Richard Stoddard Ewell and his men, preventing them from advancing beneath its cover to take the Union flank. As a result, Captain Steve says with visible discomfort, he and the other brave men of the First Maryland didn't attack until much later, when Colonel Joshua Chamberlain was in place on the ridge ahead, which lost them the battle and led to the cause's ignominious defeat.

Under our gentle questioning, Captain Steve admits that he's actually a modern-day, fifty-two-year-old, college-educated "safety professional" from Waynesboro, PA, but that he spends more than six hundred hours per year on his hobby. His authentic-looking uniform was handmade from rough gray cloth by a "suttler," and the buttons and seams have been weathered by all the time he has spent outdoors, reenacting battles and living in the field.

Steve says that he and his Civil War buddies attend these reenactments to have some fun and recall the sacrifices made by the men who fought at Gettysburg and elsewhere. Other groups, which he calls "the hard-cores," arrive early at the battle sites, sleep on the ground, and eat dried rations from their haversacks. "They hate us because we always ask 'em, 'How did you get here? By car, just like we did,'" says Steve. "The hard-cores will sit out in the field, starving themselves, eating 'green bacon.' Rancid bacon. Why?"

Politics affect the community of reenactors, just as they affect every other human endeavor. In fact, says Captain Steve, there are "three Robert E. Lees and four Grants" in the area, and the men who get to portray these august gentlemen at Gettysburg are not necessarily those who most resemble them in appearance and bearing, merely those who've developed the best connections. Shaking my head, I glance over at Surfer and say, "Even in the Civil War, it's who you know."

While we're talking, a station wagon arrives on the scene, and the occupants swarm out of the car and begin firing questions at Captain Steve and taking his photograph. They're tourists from Michigan, and they take turns posing beside the Confederate officer, who stands at parade rest with a historic scowl furrowing his brow. Surfer and I mount our bicycles and ride off. But as I take a last look at Captain Steve, what David Amram said at the train station comes back to me, and I have to laugh and shake my head. Surfer and I are not trying to imitate Sal and Dean or reenact the frenetic journeys they took up and down and across the continent in 1947–1949. We're merely digging the scene and getting our kicks, having a funkitissimo time of our own.

6

By 5:30 p.m., we're highballing down I-81 through Chambersburg, PA, across a snippet of Maryland and then a piece of West Virginia into Virginia itself. In the slanted evening light, Woody Guthrie is singing "This Land Is Your Land" as we approach the Blue Ridge Mountains. At a crossroads, we take U.S. 522 through North Virginia, heading for Charlottesville, with giant cornfields, cow pastures, and low brown fences stretching away as far as the eye can see. Surfer and I've been all over the world together, in more than twenty countries, and when we get to this hour, with fading light and dry air and familiar old songs pouring from the radio, we just want to keep going, into the night and what's out there.

Surfer turns onto 231 South, through hillside farms and deep green valleys, as lush as the African veldt. It's unseasonably cool, only seventy degrees, and at 9 p.m. we drive into Charlottesville. Across from the University of Virginia campus, we stop at a small, cozy restaurant called the Virginian, established in 1923. Wooden booths line the right-hand wall, and a huge mirrored bar occupies much of the left side of the narrow space. In the twenties they jitterbugged in the aisle, and in the 1950s letter sweater–wearing heroes piled in after the football games with their bouffant-haired sweethearts in poodle skirts and angora sweaters.

We order a pair of tall, sweating bottles of Star Hill Pale Ale and sit listening to James Brown and Archie Bell and the Drells. A picture of the joint in the old days hangs above us on the dark wood wall, the bartenders in jackets and ties with their hair oiled and shiny.

Our waitress is a syrup-voiced girl with brown hair and a heart-shaped face and deep green eyes. "How do y'all like Virginia so far?" she asks, bringing us another round of beers. Her sunny disposition reminds me of Cassady's pronouncement in *On the Road* after leaving what he called "frosty fagtown New York," highballing toward William Burroughs's place in Louisiana: "I mean, man, I dig the South. I know it in and out—"

"I like it just fine," says Surfer, grinning at her. "Real fine."

7

At six-thirty the next morning a corpulent young woman unlocks the gate to the dank little pool at the Econo Lodge where we're staying. Pulling on my goggles and flapping my arms to stay warm, I dive into the pool and begin swimming laps in the cold, overly chlorinated water. Around 7 a.m. a middle-aged black man begins loading his sales cases into an old station wagon beside the raised concrete berm of the pool. As I swim, the man heads back for another case; his image recedes with each stroke, each breath, my head tilting out, creating a series of still photos of the man, dressed in a pair of brown slacks and a cream-colored shirt, moving away from me toward the office. I'm creating some kind of folk art in my head: waterborne, time-lapse photography, featuring this anonymous, hardworking man and how he honors God and his family with the elbow-breaking labors of his sad career.

When I emerge dripping and invigorated from the pool, the salesman is gone, and Surfer is back from his morning run and is talking to one of our neighbors. David is a wizened old West Virginian in a foam-billed USA ball cap with an eagle printed on it. Dressed in khaki overalls and a work shirt, he's half-buried in the engine of an old pickup truck, trying to remove the starter. David has already explained to Surfer that twice a month he drives the three and a half hours from Oak Hill, W. VA., to bring his wife here, to the teaching hospital at the University of Virginia. Although the rebuilt starter in his truck is fairly new, it has gone bad, and the couple is in danger of missing their appointment.

David's wife, Joanne, is sitting in the cab of the truck patiently reading a magazine while her husband bangs away at the starter. A large, soft-faced woman with eyeglasses on a chain around her neck, she wears a baseball cap over her wispy hair. I'm shivering on the pavement in front of our room, and as I go inside to clean up, I hear Surfer offering David and his wife a ride to the hospital.

"No, thank you, sir," says David. "I gotta get this ol' truck of mine goin' and get my wife to the horse-pull [hospital]."

Near the start of *On the Road* Kerouac talks about his first great ride, in a flatbed truck across the rangelands of Wyoming and his encounter with Mississippi Gene, a small dark wiry gent with a soft, countrified way of speaking. David is a lot like him: the kind of guy you meet on your way to nowhere special, someone you might talk to for fifteen minutes, but in that quarter hour and long afterward it feels like you've known him your entire life.

A while later, we notice David's wife is still sitting in the truck, but he's nowhere to be seen.

Through the open window, Joanne says that the truck needs another starter and that her husband has "set out walkin'" for the auto parts store two and a half miles away. They're more than an hour late for Joanne's doctor's appointment, and looking at her now, it's plain that she's suffering from cancer. Surfer and I jump into the Volvo and go looking for David.

The commercial strip beyond the hotel is crowded with fast-food restaurants, tire stores, and warehouses. It's six lanes across, with a steel divider in the center and no pedestrian way. Searching on both sides, we finally come upon David more than a mile from the Econo Lodge, his lean figure bent slightly at the waist, plodding along in the breakdown lane.

Surfer pulls to the curb just ahead of him, and I wave from the passenger side. After he recognizes us, David climbs into the backseat, wiping his face with a handkerchief. "Twenty-three minutes I been walkin'," he says, consulting his watch. "I was gonna make it, too."

It has grown quite warm by mid-morning, and David is grateful for the ride. The starter in his truck is only a few months old, and he's hopeful that the computer at the parts store will bear that information and that he'll get another one at no cost. "Already paid for it oncet," he says.

David is more talkative now, and he tells us that he drives a cab and a school bus back in Oak Hill. He pronounces the word *fire* as "fa-hr" and *arrow* as "ar-rah"; and, of course, the hospital is the "horse-pull." He's a crusty old gent, his Adam's apple protruding from his neck and his torso shriveled to the size of a boy's through a lifetime of hard work. He wears a little moustache that hangs over his lip, disguising a set of dark and broken teeth. And there's a wiry tension to his limbs that keeps his hands moving up and down on the caps of his knees while he sits there, gazing straight ahead. When asked how old he is, David says, "Well, I'm past the halfway point, I can say that."

I persist in asking him, and finally he replies, "If the halfway point is fifty, I ain't gonna see that again."

Originally, I thought David was in his late sixties or early seventies, and I'm surprised to learn that he's only a few years older than I am. It's the condition of his teeth and his eyes, which are small and weak and sunken into his head, that's deceiving. When I look at him closely, he's got the lean, vascular body of a master athlete, every ounce of fat squeezed out of him by the constant motion of his Herculean endeavors, which occupy him from sun up to sun down. But he's not running in a race or crossing the ocean in a kayak. David is up there in the hills of West Virginia, fighting for his life.

When we reach the appropriate strip mall, Surfer goes into the auto parts store with David, and I cross the huge parking lot toward a natural foods market where I can replenish our supply bag. In a half hour, we reconvene beside the Volvo, and David is already in the backseat, cradling a rebuilt starter in his arms like an infant.

"The one feller said I had to pay for it," says David. "But I went straight for the manager. I told him to look in that computer of his and keep looking." The old West Virginian nods his head. "I was right."

Clutching the starter, David hums in a low, melodious tone that reminds me of Mississippi Gene in the bed of that rusty truck, singing about the "purty little girl" he left behind somewhere. Like that old '40s hobo, David's prospects are slim and his worries proliferating.

Back at the motel, David spreads a plastic apron filled with his tools over the side of the truck and leans into the yawning space beneath the hood. His feet dangle in the air. Within minutes, he has bolted the new starter into place and emerges, wiping his hand on a rag.

"Y'all have a safe trip to North Carolina," he says. "How much do I owe you?"

Surfer smiles and tells him, "Nothing," and begins loading up the back of the Volvo. While David fusses with the truck, Joanne gets out and comes around beside me, where I inhale her scent: cherry lozenges mixed with perspiration.

It's been a tough stretch, she admits. They lost their thirty-one-year-old daughter in a car wreck last year, leaving their two young grandchildren with no mother. With little inflection in her voice,

Joanne says that she has terminal cancer, melanoma, and that it's been "spreading like wild fa-hr."

Joanne is three hours late for her appointment at the hospital, and David has gone double-timing to their room to fetch the one suitcase they have brought with them to Charlottesville. "I just want to thank you boys for helping us," says Joanne, turning to me.

I take her weak-limbed, puffy body into my arms. "You and your family will be in my prayers tonight," I tell her.

8

We're traveling east on I-64 toward Rocky Mount, North Carolina, where Kerouac often visited his sister and her family. Caroline "Nin" Kerouac Blake was three years older than Jack, married to her second husband, Paul, who had played college football like his brother-in-law. Kerouac's visits to their home with Neal Cassady and Al Hinkle in *On the Road* illustrate the manic sense of motion that possessed Cassady, as they drove back and forth to New York City with a carload of furniture in less than thirty hours.

It's much hotter today than yesterday, and there's bluegrass on the radio. On a nondescript stretch of highway just outside Richmond, Virginia, we pass the corporate headquarters of tobacco giant Phillip Morris, with a huge Marlboro obelisk on the front lawn. It brings back Kerouac, in his '48 journal, railing against IBM and factories and punch clocks. My mother died a long, slow death from emphysema, and I have about as much tolerance for the tobacco purveyors in this country as I have for the Nazis. "They should put up a sign, like at McDonald's. 'Hey, Philip Morris, killing Americans ten thousand at a time,'" I say, and Surfer knows me well enough to let it pass.

Not long after suppertime we enter Rocky Mount, which Kerouac refers to as Testament, Virginia, in the 1957 version of *On the Road*. "You have arrived," says the GPS lady.

"Yeah. In the asshole of the Western world," says Surfer, peering over the wheel.

It sure doesn't look like much, but here Kerouac enjoyed several brief respites from his travels—the sort of humble home life he sought but never really found. Low brick homes fronted by weedy lawns and abandoned-looking shotgun shacks line the roadway on either side. A short way along is the beat-looking downtown, made up of empty storefronts, ratty old men's bars, and roofless, burned-out department stores. A railway line runs straight along the main drag, and we get hung up for ten minutes at one of the crossings as a freight train roars past: dozens of greasy CSX cars, their wheels groaning, bells ringing, and the heavy *clack-clack-clack* of the weighed-down coal cars bumping over the traverses.

Surfer parks in front of a Rexall drugstore, and we go inside to look around. My first job ever, I worked behind the counter at the Rexall in our little town square. My shift was all day Sunday, nine hours total, for a measly $1.25 an hour. My hockey teammates would come in to steal cigarettes and goof on me; the ninth-grade girls I coveted in their hip-hugging bellbottoms and tight tops, their eyes outlined in blue mascara, laughing at my "professional demeanor" and the monogrammed smock I was compelled to wear. When the place was empty, Ted, the substitute pharmacist, an aging, silver-haired Don Juan who dressed like a swell, would come down from the raised poop deck of the pharmacy. Propping open the back door, he'd smoke Winstons like they were going out of style and tell me about all the housewives he was banging on his days off. Those Sunday afternoons in Methuen were as long as hell.

Inside the Rocky Mount drugstore, two elderly black women are working behind the counter, which is crowded with red-and-white-striped packages of tobacco, dusty Mars bars, Sen-Sen, foil tubes of antacid, and various sizes and shades of panty hose stacked up in little plastic eggs. There's one long aisle down the center that stretches away into the shadows, past the rotating wire rack filled with Harlequin romances, the boxes of electric fans and tipped-over prosthetic limbs, and the mannequins dressed in fishing vests and waders that crowd the rear of the store.

"Welcome to the land that time forgot," I whisper to Surfer.

He approaches the two women, smiles about twenty grand's worth, and asks, "Can y'all tell us the best place to have barbecue in town?"

After extensive parliamentary debate, the two women behind the counter reach their decision: we must proceed to Lee-roy's Big Pit BBQ, on the far side of the railroad tracks. Surfer thanks the ladies for their advice, and we exit the premises.

Four blocks from the drugstore we find Lee-roy's Big Pit, a tiny white-brick place with cows and chickens painted in a row across the front windows. Surfer turns into the lot, and just as we're about to disembark, I throw my arm across his chest and point to the hand-written sign on the front door that says "Close," and Surfer curses and then restarts the car.

On the way out of town we drive by a group of idle teenage boys in front of Asso Grocery and on past the Freedom Temple of Inner Peace and the Gus Z. Lancaster Junkyard and the Nahunta Pork Center, a crowned pig adorning its sign.

A few miles away on Highway 301 is Parker Barbecue, a low-slung clapboard building with a parking lot that's nearly full. "That's it," says Surfer. Inside, a half-dozen teenage waiters in paper hats and long white aprons stand against the far wall, detaching, one by one, to escort patrons to their tables. The smell of broiling meat emanates from the kitchen as we're led to a wooden table with a white Formica top.

Our waiter is a tall, shy kid with glasses and blotchy skin who says, "Yes, sir," a lot and brings us tumblers of sweet tea without being asked. Five minutes later he carries out a tray loaded with pulled Southern barbecue. As our stomachs fill up and we ascend Maslow's Hierarchy of Needs, the local color begins to bloom. A short distance away, there's a gigantic man in bib overalls with his plain-faced wife and three silent young daughters, eating barbecued ribs in synchro-nization and wiping their mouths with paper napkins. A minister in a frock coat enjoys a glass of iced tea with a lady from the church, and three athletic-looking high school boys go sauntering past our table, headed for their favorite spot by the windows.

There's a lovely young girl working the cash register, green-eyed and buxom with honey-colored hair and soft red lips. She's our hostess for the evening, and, somehow, in our minds and the minds of the lanky young waiters who cast surreptitious glances at her, the crowned princess of Parker Barbecue, the axis on which turns the whole experience of sweet tea and cornbread and turnip greens. I secretly believe she is the sweetest and loveliest of the wild Parker girls, the primary heiress to this pork-filled gold mine. And for however long she has held sway here, this twenty-five- or twenty-six-year-old beauty has uttered her soft commands and marveled at the result. Hearts leap, eager boys run to the kitchen and back, customers tip their hats and return in droves.

As we hover there by the little counter, waiting to settle the bill, even two experienced hands like Surfer and me fall under her spell. Kerouac himself announced in his journal that he was tired of being a "subway street corner romeo" and was looking for a girl like the princess of Parker Barbecue. She's wearing a man's white dress shirt with the top three buttons undone and we can't help but stare into the dark sweet shadow between her upright breasts.

"How did y'all like the barbecue?" asks the princess, handing over our change.

"Just fine," says Surfer, grinning like an idiot. "Real fine."

Crossing the parking lot, we're each occupied by wistful Carolina thoughts. Chewing his toothpick, my old roommate unlocks the car door, swings into the driver's seat, and fires up the engine.

"Those things were singing to me," says Surfer, who on previous occasions too numerous to account for in this record has heeded the siren's song.

9

From Parker's Barbecue we drive a straight line to Dunn, North Carolina, a little town outside Fayetteville where Jack and Neal and Al Hinkle and Louanne stopped in 1949. There was a young kid who they'd picked up hitchhiking, and he said his aunt had a grocery store and that he could get some money from her. There was a store but no aunt, and they left the kid there, with his "disordered feverish mind." We creep along the broken pavement of the main drag, looking for a place to restock our bag of supplies. The Stop 'n' Go is a bright green cinder-block building with a crooked door and a little bell that erupts when you open it. Inside is a warped wooden floor and dingy shelves lined with pork cracklings, malt liquor, and chewing tobacco. I reach deep into the cooler for bottles of water and green tea and open up a jar on the counter and take out a handful of dusty pretzels.

"What's new?" I ask the fellow at the register.

"Same old, same old," he says. The proprietor is a tall man in his early sixties, his belly hanging at his belt like a sandbag as he tallies up my purchases. He's wearing a gray sweater vest, and when he bends over, I can see the leather strap of a gun belt running beneath his armpit.

When I emerge from the store, Surfer is facing a predicament of his own. Somehow a panhandler has gotten between him and the open door of the car. She's a chunky black woman, somewhere around forty years old, dressed in a stained cotton tank top and fluorescent pink bicycle shorts. The woman has two teeth missing in front and reeks of alcohol. She insists she needs money to buy her child some medicine, and Surfer is being polite but firm in saying that he's not going to give her any.

A short ways down the block two young black men in do-rags hear the rising tenor of the woman's voice and begin to stare in our direction. The panhandler sees them walking toward us, and her entreaties grow more urgent; it's unclear what action the interlopers are going to take, but we don't want to stick around to find out.

Although the panhandler is intent on keeping Surfer from getting into the driver's seat, with a nifty little move he opens the door a few inches wider, lifts her hand from the window top, and ducks inside. He shoots a look over at me, and I jump in the other side, and he immediately backs out of the parking space and drives away.

"I'm done with Dunn," he says.

10

We're back on the road by 7:30 a.m. on a beautiful, sunny Fourth of July. We pass over the slow-moving gray-green band of the Shenandoah River, the hazy emerald hills of central Georgia stretching away on either side. Of course, music accompanies us everywhere. Like a couple of footloose bastards out of Carolina, late into the evening we heard the syncopated breathiness of "Time" from Pink Floyd's *Dark Side of the Moon*. We drove into Georgia as the sun came up, and it was "Fat Bottom Girls" by Queen, long green fields stretching into the shadows, delineated by rows of ancient mossy trees. Then I turned up the volume on an old hit by Boston, and sang along with Iggy Pop's "Lust for Life."

When people ask me what I would like readers to think or do after they're finished with something I've written, the question always throws me a little, because I don't want them to "think" or "do" anything. In his journal, Kerouac said that he admired guys like Mark Twain, who had piloted steamboats and dug for silver and roamed the West, writing what he felt like writing and not what "literature" demanded of him. When I read something that's really good, it reminds me of driving in my car late at night when suddenly a tune comes on the radio that I haven't heard in a while, and that calls to mind a specific period in my life and the people and events from an era that I love and cherish, even if I haven't thought about them in quite some time. The perfect song at the perfect time makes me *feel* a certain way; I can't quite describe it, but I know that when I read *On the Road* those many years ago and an hour or so later heard Springsteen's "Thunder Road" coming in from some obscure radio station in Maine, I was filled with homesick longing, as well as a type of understanding about the world and my place in it that was neither cognitive nor operational.

So far, we've traveled over a thousand miles, deep into rural America, and haven't seen a single hitchhiker. In Kerouac's time, the roads were filled with victorious ex-GIs, and motorists were happy to give them a lift. Today, conditions are perfect for these hoboes of the open horizon: rural towns a short distance apart, day laborers on the highway and in the fields, and hardly a sheriff in sight. But there's this feeling that we have the road all to ourselves.

We turn south on 441 in Madison, GA, a two-lane road slicing through the dense brush of the country. Live oaks are draped against the façades of graceful homes, and farmhouses equipped with ironbound water tanks and wide front porches appear here and there in the thickly wooded landscape. At a bend in the road comes Pettigrew Service, a tin shack painted white and rusted at the seams; an abandoned one-pump gas station with a gigantic Rorschach of cracked asphalt and weeds growing in the doorway. *O, where have you gone, Mr. Pettigrew?*

Entering Putnam County, we pass a sign marking the population with the words "Pecan Syrup" underneath. A short while later, Surfer pulls up at a ramshackle fruit stand on the side of the road in Eatonton, advertising "Syrups, Jellies, Peaches, Apple Tomato Cider" in giant red letters across the bottom. The proprietress is a wily, gray-haired woman "name Teri-Lynn" with one pair of glasses perched on her nose and another pair on her head. There's something asymmetrical about her face—she looks like a remedial Picasso.

Surfer has a weakness for boiled peanuts and buys a cup while asking Teri-Lynn to point out the best route to La Grange, Georgia, over on the border with Alabama.

"Go back yonder-way to Route Sixteen," she says, indicating that we should turn around and backtrack several miles when our map shows there's two other routes waiting just ahead. "That'n be your best way."

When I ask her how much the peaches are by the pound, Teri-Lynn shakes her head. "It's got to come in a bag, a bin, or a basket," she says, stirring the giant steel vat of peanuts.

Dressed in a sleeveless plaid blouse and black shorts, Teri-Lynn is in her early seventies but hale and strong, with a loose wattle hanging from her neck and a birdlike demeanor. After handing over a couple of dollars, I reach into the bag and eat one of the small hairy peaches and then wind up and fire the pit across the road into the trees. With a sly wink, Teri-Lynn tells us to watch out for the "po-lice" over in La Grange. When I ask her why two law-abiding citizens would ever have to worry about law enforcement in any city or town in America, she gives me a cagey look, like I'm trying to deceive her.

"They country," Teri-Lynn says. "They got no law 'cept what they do their own-selves."

It's funny when Kerouac says in *On the Road* that the police are involved in psychological warfare against those who aren't frightened by them and their "imposing papers and threats." Teri-Lynn is friendly enough, as far as that goes, but there's something odd in her manner. While Surfer is talking to her, it occurs to me that all the *wonder* and the *love* and the *joy* peculiar to the human race have been pressed out of her by a machine like the ones that press the oil out of olives. Standing here all day by the side of the road has done it to her. She's been flattened somehow.

Stirring her vat with a wooden paddle, Teri-Lynn tells us about a chipmunk living under the shack that comes up and "takes a lil bite out of each of them peaches, if'n I don't watch for him." With a sinister laugh, she brings up the paddle and gives it a little shake, leaving the distinct impression that she's no animal rights activist.

Apprised of our notion to go swimming in La Grange, the fruit-stand lady warns that there are snakes and bull gators in that region of western Georgia, which Surfer rolls his eyes at. Furthermore, she no longer swims in the local lakes because the catfish have "heads as big as shovels" and have been known to eat people. "I never swim less I can see the bottom," she says, which seems to be her life's philosophy as much as her bathing policy.

We leave her sorting the peaches in little baskets and tending her peanut vat, ever watchful of marauding chipmunks on this hot Georgia Fourth of July morning.

But before we go, Teri-Lynn warns us again about the po-lice. "They con artists," she says. "The law is whatever they say it is."

"That's all right," I reply, winking at her. "I was born on a Tuesday, but it wasn't last Tuesday."

Teri-Lynn huffs at this declaration. "I hope you wasn't," she says.

11

The road winds through scrub and swale and piney woods—cows grazing in squared-off pastures and diving floats sitting peacefully in the middle of still, grass encircled ponds. Before noon, we enter the quiet town square of Monticello, Georgia: "Home of Trisha Yearwood," the country recording artist. Large, whitewashed homes framed by Ionic columns line the streets, terminating at the four-story brick courthouse and a grassy town square that contains the obligatory CSA monument.

Surfer and I emerge from the car to stretch our legs. The square is deserted, and all its shops are closed, including the diner, coin laundry, and tobacco store. Although it's still quite early, wooden DPW horses and spent firecracker casings and the confetti that litters the pavement indicate that the July 4th parade has already taken place. On their way to Louisiana in *On the Road*, Kerouac and Cassady had to wait for Harry Truman's inaugural parade to pass and were touched by the final item in a long line of war matériel: a tiny, forlorn lifeboat. "Good old Harry," said Cassady. "That must be his own boat."

Here in small-town Georgia, the war monument is a granite spire flanked by the statues of an enlisted man and a Confederate officer standing on a pedestal halfway up. The base contains four oxidized panels engraved with the names of Monticello's honored dead from the War of the Rebellion. Examining the list, Surfer points out that there's no accompanying tribute marking those who served in the Great War or World War II.

"I'd have to guess that a lot of boys from around here died in France, and on Guadalcanal, or at Khe Sanh, for that matter," says the ex-Marine, who has visited the military cemeteries at Normandy and elsewhere. "Where are their names?"

On the way back to the car, Surfer says, "It's always that way in the South: like there was only one war."

The sky is filled with high, puffy cumulus clouds against an indigo sky. A sign on the side of the road says "Sons of the Confederate Veterans. Join Now!" and is emblazoned with the battle flag. Every town along Route 16 has a six-story water tower and a Confederate monument. In Griffin, we pass a restaurant named the "Chick-Fil-A Dwarf House," and on the strength of the name, I shudder to think what goes on there. Wild horse and burro adoption services are advertised on the radio. In Newman, which is nicknamed, somewhat redundantly, "the City of Homes," antebellum mansions protected by shade trees line the roadway, interrupted by occasional stucco homes that look like something straight out of a movie about Texas.

Nearing La Grange, we drive alongside banks of red Georgia clay and end up at Pyne Road Park for the 27th Annual Fireworks Show, sponsored by the Parks and Recreation Department of Troup County. At the outskirts of the park, we pay the five-dollar entry fee, and a policeman wearing a flat-brimmed hat waves us through. Surfer and I arrive in early afternoon and decide to take a long swim across West Point Lake, Teri-Lynn's warnings be damned. After changing in the car and ditching the keys beneath a rock, we choose a spot on the opposite shore about a half mile away.

"Maintain situational awareness at all times," says Surfer. He indicates the power boats and Jet Skis that are zooming up and down the lake. "They're not looking for you, so you have to look for them."

We wade in to our knees, reach down to splash ourselves like it's holy water, and then don goggles and set off. A hundred yards out, staring into the gray-green abyss, I imagine catfish as big as manatees, sinister water snakes, and renegade bull alligators that have crept into West Point Lake from what Teri-Lynn had called "swampy Alabama."

It doesn't help that the water is as warm as pea soup, and I'm crossing a boat channel that's at least forty feet deep by the sounding ropes. Jet Skis buzz at the edge of my consciousness as I stroke through the foamy green water. I have to keep popping my head up, scanning for boats, and that exercise, combined with the chop from their wakes, interrupts my rhythm. Halfway across the inlet, I swim too close to a rocky point and smash my foot on a submerged boulder and then stand up for a moment in the waist-deep water. My big toe is bleeding profusely, and I can't see John anywhere.

He's a big boy, having completed many open-water swims in various triathlons up and down the East Coast. So I rub the fog out of my goggles and resume swimming. There are no turns to make, but after all the time I've spent swimming in a pool, I have trouble remaining on a straight course. When I reach the far side of the lake, I wade up on the beach and look up and down the channel, as well as the broad plain of the lake, searching for John. No luck. Then I dive back in and begin heading for the rocky beach where we originally launched ourselves.

A hundred yards out Surfer comes swimming up alongside, and we break off and start treading water, our heads bobbing on the surface just a couple of feet apart.

"It took me awhile to find your head sticking out," says Surfer. He points at the beach he has swum to, which is quite a bit farther along the inlet than where I landed. "Twenty minutes to there; I figure that was a half mile," he says.

We look across nearly that much dark open water to where we have to go. "Every time I hear a Jet Ski, I get paranoid and have to stop and look around," I say.

"Nobody swims anymore," says Surfer. "They just splash."

He kicks once, powerfully, and rainbows into the water like a dolphin and starts for the other shore. I trail after, following his advice to swim farther out where the lake is deeper and colder. This time I keep up a steadier free style and make myself "longer," using my back muscles instead of my shoulders. "Keep your belly button pointed at the bottom and your head lower," John had advised. "Swim downhill."

I can feel my hands, with each stroke, dipping into the thermo cline, pulling up the ice-cold water below me. My banged-up toe aches from it. Twenty minutes later, I emerge from the water and lift my goggles.

John squats on shore, grinning at me. "Aqua man," he says.

After a quick lunch, we park the Volvo on the edge of a gigantic field overlooking the western expanse of the lake. We're in a long line of cars, pickups, and RVs facing a makeshift stage at the water's edge that's draped with a giant American flag. Above is a canopy of pine trees and then the sloping park that contains a baseball diamond on one side and some volleyball courts and concession stands opposite.

With all the windows rolled down in the car, I tip the seat back and turn up the radio when the disc jockey plays "Smoke on the Water" by Deep Purple. "Having fun and doing nothing all day is pretty tiring," I say to John and begin to doze off.

When I wake up a short while later, the field is crowded with teenage boys throwing footballs to one another, their long-limbed and tanned girlfriends in bikini tops and tiny cut-off jeans, and an array of beer-drinking, cowboy hat–wearing men folk and women in maternity blouses pushing strollers. Our neighbor, a goateed and gray-haired fellow named Roger, ambles over to introduce himself and immediately launches into conversation.

"They say that life's a circle. I started down here in Augusta in 1965 on my way to Vietnam," says Roger, who explains that he's traveling over the Fourth of July weekend in the RV parked beside us, accompanied by his and his girlfriend's blended families.

The retired infantryman fought in the Ia Drang Valley in '65, where he operated a grenade launcher. It was a particularly bloody battle, and looking into Roger's friendly brown eyes, I can see traces of an old sadness there, a toll that has been taken.

Roger suffered a pretty bad wound in the Ia Drang and received eleven months of critical care in Vietnam, and then six additional months were spent recuperating in a hospital in Japan. "Japanese protesters would march outside every day," says Roger. "Pissed-off GIs would throw chairs off the roof, shouting 'Remember Hiroshima.'"

Roger and his son Tom, an Indiana native in his mid-thirties, invite us over to their RV for a barbecue. Standing over the little round grill, Tom, a wholesome-looking fellow with thick brown hair and a ready smile, is cooking hamburgers, hot dogs, and skewers of local vegetables. Although our supplies are few because of the improvised nature of this endeavor, we contribute a bag of peanuts from Teri-Lynn's stand, a carton of blueberries, and homemade licorice from the Kutztown German Festival.

"We're neighbors," says Tom, a cheerful, blue-eyed man wearing an Indiana Hoosiers T-shirt. "Help yourselves."

Gamboling around the RV is an assortment of blue-eyed kids, handsome teenagers, and Roger's middle-aged girlfriend, a calm, pretty woman with good manners.

"A reconfigured puzzle of broken family pieces," I say to Surfer John. "Like most of America these days."

After dinner, father and son go off into the woods to smoke a joint. "That's weird, with his grandkids and step-grandkids and everyone around," I say to John. "He was a military man."

"He's an old hippie," explains Surfer. "He's from the sixties."

At 8 p.m., John and I take another swim in West Point Lake to cool off. Swimming out forty yards or so, we talk about one of our rugby friends, Bill Bishop, who also plays for the Vandals RFC. Straitlaced, blue-eyed Billy Bishop, a hard charger on the rugby field, a swashbuckling center who's a treat to play alongside. Once, when we were in Las Vegas, Billy was spotted at three in the afternoon in a hotel lobby, where he proceeded to slide belly-first down the shiny stainless-steel chute that lies between the up and down escalators. It was one of the grand hotels, and the run was about three stories up and quite steep. They called him Wild Bill after that, and he's one of the great characters in the game.

"I wish ol' Billy was here right now," I say, spitting out a plume of lake water.

A quarter mile away, the reigning local cover band is pounding away at an old Hank Williams Jr. song. Surfer and I start singing a song from an old cartoon after I say, "Ah, this is the life": "Working can wait/Life is paradise/With no work to do . . ."

Shortly after dark, we change our clothes and join Roger and his family atop the RV for the fireworks show. As each one goes fizzing upward, a loud *shhh-wwooop* echoes across the field, and then a concussive report shakes in our throats. As colors bloom in giant circles overhead, Roger whoops and hollers. "That's a beauty," he says, and, "Wow. Look at that one."

On witnessing the finale, most of the revelers sigh and yawn and get back in their cars and head out of the park. With the stream of their headlights winding through the forest, I take out my sleeping bag and spread it over the roof of the Volvo and crawl inside. When the last amateur rocket sizzles and fades against the black tarpaulin of the sky, there's one constant and uninterrupted light in the firmament: Venus.

Man yelps and yawps and the planets merely endure.

12

Swinging toward the Gulf Coast now, with early morning heat rising from the surface of the highway. Everything we've purchased and everything we've eaten on this trip was carried to us on the trucks we see bombing down the highways of America. Right now we're listening to Charlie Parker's crazy horn, as the sun tracks toward its zenith. When Kerouac and Cassady traveled this same highway, they listened to a radio show called *Chicken Jazz'n Gumbo* emanating from New Orleans that featured the Bird and other jazz luminaries. If Neal Cassady were alive now, he would be listening to hip-hop and sagging his pants, as the music that sprang from the stoops and alleys of the inner city is the "bop" of today: loud, sharp, carnal, and omnivorous.

We turn onto a rural road and drive past the Tuskegee Airmen National Historic Site. The area is an enclave of rural poverty: dented trailers, little stores made of cinder blocks with jailhouse windows, an overgrown cemetery surrounded by a crumbling brick wall; past the Tuskegee Swifty Lube and into the neighborhood that contains the Tuskegee Institute, founded in 1881. Kerouac famously observed in *On the Road* that he wished *he* were a Negro, that life as a white man did not include enough joy, kicks, darkness, or music. What depressed him the most was what he called his "white ambitions," the trappings of success that are prized by the shot callers of the ruling class: money, cars, a straight job. After dropping out of Columbia, Kerouac attended the New School in New York; had he lived in the South, it's easy to imagine him signing up for classes at the Tuskegee Institute under the GI bill, listening to the hottest jazz, and attending late-night bull sessions with his classmates.

The educator, innovator, and orator Booker T. Washington was the first principal of the Tuskegee Normal School for Colored Teachers and developed the place into a world-renowned center for learning. He was the first African American to earn an honorary master of arts degree from Harvard, and the school that he and his students built from bricks they fashioned with their own hands is now a National Historic Landmark.

The present-day campus is a neat arrangement of large red-brick buildings, well-maintained lawns, and wide, smooth concrete walkways. After parking the car out back, John and I walk up to Booker T. Washington's residence, "the Oaks," a Queen Anne–style brick home that was designed by a man named Robert R. Taylor, the first black graduate of the Massachusetts Institute of Technology. It's not open today, but we peer in the windows at the dark mahogany walls, rattan chairs, and formal dining room, set with elaborate china.

Nearby is a sign for the George Washington Carver museum. "He invented the peanut," I say. Chained to an old piece of wrought-iron fence behind the house is a rusted Tek bicycle with two flat tires. "That was Carver's ride," I say. "He was way ahead of his time when it came to bicycle technology." I reach over and grip the handlebars. "If you look closely, you'll see it's made of peanuts," I say.

"Generally speaking, Professor Washington probably didn't get much support from the locals," Surfer says.

"To put it mildly. If he was just an ambitious guy, he could've gone to MIT and that would've been a major achievement. But founding his own college was pretty damned ballsy."

Outside Tuskegee, spacious farms line either side of the two-lane, the trees draped over with Spanish moss. A small store called Blues' Old Stand appears on an open stretch of road, advertising "Groceries" beneath a giant shade tree. In preparation for our trip, Surfer reread the original published version of *On the Road*, which he hadn't picked up in twenty years or more. Here and there along the road we have mentioned the reason for this trip and been greeted with mostly blank looks. "The average Joe doesn't know who Kerouac is," says Surfer.

"The average Joe doesn't know who Dickens is," I say. "Nobody reads books anymore. They just splash around on the Internet."

We're following a truck piled high with thirty-foot pine logs. Red flags are streaming out from the back of the truck, and I can smell the resin in the air. George Shearing—Cassady and Kerouac called him "Old God Shearing"—is playing from the stereo, but I don't recognize the song. Jazz, like scotch and crudités, was something I thought I was going to mature into, but I've frittered away my adult life on rock music, cold beer, and chicken wings.

A short while later we pass through Brantley, Alabama, "the Front Porch City," a collection of small white clapboard homes and white picket fences. Traffic stops for several moments when a thin, gray-haired man wearing a blue work shirt crosses Main Street in his wheelchair. For lunch, we pull off at Hook's Pit Bar-B-Q in Andalusia, Alabama, where I'm treated to the best meal I've ever eaten from a paper plate. While we sip our iced tea, Surfer notes that Hook's Pit is actually a chain restaurant: Andalusia, Opp, Dotham, Troy, and Luverne. "I think they're on to something," I say, sopping up the beans with a square of cornbread.

Down the road is a giant antebellum mansion with a massive gate, long curving drive, and wrought-iron fence encircling the multiacre estate. Right next door is what Surfer calls "a real shithole" of a trailer park, and the gap between America's haves and have-nots is comically demonstrated.

Just as Kerouac and Cassady did in '49, we note the signs for Flomaton, Florida, and turn onto Route 90, the old coast road. Piney woods and intermittent swamplands appear on both sides of the cracked asphalt, dotted with signs for Butts TV Repair, Florabama Loans, and Crazy Carter's Fireworks.

We travel over the raised causeway of I-10 across Mobile Bay in a pelting rainstorm, with the rolling gray waters of the Gulf to our left and marshlands dotted with low buildings to the north under ominous skies. Off the ramp, with the water on both sides, Surfer aims the Volvo toward Battleship Park. The USS *Alabama* is docked next to the bridge, rising out of the mist like Tojo's worst nightmare. We take a short break and examine several of the aircraft on display: a Corsair Navy jet; the F-4 Phantom, which was the workhorse of the Vietnam War; and the spy plane SR-71, the Blackbird, a jet that the U.S. government said didn't exist until it went out of service. After the rain lets up, we drive through a tunnel and get back on I-10 past Mobile, Alabama, while Surfer tells me about a rugby tournament he played in a few years ago, on the low-lying field beside the old warship.

We follow a battered pickup truck into Cloud Bay, Alabama. By 4 p.m., looking at the map while Surfer drives, I can see that we've passed into Jackson County, Mississippi. Radio towers loom by the roadside, while stunted trees cover the flatlands, and evil black clouds scurry overhead. A lane of tall pines runs along either side of the road, stubby trees with no branches 'til they flare out at the very tops. The air is dense and warm, sickly sweet. Pascagoula is dead ahead. Giant yellow cranes mark the port to our left, alongside the black silhouettes of giant cargo ships.

With the Gulf of Mexico yawning off to the south, we decide to take an open-water swim. Down a side street off the coast road we're looking for Shepherd State Park, which appears on the map as a little green square beside the ocean. John pulls over by a brick building called Mississippi Mosquito Control and hails a tall, ropy-muscled black man with white hair and a string of puka shells around his neck. The man ambles over to the car and provides directions. When I ask if there's good swimming at the State Park, the man shakes his head solemnly.

"No," he says. "Ain't no swimmin' there."

He's right. The park is situated on alligator-infested lowlands, across a span of brackish water from the gigantic cranes of the port. Swimming here would satisfy the spooky scare dream of my aquatic childhood, and even sitting in the car, I'm afraid that an old bull gator will look at me with his veiled ancient eye. Fuck that, I tell Surfer.

Down Highway 49 through the decrepit section of Gulfport, Mississippi, the landscape shattered by hurricanes; poor people are shuffling back and forth between check-cashing bunkers and legal-ized loan sharks. It occurs to me that America is one big pawnshop. At the end of the main street we turn onto a coast road that fronts the beach, silent and empty at dusk. Not even a dog walker or a kid riding his skateboard, just a vista to the brownish-black waters and an occasional giant oil tanker steaming offshore. Facing the gulf is a huge luxury hotel that's been blown partway off its foundation. It looks like a giant cake that's been halved by a falling blade, the walls sliced away on all seven floors and the tattered ends of the wallpaper rotten with water and flapping like shrouds.

It reminds me of that hotel in Beirut, Lebanon, where all those Marines were killed in '82. I know a retired USMC master sergeant, Jeff Turner, who was there and who wakes up at night, still, with the sound of men screaming and automatic weapons fire echoing through the nearby streets. The rules of engagement in that fucked-up operation meant the Marine Corps guards had no rounds in their M16s, Turner said, and when the suicide bombers came smashing through the paltry gate, they had no way to stop them. By sheer luck, Jeff Turner had drawn sentry duty that morning and watched the truck with the bomb in it racing by his position.

Empty foundations line the beachfront, vacation homes that no longer exist. Ruined piles of brick. Houses with no bottom halves, just rickety pilings, or with the roofs blown off. The golden arches of McDonald's are intact, but there's no restaurant beside them; the whole area has been "stripped clean," John says. An empty and deserted prep school, yellow stucco buildings with gaping holes where the doorways and windows should be. It looks like the University of Ghost Studies, and fragments of T. S. Eliot's "The Wasteland" fill my head: "O you who turn the wheel and look windward/Consider Phlebas, who was once handsome and tall as you." Disembodied poetics, indeed.

Here and there, homeowners are rebuilding, but most of them have gone somewhere else, given up, even the moneyed ones. "I have no idea what's ahead," Surfer says, driving around bundles of wreckage and heaved-up spots in the road.

We're fixed on the idea of swimming in the gulf, and the sun is going down fast. On a desolate stretch of beach in front of the ruined hotel we park the car, bury the keys in a plastic sandwich bag, and change into our trunks by the side of the road. There isn't a soul around.

"This was ground zero for the storm," says John as we lower our goggles and wade into the flat, brackish water.

The sky is gray and gloomy, and the water is gray-brown and tepid. An old song comes to mind, a mournful tune about lost chances and luck that went bad. We slog through the shallows until the water is chest deep, one hundred yards from shore and less than ten yards from the buoys that mark off the channel.

They are square black pillars of oiled wood that have been driven into the ocean floor. The buoys are spaced evenly across, a distance of approximately forty yards from one another. On the other side of them is the shipping channel, deep enough to accommodate the giant tankers that cruise off shore.

Something brushes against my leg and I jump out of the way, only to be touched again by another tiny fin under the water. Surfer dismisses them as "little fishies" and zeroes out the timer on his watch and takes off swimming as I fall in behind. The big toe on my right foot has been weeping all day, and I can feel it leaking a thin trail of blood into the water. When I was a kid, I swam across an inlet at Plum Island that contained a sunken ship, and just passing by the jutting prow filled me with dread.

Only six feet deep here, but the water is so dark and silty I can't see the bottom—I can't even see my hand on the downstroke. Swimming along with no direction indicator, I poke my head up after ten minutes and find myself on the wrong side of the buoys. Out here, I can feel the channel yawning beneath me. I'm perilously close to very deep water, and I imagine a ribbon of blood flowing from my banged-up toe into this trench, like an urgent memorandum to the hungriest sharks. A quarter mile out, though it looks much closer, an oil tanker the size of a small city is cruising past, and I get that same feeling I had on Plum Island when I was a teenager.

Charged with adrenaline, I swim in a head-out crawl back toward the nearest channel marker, which has the word DANGER emblazoned on its side. I'm zigzagging back toward the shallows when something brushes against my leg. I kick away furiously, swimming like a madman. In the depth of the western sky, the bloated sun is like a ghost behind the cloudbank, sinking into the gulf. All around me, the water has turned black.

Less than halfway to the final buoy, which had been our goal on setting out, I catch up with Surfer, who's already past the turnaround and coming back. We stop for a moment, treading water, our heads turned toward the empty beach and the deserted parkway beyond. No joggers pass by. No cyclists. Nobody.

"Like swimming on the *Planet of the Apes*," says Surfer.

Surfer continues on, gliding along in his smooth, efficient stroke, while I thrash toward the halfway mark. It takes me thirty minutes to get there, and on the way back, something stings me on the neck as I turn my head for a breath. It sends me gulping for air, speeding up beyond my capacity for oxygen transfer, and I go sputtering into the shallows. Popping up, I search the air for Najeeb's missing honeybees, but there's nothing there. I compose myself and continue grinding out the mile course.

I check my watch at the starting buoy and see that I've been swimming for an hour. It takes a long time to wade back out on my weary legs, and mounting the beach, I meet Surfer by the Volvo, and he tosses me a bottle of energy drink.

"I got stung by something," I tell him.

"Yeah, there's jellyfish everywhere," he says. "I saw them straight off but didn't want to tell you, 'cause I thought it would freak you out."

13

Passing through Bay St. Louis just west of our swimming spot, we drive along beside the devastated ruins of St. Stanislaus Preparatory College, founded by the Brothers of Sacred Heart in 1854. A few of the buildings have been renovated and are back in use, but most look like they were bombed and left in heaps during some forgotten holy war. The graceful stone halls of the main campus are hollowed out, the windows broken and doors hanging from their frames. There's something particularly sad about all those empty classrooms, the sodden books in the library, heaps of overturned desks piled up outside. It looks like a monastery that's been ransacked by the Huns.

Wrecked homes line the street, amid piles of rubble. "This reminds me of Nicaragua," says Surfer. "It's wiped clean." Crumpled mansions appear by the roadside like heaps of garbage. Surfer notes that a twenty-five-foot wash blew through here, like a tsunami. The smart ones got out; the rest drowned. "You'd just be a speck floating amidst tons of wreckage and garbage," he says.

"Katrina was big but God is bigger" says a sign outside St. Clare church, which lies in ruin but has been replaced by a Quonset hut. We pass by a tall black man, throwing a net over a brackish pool. Then another fellow standing on an abbreviated pier, casting his fishing rod with a disconsolate look on his face. The waters look fished out; nothing but parasites and predators remain.

"If you stayed here when the storm came through, you died," says Surfer. "Those giant houses were blown off their pilings like twigs."

At the end of this Road of Sorrows is a massive new building lit by klieg lights, shining against the gloomy dusk when we're still a half-mile off. At least something has been rebuilt; a bastion of hope that casts its light over the savage landscape that surrounds it. In the old times, it would've been a mission, built by the indefatigable Brothers of Sacred Heart or the Little Sisters of the Poor. A sanctuary for weary travelers and, despite all the ruin, the one true symbol of God's dominion over heaven and earth.

Creeping toward it over the broken pavement, we come within range of a thirty-foot neon sign that reads: "Silver Slipper Casino." After two miles of empty lots and deserted side streets, the giant stone box of the casino is teeming with people, lights, music: the action.

"Your house and hearth are gone, but you can still play blackjack," I say, as Surfer bangs a U-ey in the parking lot. "At the end of the holy American road is Sodom and Gomorrah. What a fucking surprise."

14

It's a sultry hot morning in Bay St. Louis, Mississippi. Old Town is comprised of small neat clapboard or brick homes alongside piles of soggy ruin; the day of the big blow, it was like a pair of enormous dice rolled down Main Street and some won, some lost everything. A halved church appears on the side of the road—a house divided against itself—the altar exposed, the rest gone for good. An old savings bank has been destroyed, except for the thick rusted vault door and part of a brick wall that remains. Then there's the upper floor of a house, perched crookedly on the thin iron girders; no windows, big holes in the roof, and the lower floor missing; you can see right through to the weeds on the other side.

By 6:30 a.m., we're on Route 90 going west toward New Orleans. Usually, Surfer and I avoid talking politics, as my old buddy is an ex-jarhead and right-winger and I'm a violent and dreamy iconoclast who would rather climb a tree or bike the gulches of some landfill than read the editorial page. But for some weird reason, Surfer has latched onto the legacy of Bill Clinton this morning, lecturing to the former president as one seasoned womanizer to another; in fact, my old roommate has gotten himself quite worked up over it.

"He's a disgrace to his party. I mean, Jack Kennedy had *Marilyn Monroe*, for chrissakes," Surfer says. "He shoulda been boning some major league babe, not some fat intern. Bill Clinton was the most powerful man in the world, and chicks really dig that. *Hot* chicks." There's a pause as this self-evident proposition is allowed to sink in, which it does. "I have to question the man's ability to see what's right in front of him," says Surfer. "We all should. How can he be trusted to deal with the Palestinian question, let's say, if he can't discern between a hottie and a fat chick? Poor fucking judgment works both ways."

At this hour, we're alone on the coast, a two-lane road cutting across the saw grass plain. There's the incongruous sight of a big shrimper with its rusty spire pulled right up near the shoulder in a tiny inlet. Farther along, a huge pile of rotten couches, old tires, and garbage rises from the side of the highway like some profane monument. We're in bayou country now.

"This is where if you marry your *second* cousin you're the mayor," I say.

Crossing into Louisiana, there are brand-new houses on stilts right on the shore of Lake Catherine. We cross the Pearl River on a narrow two-lane bridge; workers are building a gigantic one right beside it, thirty or forty feet higher, at their peculiar, lugubrious pace. The "bayou," or swamp, is right up to the road on both sides. The air smells of rotting vegetation, exposed muck, and discarded sea shells.

Coming into New Orleans from the east, we embark on what Surfer calls the "slum tour": abandoned strip malls, closed-up businesses, shuttered homes, and piles of scrap metal and tires. When Kerouac and Cassady entered the city in *On the Road*, Cassady exclaimed, "Oh, smell the people!" That much hasn't changed: the place reeks of low tide and rot. The abandoned LSU health center, thirteen ghostly stories of empty rooms. There's an enormous clarinet painted on the side of the Holiday Inn on Loyola Avenue, running vertically. The Voo Doo Liquor and Beer Store on Canal Street. Assorted vagrants in stylish hats. An army of mangy-looking dogs.

We take a couple of rooms in a funky old hotel in the Garden District and head over to Slim Goodies diner. A large oil portrait of blues man Robert Johnson and his guitar occupies a place of honor beside the grill. Polaroids of various guests, famous, infamous, and unknown, are taped up everywhere on the pale yellow walls. Over the stereo system, Marvin Gaye keeps insisting "Let's Get It On," in his smooth, soulful voice.

Occupying many of the cracked red vinyl booths are shaggy-haired kids in smoked glasses reading the *Times-Picayune* over mugs of coffee and crawfish omelets. Tulane girls in tight shorts and painted-on white halter tops are ubiquitous, whispering and laughing and stirring their tea with dainty strokes. I order a Cuban omelet with grits and iced tea from our waitress, who's shorthaired, tattooed, and butch. She's wearing an orange T-shirt emblazoned with "Jesus Christ Fan Club" and a drawing of our bearded Savior.

"Are you really a fan of Jesus Christ?" I ask the waitress, poised to give my four-hour commercial lecture on the subject.

She looks down at her shirt. "Not really. Somebody gave me this."

After the meal, Surfer buys a Slim Goodies T-shirt for Giz that features two strategically placed fried eggs on the front, and he also picks up the tab and leaves a good-size tip. Surfer has always been generous to a fault. In one of my first journal entries, dated November 9, 1980, I wrote,

You can tell what kind of day I had yesterday by what I ate. It started with an unassuming hot chocolate and toast at

6:30 AM with Surfer and Noel at the Bunker. Sandwiched around a rugby game at Jacksonville (played for the A-side, we won 21–17, I broke a long run and pitched to Norman Litwack for the winning try) were 7 or 8 pieces of pepperoni pizza, a McChicken sandwich with a small fry, a dozen raw oysters: one with a cockroach garnish fresh killed from the Winjammer bar top, and a bathtub of beer.

Went to a Gainesville bar after and met a brown-eyed girl from Illinois.

me: If you were a dog I'd bring you home.

her: Woof.

We went to my house and sailed the mansion seas on the waterbed.

I owe Surfer John twenty bucks.

15

On the street outside Slim Goodies, an angry, red-faced young man looks over at me and shouts, "Fight!"

"No!" I yell back, shaking my fist at him, and Surfer laughs. Surfer and I rent mountain bikes from Michael's Bicycles on Frenchmen Street, passing by a legless man in a wheelchair panhandling out front. Several other bike shops have gone out of business, and Tim, the proprietor, a tall, pudgy, balding man with a long ponytail, relates how they all took "evacu-cations" when Katrina hit. He bounced right back after the storm, renting bicycles from a nearby parking lot to the "voluntourists" who flooded the city in the wake of the hurricane. The neighborhood where the bike shop is located was spared most of the destruction wrought by Katrina, Tim says, calling it "the isle of denial."

While getting our bearings, Surfer and I pedal by the giant white bubble of the Louisiana Superdome on Poydras Street, the one true symbol of what a colossal fuck-up the aftermath of the hurricane turned out to be. My mind works in pictures, and I recall my visit with David Amram last month; we were heading into the train station, Uncle Dave's lean, Western-style face in profile, with the areola of gray-black hair and that wry glint in his eye, like he was twenty again, sauntering into some joint in the Village wearing his red-and-black hunting cap with the ear flaps. Somehow we'd gotten on the topic of upper-class indifference and were talking about Hurricane Katrina and how the refuge of last resort for the city's poor was the Superdome. Chuckling at the inanity of it, Amram paraphrased former first lady Barbara Bush, who, when asked to comment on these pitiful accommodations, said, "This is a step up for them. This works well for them."

Cycling through the French Quarter is the most dangerous thing we've done so far: weaving in and out of hooting taxis and buses and tourists from Ohio and Delaware; past five tap-dancing black adolescents in long white T-shirts, performing in unison for fugitive quarters. Finally, we turn off the main thoroughfare and roll down a long smooth stretch of road to the embarkation point for the Algiers ferry.

After the passenger cars load on, Surfer and I and a tired-looking man wearing a Vietnam veterans ball cap walk our bikes onto the double-decked ferry. It's a short, free ride. The murky depths of the Mississippi lie before us—in *On the Road*, Kerouac called it "the great brown father of waters"—the ferry churning its way toward the shore a quarter mile distant. Halfway across, I pull out my phone and give my rugby buddy and physical therapist Chris Pierce a call; he's working in his clinic back in Windham, New Hampshire, and jumps right on the line.

"Piercey! I'm crossing the mighty Mississipp'! Man, too bad you weren't here."

"Atkinson, you son of a gun! What's it like?"

"I just saw Huckleberry Finn go by on a fuckin' Jet Ski. I'm gonna call you every time I cross a big river on this trip."

"You do that, brother. Good luck!"

We roll over to the Algiers courthouse in the suffocating heat, the first real scorcher we've endured, even here in the Deep South. While Surfer locks up the bikes, I go inside to join a queue of sorry-looking folks being herded through the metal detector. I want to visit the Assessor's Office to look at property records and see if I can find William Burroughs's old house, where Kerouac and Cassady visited in 1949. It's cool and dark in the vestibule, and we go speedily through the line, but when Surfer and I get to the front, a short, stocky black woman in a bulletproof vest announces that the Assessor's Office has closed so the staff can go across the river for the last day of something called "Essence Fest," which celebrates African American music.

"They close up to go to a fuckin' party?" I ask.

But Surfer is philosophical. "You can't penalize a bear for shitting in the woods," he says. "After all, this is the party capital of the Western world."

There's a New Orleans police officer right outside the courthouse, talking to a black woman and her two children. He's a small, chunky red-faced guy with a mesh hat pushed back on his head and a pair of mirrored sunglasses. When the patrolman finds out what we're looking for, he obliges by taking out a laminated map of the parishes. The cop is an old-timer but not that old, and he can only speculate where Burroughs lived when I describe the neighborhoods of 1949.

Apparently, there's a string of old, rundown houses with good-size plots of land about a mile and a half from where we're standing, in Lower Algiers. "Y'all might try out he-ah," says the patrolman, indicating the line on his map that signifies the levee. "It kinda sounds like what you're saying, and it's been around a long time."

Ten blocks away is the public library, where the cop told us we might find some old property records, but there's a sign on the door that says "Closed for Essence Fest." Riding through the dense, superheated air is like touring a blast furnace, especially for a New Englander like me. While I take a rest in a leafy city park, Surfer runs across the street to a corner market for more bottled water and energy drinks. A rusty pickup rolls past on Opelousas, its tail pipe dragging behind and throwing up sparks. Rickety two-story homes line the street, with open porches on the top floor. There are very few white people here, but nobody pays me any mind. A boy comes by with a basketball and just detours around me without a word or signal. I'm like the ghost of Opelousas.

Refreshed for the time being, we take a long slow ride back across town, up the steep edge of the levee and along its length. Off to our left is the churning brown water of the Mississippi, and to our right, down the grassy bank, is the perimeter road and a series of tiny cottages and trailer homes separated by mossy trees and overgrown lawns. After twenty minutes of riding, we reach a place where the levee is blocked by a ten-foot chain-link fence. There's a sign warning us away from "United States Government Property," and we're forced to detour around a U.S. Navy base by going through a couple of small, tidy neighborhoods.

Surrounded by fencing, the base contains a large number of low wooden buildings and dozens of Quonset huts. Halfway back to the levee, we encounter a huge collection of shiny white FEMA trailers, which Surfer explains is "temporary" housing provided for those families uprooted by the hurricane. A good percentage of the trailers look empty, but more than half of them are occupied; SUVs and other upscale cars are parked in some of the driveways, and, within the fencing, clusters of men and women are sitting in lawn chairs or standing idle.

It's been more than two years since Hurricane Katrina ripped through here. "Shouldn't these people be doing something by now?" I ask.

"Your tax dollars at work," Surfer says.

Back home in Florida, Surfer often trains in this kind of heat, running on Cocoa Beach, swimming in the Intercoastal Waterway, and going for fifty-mile bike rides on the paved roads that crisscross the Space Center. But I'm getting shaky: my mouth is dry, and I feel like I'm going to throw up. After circumventing the navy base, we mount the berm again, and I have to pause to drink another pint of water and consume one of the energy gels I'm carrying in my backpack. The masts of a gigantic tanker are visible above the levee, and I get that same queasy feeling I had when I saw the USS *Alabama*.

Surfer busies himself with the map and doesn't appear to have broken a sweat. "You look like hell," he says.

"You don't say?" I reply, downing another sports drink. "I feel like a hundred bucks."

The levee, which is smooth-packed clay at its apex, drops in a steep grassy slope for about seventy-five feet. At the bottom is an irrigation ditch and, just beyond it, a two-lane road that bounds a weedy rural neighborhood. Gazing across at the nearest plot of land, I call to Surfer, who has cinched up his pack straps and is rolling away. "Hey, bean, look at this," I call, and he doubles back.

It's a modest estate, consisting of a large long plot of land, several overgrown willow trees, and a rambling one-story house that looks like a bunch of shacks cobbled together. There's some kind of rusty old car pulled up beside the house and a barn that leans so far over, it's impossible to figure out what's holding it up.

"That's it," I say to John. "That's old Bull Lee's place."

Immediately, I conjure up William Burroughs as Kerouac knew him: tall, gaunt, and jaundiced, with his nasty morphine habit and seven distinct personalities as revealed by "narco-analysis," including an English lord at the top and a drooling idiot at the bottom. Gazing over the land, I'm convinced that the author of *Naked Lunch* and *Junk* roosted here, bustling around in the morning, throwing knives, reading the Mayan Codices, and lecturing his guests on various esoteric subjects. Inevitably, this would all culminate in Burroughs's noontime fix, whereupon he nodded through the hot sultry afternoon, his cat dozing beside him. In *On the Road*, Kerouac transformed his old friend Burroughs into W. C. Fields, a cranky old gent whose humorous asides lighten the mood of the serious young travelers.

Surfer sees everything through the lens of science. Straddling the bicycle, he measures the swampy field with his exacting eye, taking stock of the barn, the willow trees, the stretch of empty road where Jack and Neal demonstrated their athletic prowess, and a big hunk of wood that might've been the shelf Burroughs was making, the one that was supposed to last a thousand years. While we're considering all this, a swaybacked white horse enters the property, grazing on whatever savory weeds are growing there.

"It sure looks like it," says Surfer.

Halfway through Burroughs's ladder of personalities was an old black man who waited in line with the rest. He lived by a certain principle, and Surfer repeats it now: "Some's bastards, some's ain't, that's the score."

John swings his pack to one shoulder, digs around in there, and pulls out his camera. Motioning with his hand, he places me in line with the backdrop and creates an instant digital image of the house, the barn, the willow trees, and the overgrown yard. I've already committed it to memory and don't even look back.

16

We catch the Lower Algiers ferry on the return trip, loitering in the shade of the lower deck. Within minutes, a giant thundercloud darkens the sky, and it begins to rain. An oil refinery looms as we approach the far bank, and the stench of gasoline and its greasy taste fill the air.

Only a few cars occupy the ferry, and Surfer and I wait until they rumble up the ramp and disappear into the blowing mists. I zip up my windbreaker and peddle off the ferry into a deluge, happy about this break in the weather. Laboring up the incline, we pass among the giant storage tanks, studded spires, and catwalks of the refinery. Against the blurry gray backdrop of the rainstorm, it looks like Satan's amusement park.

Half a dozen miles south of downtown New Orleans lies St. Bernard's Parish, which still resembles a war zone even though it's been years since the big storm. In the once middle-class neighborhood abutting the Jean Lafitte National Historic Park and Preserve, abandoned ranch-style homes line the streets, marked for demolition by the government. Spray-painted on these facades are numbers and letters in a peculiar diamond formation; they look like an alchemist's symbol or warnings of a plague. Here and there, isolated homeowners are trying to renovate and regroup, but the absence of children gives the place a silent, threatening atmosphere. It's like a crack house development.

While we're riding through, a jet-black Cadillac Escalade with tinted windows comes toward us the other way. The windows of the

SUV go down, revealing four young black men wearing sunglasses and blue bandannas. They stare at us, we stare at them, and they go gliding past without changing the blank expressions on their faces.

Riding ahead of me, Surfer turns around and says, "They must be from Welcome Wagon."

"Forcing you to join the Chamber of Commerce at gunpoint."

An hour later, we return the bikes and go back to the Lake Pontchatrain Hotel and get cleaned up. Igor's Bar and Laundromat is right down the street, a dark, narrow joint with red canvas awnings and strings of Christmas lights strewn along the wall. Every good bar has a history, and, while we're waiting for the barmaid to top up our pints of Guinness, I regale Surfer with details of my previous visit to Igor's a few years ago.

Surfer missed that particular trip; he and I've been playing rugby with the Vandals for several years, an invitational team captained by Frank Baker, an old pal of mine who works for the Associated Press and lives in Long Beach, California. On a cold, rainy afternoon in February, the Vandals eventually played the host club in the championship of the New Orleans rugby tournament and lost 23–8. Afterward, we went to Igor's to wash our muddy uniforms in the large stainless steel machines out back. I was standing around in my boxer shorts with Super Dave LaFlamme, Baker, Crab, Solly, and the other Vandals, drinking beer and laughing. An effeminate, chubby man in a Hawaiian shirt was nearby, listening to some barroom acquaintance complain about the vicissitudes of life. In his Louisiana drawl, the chubby man said, "Every day that I wake up, and the sky is up there [points at ceiling], and the ground is down there [points to floor], is a pretty goddamn good day."

Baker and I were about ten feet apart in a sea of people, and when he caught my eye, we exchanged a long series of deferential bows, salutes, and hand gestures with each other. Every flourish was more elaborate and respectful than the immediately previous one, the two of us smiling and then laughing, amazed that we were still playing rugby together so many years after our first acquaintance, playing in championship finals no less, all of it a bonus and all too rare, like old good times, visited and revisited, again and again.

• • •

The barmaid hears the tail end of my story and comes down to flirt with us. Alicia is a pretty blue-eyed blonde from Phoenix, and her partner behind the bar is a petite brunette named Sam, a local girl with a tight little body and a rose tattooed on her upper arm. Alicia and Sam buy us shots of tequila, while the other customers gamble on the poker machines and heavy, loud music fills the room. In New Orleans, Cassady nearly went insane from the air, wafting in from the Mississippi like "soft bandannas," and from the torrents of local women roaming the sidewalks, with their scent of mud and molasses and their tender, intimate way of speaking.

Surfer wants to know where the action is, and Alicia says there's a hot band playing just a few blocks away. Since the hurricane, the neighborhood right behind Igor's has become crime-infested, and Sam advises us to take a cab to the other bar. One of Igor's bartenders was mugged just a few nights ago, and "they usually don't pick on the locals," Alicia says, but things are getting pretty bad.

After a couple more drinks, we walk next door to a soul food place and have supper. "The girls at Igor's are digging us," I say. "We should go back there."

"The bars are open all night," replies Surfer.

I wipe my mouth with a napkin and drink some of the cold, sweet beer. "Bird in hand, amigo."

Following Alicia's tip, we take a cab to Frenchmen Street and saunter into a little blues club called d.b.a. The band that's playing has a black drummer named Cedric "Mississippi" Burnside; a white guitarist in a long white T-shirt known as King James, who sings in a gravelly, throat-coated baritone; and Lightnin' Malcolm, a husky guy with dirty blond hair who plays rhythm and lead on the same six-string guitar and announces, "Welcome, boys and girls. We play this song in the country in juke joints and we're gon' party tonight New Orleans style, all night."

The drumbeats thump off the walls and pound inside my chest cavity, while King James's guitar goes *brang, brang, BRANG* and stringy-haired girls in cats-eye glasses and reed-thin men wearing little straw hats wriggle and groan along with the music. Surfer maneuvers his way to the bar and returns with two sweating bottles of Sierra Nevada, and we lean against the wall drinking beer and snapping our fingers while the dance floor fills up.

Lightnin' Malcolm and the boys play for two hours straight and then take a break. When the house music comes back on, a small but well-built woman comes over and stands next to me. She's in her forties, wearing a black leather corset that grips the underside of her protuberant breasts like a form-fitting rubber glove. She stares at me and smiles, and I introduce myself, but in the midst of all the racket, I don't catch her name. Surfer jabs me and says she looks like a hard-luck version of Kitty, from the old TV show *Gunsmoke*.

Kitty says she's in the oil business, a former local who now lives in Alabama and wants to party. She's drinking Crown Royal, straight up. "I'm a New Orleans girl," she says. "When I hit it, I hit it *hard*."

After we buy her a drink, Surfer and Kitty and I hustle across the street to another bar. In *On the Road*, Burroughs's character, Old Bull Lee, tells Kerouac that the bars of New Orleans are "insufferably dreary" and then proves it by taking them to the lowest, meanest, and dullest ones. It's the witching hour, and we enter the small crowded establishment just as the Claim Jumpers rip into their first number. This place feels different than the other bar, and there's a vibe I can't quite put my finger on that I don't like. I get bumped to the side by a man passing on his way to the head, and he doesn't even acknowledge it, and I shoot a look around the bar itself, which is filled with thin-skinned skinflints and haughty young hotties. The bartender is a mannish, horse-faced woman in a red cocktail dress.

Even Kitty takes on a darker mien. When I ask her why she's not partying down on Bourbon Street, she sneers and says, "You mean Nigger Fest? Oh, pardon me: Essence Fest. Why would I want to go there?"

Kitty's remark shocks me, and just as I'm about to act out that scene from *White Hunter, Black Heart*, where a drunken woman utters an anti-Semitic slur and Clint Eastwood rips into her, Surfer buys a round with a hundred-dollar bill, and the barmaid palms it. I see it all like it's in slow motion. Making change, the barmaid hands over four banknotes and a couple of quarters, and Surfer sticks them in his pocket. Half a second later, when he pulls the bills out to examine them, Surfer notices that the barmaid has given him four one-dollar bills instead of four twenties.

"You shortchanged me," he says.

The barmaid says, "Fuck you, I did," and goes around, lifts the trap, and leaves the bar for a moment.

Kitty taps me on the shoulder. "She's going to ditch the hundred, so it doesn't turn up in the cash drawer," she says.

"She took the money," I tell Surfer. "Don't let her get away with it."

When the horse-faced barmaid returns, I pitch my voice beneath the music and say, "I know you stole that money and you better give it back, or I'm calling the cops."

"I didn't steal nothin'," says the barmaid, her eyes turning sixes and sevens.

The barmaid keeps insisting that Surfer has made the mistake, so I go outside to look for a cop. The back streets of the Garden District are quiet at this hour, and I pass among the columned and balconied private homes, many of them still tricked out in the faded green, purple, and gold of last February's Mardi Gras, with spiked wrought-iron fences and small metal signs advertising "Bad Dog."

Down the block are gritty apartment buildings with their chained-up wheelchairs and bicycles; the little corner markets and plain stucco offices for doctors and aluminum window companies, homogeneously arranged and looking and smelling the same way that Gainesville, Florida, looked to me in 1980, when I lived in the student ghetto there; the same flowering trees, the subtropical heat, the same empty husks fallen from the trees and crushed together, lying in the interstices of the sidewalk like God's good grout.

I find a police officer sitting on his motorcycle a few blocks away. He tells me to insist on seeing the manager. "By Louisiana law, he or she has to be on the premises," the cop says. When I return to the bar, Doug the manager is there, an aging party boy with long strands of gray hair hanging from under his baseball cap and two or three days' worth of stubble. He takes the cash drawer into the back and counts the money and then returns to the crowded bar with the drawer under his arm.

"It's not eighty bucks over," Doug says. "So it's your word against hers."

Surfer is becoming irritated. "She stashed the hundred out back somewhere."

"So you say."

"Do you have surveillance cameras pointed at the bar," I ask, "as required by law?"

With his gray hair and spindly shanks, Doug looks like an old frat boy who caravanned down from Tennessee in the '80s and never went back. He stares at me but doesn't answer. "Let's get a cop and ask him or her to figure this out," I say.

"Be my guest," Doug says.

Every road trip begins in joy and ends in sorrow. I make the call on my cell, and fifteen minutes later, a huge cop in a motorcycle jacket arrives and ushers the bar manager, Surfer, and me onto the sidewalk. Doug tries to take the patrolman by the arm and lead him out of earshot, but he resists. "We're all grown-ups," the cop says. "Let's act like it."

When the policeman asks me what happened, I explain the incident and then point at Surfer and say, "He's an aerospace engineer at NASA, and I'm a college professor. We don't go around trying to beat bartenders out of a hundred bucks. She stole it from us."

The cop shifts his impassive gaze to Doug, whose tiny pupils are shifting from Surfer to me and back again. "I don't believe your story, but I'm going to give you the eighty bucks," Doug says, reaching into his pocket for a roll of bills. He peels off four twenties and stuffs them into Surfer's hand. "Don't ever come in here again."

The next morning Surfer and I get up and take a drive out to Lake Pontchartrain, stopping by a ruined arcade with the wind driving the surface of the lake into a blue-black chop and not a soul around. We stand on shore, counter passant to each other, staring at the waves and into that pool of gloomy notions that usually follows a night on the town. There's some talk of pressing on toward

Oklahoma and Texas, but we both have stuff to do back home, the weight of responsibilities. I have a teenage son, and when I hit the road like this, I miss him terribly. Certainly, Kerouac's biggest moral failing was not being there for his daughter, Jan, who inherited her Dad's crystalline blue eyes and intolerance for alcohol and died young, at forty-four.

"Once you get moving, it's hard to stand still," says John.

PART THREE

MEXICO

1

On my way back to Massachusetts from New Orleans, I split up from Surfer at the Orlando, Florida, airport. "What's your road, man?" he asked, slinging his pack over his shoulder with a sad grin. A month later, I'm flying through the cloud canyons, thirty-five feet above that old road, connecting through Chicago and heading for Denver. All the swimming pools in that part of the country are above ground for some reason; you can see their shimmering blue orbs dotting the neighborhoods when you fly out of Midway. They look like the uncounted wishing wells of Illinois fortune-tellers.

When I arrive in Colorado, it's 3:30 p.m. local time, hot and dry amid the thin air of the Rockies. Keith Bowden, my old Acadia pal Bongo, is wearing khaki shorts, a gray Laredo Baseball T-shirt, and a pair of 1960s-style wraparound sunglasses. I haven't seen him in four years, and this summer he's been crisscrossing the map of the U.S. by car, in his 2000 four-door plum-colored Mazda 626, covering more than twelve thousand miles. Every summer for the past seventeen years, he's driven up from Laredo, Texas, visiting friends from Maine and Nova Scotia to California and British Columbia. If he's not in his car, he's river rafting somewhere, always on the move.

"Let's go," Bongo says, heading out through the vacuum doors of the airport.

The famous 1952 photograph of Kerouac and Cassady with an arm slung over each other's shoulders is sitting on the Mazda's console. Unlike my last ride, Bongo's car has no GPS, no air conditioning, no sunroof, and an old AM-FM radio. Besides that, Keith Bowden is a man of very few words, and after the perfunctory exchange of recent facts, we just get in the car and start heading south. The plan is to drive down through New Mexico and Texas to the border and all the way to Mexico City, following roughly the same path that Kerouac and Cassady took in 1949. Then we'll head

100

back up to San Antonio. In the end, we'll have logged approximately twenty-five hundred miles in a little over six days, so I can make it back home for my son Liam's thirteenth birthday

Bongo is a writer, and for the last few years, we've been torturing each other with good ideas. I suggested he take a mountain bike-raft-canoe trip the length of the Rio Grande, and he did, producing a first-rate adventure story, *The Tecate Journals: Seventy Days on the Rio Grande*, from this grueling 1,260-mile trek. Then a year or so ago, seeking his revenge, Bongo phoned to say I should recreate Kerouac's trips from 1947 to 1949, even offering to drive the critical leg from Denver to El Jefe, in Mexico.

On his two-and-a-half-month journey down the Rio Grande, Keith was spooked by mountain lions, pelted with rain and biblical hailstorms, pestered by drug traffickers, and hounded by the Border Patrol (until they got to know him and began to help him along). When I acknowledged the lure of his Kerouac idea, I knew I'd be stranded on the side of the road in lousy weather, marooned in fly-blown Midwestern diners, and generally harassed and harangued by bus station lurkers and leeches. But in the end, I couldn't resist.

Healthy, attractive Colorado families are passing on the highway in their jeeps and station wagons, and we see an eight- or nine-year-old girl with an angelic face, bronzed by the sun, her auburn hair streaked with threads of gold. She smiles at us in benediction, a good omen for the trip.

Keith is tall with dark hair and blue eyes and the prominent cheekbones of an old cowboy. Dipping tobacco and occasionally hemming to himself, he ruminates sadly upon the world. This has been his way ever since I first met him in 1977, but it has become even more pronounced in the eighteen or so years since his young daughter, Ana Luisa, died from cancer. One story he tells captures his feelings on this subject: he was in Nova Scotia a few years after his daughter passed away, visiting an old friend, Eric Clem, whom we both met back at Acadia University more than thirty years ago. One of Clem's sons took Keith fishing on a snowy afternoon in early May. They went down through the trees to the brook that meanders across Clem's land and caught a mess of small brown trout, which the boy skewered through the gills on a sapling. When they were done for the day, the boy sized up the trout and just threw them into the tall grass, where they lay struggling for breath, still bound to the stick that had been threaded through their gills.

"I haven't been fishing since," Keith says.

2

We're driving along I-25 at dusk, with the misty blue Rockies on our right and what appears to be one long strip mall on our left. Keith has spent a total of four weeks rafting in the wilderness this summer, Maine, Montana, California, and BC, and his disgust for suburbia is palpable. "I could knock you out, and when you woke up, you wouldn't be able to tell where we were within a thousand miles," Bongo says. "Every town in America has a Pet-Smart, a K-Mart, and a Jiffy Mart. They built this whole country around Bed, Bath and Beyond. It turns my stomach."

By the time *On the Road* was published, Kerouac had given up the life of the hobo, complaining that stories of dangerous strangers with backpacks had ruined the prospects of the profession. And he did consider hoboing a profession, and his own wanderings part of an American tradition of the "Homeless Brother" (descended from the "Brueghel bums" of Europe) that included Johnny Appleseed and Jim Bridger and the "lumberjack bard," Jack London. To Kerouac, Buddha was just a hobo who paid no attention to other hoboes, and Christ himself "was a strange hobo who walked on water."

Heat is blasting in the open windows as we go rocketing south. "We're not going to get much more of the 'coolness,'" says Bongo, cackling to himself. "That party is *over*."

Keith is following a hearse down I-25, as the purple dusk spreads over the mountains and the world we're riding through grows solemn. When the limousine turns off, I can see that it's all beat up, patched with rust and cheerful yellow flower decals on the quarter panel, driven by a shirtless, tousle-haired kid who waves as he ascends the ramp, and suddenly our prospects seem bright again.

When Kerouac took this same trip in 1949, along with Cassady and Frank Jeffries, whom he refers to as Stan Shephard in *On the Road*, Cassady was looking for a Mexican divorce from his second wife, Carolyn, or "Camille," as she's known in the book. For this, he needed Kerouac's cash and companionship, but traveling with Keith is just the opposite: he doesn't say much, and I'll have to move fast when we approach a cash register, or he'll quietly pay my way and wave me off when I stick out a handful of banknotes. The landscape is being shaded in by degrees, the foothills of the Rockies just off to my right and draped in blue-gray shrouds. Keith hates driving at night and follows the signs for the Prentiss Motel, located right off I-25 in Trinidad, which is the last stop in Colorado. It was built in the 1950s and has served four generations of truckers, vagabonds, passers-through, cowpokes, and yahoos. It's an L-shaped, white stucco building with a second floor piled atop the office and café, and tiny dank rooms walled in old plywood and hung with battered polyester curtains. Above the entrance to the café is an illuminated clock that says "Frontier Time" along its upper rim.

Once we register, Keith and I sit in creaking metal chairs on the sidewalk in front of our room, drinking cans of Tecate beer and talking about the road that lies ahead. (In his book, Kerouac estimated that it was 1,767 miles from Denver to "the great city near the cracked Isthmus.") Bongo is dipping tobacco, and, leaning against the hood of his car, he tells me about this summer's rafting trip on the Machias River in Maine, with Scotty Hayes and Eric Clem, whom we've both known since the 1970s and whom Keith is particularly close to.

They embarked on the river from Route 9 above Bangor, Maine, the old Airline Route and my stomping ground when Keith and I were attending school in Wolfville, Nova Scotia, and I would hitchhike down to Massachusetts for February vacation. I tell Bongo about the negative reception I got hitchhiking in New York earlier in the summer, and he says it's easier in the West, where sometimes the cops themselves will accommodate him with a ride. Just a couple of weeks ago, he packed his raft and stowed it along the Klamath River in northern California, then drove his car down river and hitchhiked back so he could run the rapids and then float to the car. He got three quick rides, including one from a sheriff's deputy, and covered the forty miles in an hour and ten minutes. It took two days to run that stretch of the river.

It's growing late. There's a convenience store opposite the motel, and I cross the flat dark pavement and enter the outrageous chill of the air conditioning. The store is empty at this hour except for the cashier, a plain, middle-aged woman in overalls and a yellow Tweety Bird T-shirt. Lingering there among the cans of pinto beans and cigars and beef jerky, I finally select a packet of almonds and a bottle of water and approach the clerk.

"There's nothing like a smoked almond," she says, scanning the packet with her wand.

For some reason, it's comforting to be alone with this woman in her store late at night. She twists the almonds and the bottled water into a little paper bag and hands it to me along with the change. Her smile is bright and genuine, an artifact of the Old West. "You take care now," she says.

When I return to the motel, Keith is passed out on the floor in his sleeping bag. Rooms are only $30 a night at the Prentiss, but the beds are small and worn out, their exhausted springs hanging nearly to the floor. After brushing my teeth, I get beneath the threadbare coverlet and say my prayers, including a Hail Mary for Keith's little girl. Beside me on the chair is my backpack and journal, the only items I've taken with me. Bongo is also traveling light: he's been gone from Laredo all summer, and everything he needs is contained in the trunk of his little car.

My life has always been portable. Back home, what few things I own are in cardboard boxes, ready to be hauled away at a moment's notice. That all started back in Canada, when I was reading *Walden* and *On the Road* and realized that Kerouac knew the old Concord maestro and was responding to him like one clarinet player to another.

In 1845, Henry David Thoreau built a tiny cabin on Walden Pond, where he grew a garden, worked intermittently as a hired man, and announced his intention to "live deep and suck all the marrow out of life." Due to his learnedness and introspection, most of us wouldn't consider Henry a man of action. But what drove Thoreau into the Concord woods was the same force that compelled Jack Kerouac back and forth across America: he wanted to be free. And while Thoreau's daily circuit took him around a pond, some of the episodes in *Walden* take readers on a much grander tour—among the naked savages of Tierra del Fuego, past a Brahmin suspended over flames, and alongside Hector as he waded toward Achilles. Read this little local story, and you understand a greater part of the world, as it should be.

A shaft of moonlight falls across our room, illuminating the patch of carpet where Keith lies sleeping. In many ways, he's the ultimate sojourner, home wherever his hat is, and not prone to materialism or fretting about the future. In *Walden*, Thoreau points out the foolishness of "making yourself sick, that you might lay up something against a sick day." During my summer of *On the Road* and *Walden*, I was nineteen and had a job at a soda-bottling plant. One morning when my father came to wake me, I decided that not only was I going to quit working at Coca-Cola, I would never labor over anything so meaningless again. To my dad, it seemed a youthful indiscretion. But a book can change a life. Since then, I've had a few lean years but managed to avoid what Thoreau called the "demon" of good behavior.

3

Right outside the hotel in the morning light a gigantic, flat-topped butte rises above the town, with the green folds of the mountain cascading downward to the first scattered homes and then Trinidad's small business district. This scene is eclipsed in the near ground by four fifty-foot metal poles supporting a quintet of large white metal rectangles with SHELL printed on them in six-foot red letters. Man has therefore put his obscene signature on the horizon and stamped "Trinidad," the Holy Trinity, with his unholy imprint.

By 6 a.m., we're going up and over the final pass out of Colorado into New Mexico. "My twenty-seventh state," says Keith. "But you can put down forty-seven, and be one of those writers who lie, like what's-his-name, James Frey."

I spit out my tea at this remark. "Fucking phony."

We turn onto 64/87, a two-lane highway through and across the northeastern corner of New Mexico. Long golden fields stretch away to the high chaparral in the distance, solitary mountains with rocky cliff faces and low-lying tables of rock where Kiowa scouts once watched for wagon trains and stoically puffed at their pipes.

"Jack and Neal definitely went through here, with Cassady chain-smoking and talking incessantly," says Bongo, who averages only about fifty words an hour himself. "And taking Benzedrine, which we would call diet pills." Keith refers to the photo of Cassady on the console. "That's why he was so skinny."

Rob Boushel was a friend of ours at Acadia, a happy-go-lucky, freckle-faced kid who ran like a deer; he and I played in the midfield together on the soccer team. Today, Rob is a PhD in physiology and lives on a farm in Quebec. Once a year, when Keith visits Rob on the farm, Rob will buy a flat of beer and try to play a game with Keith that he calls "famous person"—what famous person would you like to spend a day with?

"Nobody," says Keith.

"Come on, Bongo," Rob will say. "There's got to be somebody."

"Nope."

It wasn't always that way. When Keith was a teenager, he called a Los Angeles radio show to talk with Neal's wife, Carolyn Cassady. "I was nervous, like I was talking to royalty," he says. "I wanted to ask something that I really wanted to know. About the gap in Cassady's biography between his days with Kerouac and his time with the Merry Pranksters. What he was doing then. But when I finally got through, [Carolyn] wouldn't give me the time of day."

We drive between miles of wire cattle fences, the members of the herd like black specks in the distance on both sides. "I asked her about those years and she was a real bitch," Keith says. "Like, 'You gotta ask something better than that, kid, if I'm gonna come all the way down here.'"

Out of high school in 1975, Bongo owned a '62 Plymouth "with three on the column" and spent a year driving in a big circle around the U.S. Along the way he got directions to Ken Kesey's farm outside Springfield, Oregon. "Pulled right up to the house. There was [the Merry Pranksters' psychedelic bus] 'Further' right by the barn in a pasture. Fay Kesey came out of the house when I was standing there. I was eighteen, shy, very nervous. She walked outside and I got up the nerve to say, 'Is Ken here?' 'No. What do you want?' 'I was wondering if I—if we—could listen to some Neal Cassady tapes.' 'We don't have any Neal Cassady tapes,' Kesey's wife said. I said, 'Oh, thank you,' and left. But they had hundreds of hours of those tapes, from the Acid Tests, from the bus. I could just tell from her demeanor that she was thinking, What the hell are you doing here? I had four idols at that age: Kerouac, Cassady, Kesey, and [Grateful Dead guitarist] Jerry Garcia. It's funny to me now. There's no one that's famous I would drive across town to talk to. In those days, I would drive across the country just to talk to one of those guys for ten seconds. I drove all the way to San Miguel de Allende in Mexico just to walk on the railroad tracks where Cassady died. How ridiculous is that? I didn't even speak Spanish."

Not long after I finished reading *On the Road*, I went looking for a copy of Tom Wolfe's *Electric Kool-Aid Acid Test* so I could follow Neal Cassady and Kerouac, who makes only a cameo appearance in this watershed '60s book, into what Jack would call "later phases of our lives." It's hard to say what was sadder: Cassady continuing to *move*, chasing the ghost of his younger self into the Age of Aquarius, or Kerouac taking himself out of the game, retired to the sidelines with a cheap bottle of booze. In the end, Kerouac rejected the sort of instant enlightenment sought by the LSD generation, proclaiming that "walking on water wasn't built in a day."

Groundbreaking novels like *On the Road* are the planted seeds that, over time, become mighty trees hung with the bright shiny "leaves" of two or three hundred other good, honest books. Keith says that the best book he's read lately is *A Fan's Notes* by Frederick Exley. "Drank a lot and lived with his mom," he says. "Does that sound like anyone we know?"

It sounds like everyone we know and love, Jack Kerouac, Jim Thompson, John Kennedy Toole, you name it. When Keith was young, his relatives would say, "Don't be like Aunt Erm," who chain-smoked and drank and only ate chocolate. One by one, Keith's relatives died off. And there's Aunt Erm in her nineties, partying like a rock

star. She died when she fell down and broke her hip and had to go
in the hospital, where they wouldn't let her smoke and drink.

4

After a long, dusty afternoon, Keith and I stop on the side of the
highway to take a leak—Texas is not a bit modest.

Not far down the road is Grant Feed Lot, thousands of head of
cattle stocked in large, iron-fenced pens with a manmade watering hole
and grazing lands on either side of the highway. We pass through
Clayton, NM, the long, wide, main thoroughfare lined with small
cattlemen's hotels, empty diners, and brick churches. The Hi-Ho
Café sits vacant on the side of the road going out of town. Wild
West Trading Post is closed. The carhop burger joint looks deserted.
Remnants of the Old West are still here but fading away.

Deep into Texas and the Central Time Zone, where the clock
jumps ahead an hour on my cell phone, and suddenly it's hot. Hot
and flat. There are bulldozers and jackhammers and flagmen everywhere in Texas, grading and pushing the dirt on the sides of the
road in little work crews that appear futile against the gigantic
backdrop of the horizon. And it seems that every car in Texas has a
broken windshield. "It's the law," says Bongo, whose own windshield
features a jagged crack right across the middle.

Freight trains a half-mile long go rolling past on the endless
tracks, and the North Texas oil fields are dotted with the great tipping insect heads of the oil wells. Money comes out of the ground,
and we all go into it, from the poorest old cowhand to the chairman
of the board at Standard Oil. So I'd rather be just passing through
than counting batches of old money down at the local saloon.

Lunch is at the Sands Restaurant in Dalhart, Texas, the dining room
filled with men in straw cowboy hats and boots with spurs; where the
"Ladies' cut" sirloin is six ounces, half the size of the men's cut. The
restaurant is squared up with pale yellow walls and corny oil paintings of ghostly stagecoaches and cowboys on rearing horses. Seven
years ago, Keith says, after a rafting trip in Montana, his friend

Becky treated him to a steak dinner at a restaurant in White Sulphur Springs, and Bongo ordered his sirloin cooked medium rare. It came to the table dripping with blood, straight up raw, and he didn't bother to send it back. Finally, this summer on another river trip Becky got around to asking Keith why he did that. "Because I don't care," he said.

The great dividend from these trips is reconnecting with my old buddies, especially Keith, whom I only see every three or four years and who doesn't like to talk on the phone. In a way, losing his old friends and their youthful enthusiasm—not to mention their love for him—is what did Kerouac in. It's not easy for a middle-aged guy to leave hearth and home to light out for the territory, as Mark Twain put it. But my old true friends are just as wild-hearted and footloose as I am, favoring the vicissitudes of hard travel over the illusory comforts of a settled life.

Huge feed silos line the highway in Hartley, Texas, with dust kicking up from passing cars, and I remember driving through here with Surfer nine years ago and the same road dust swirling between the silos, rising up eighty feet from the highway on both sides. Route 87 is two lanes of empty pavement until we encounter a sheriff's deputy in a marked pickup blocking the lanes in both directions and waving his arms. Keith slows and then stops and unrolls his window. The deputy tells us that over the next rise we'll find a stalled driver and that we're to tell him that the sheriff has stopped traffic.

"Where is he?" Bongo asks.

The deputy points. "You'll see him."

Sure enough, there's a pickup truck bogged down in some high grass in the median, and when Keith slows again to inform the driver and his passenger that traffic is stopped, they run to the truck and gun it out of the ditch and take off down the road past us. The chivalry of Texas drivers and law enforcement is notable, especially to a guy like me, from Massachusetts, where everyone is giving everyone else the finger and most of the cops don't smile until they punch out for the afternoon.

Long silent miles ensue, as we cross the arid spaces of Texas until, entering the streets of Amarillo, Bongo says, "This is where

Kerouac smoked his first cigar." With all the time Keith has spent poring over Kerouac's and Cassady's letters, audio tapes, journals, books, and biographies, I don't question this pronouncement.

The temperature has risen past ninety degrees, and in Post, Texas, a little town twenty-five miles south of Lubbock, Bongo pulls off Route 84 when he spots a park containing a little greenish pond. It's nearing five o'clock in the afternoon, and at the edge of the field a collection of large, shaggy, gray-haired Christian bikers is standing around an open pit barbecue eating hamburgers and drinking Coca-Cola. Inside the fence is a sparkling, Olympic-size swimming pool, and the husband and wife who manage it are busy tidying up the pavilion and concrete deck when I approach. The woman, a pleasant young brunette with a ring of roses tattooed around her upper arm, tells me that they're closing at five, but that she doesn't advise swimming in "the lake."

All I say is thanks, but the woman reads the disappointment on my face and comes around the snack bar to confer with her husband for a moment. He's a large Mexican American fellow with a ready smile, dressed in a blue T-shirt that says "Perez Family Reunion."

"We had a lot of rain, and we shocked it with chlorine a couple days ago," he says. "If you don't mind that, you can go in."

Over at the car, Bongo puts on his sneakers and heads for a nearby baseball field. He's just been saying that Kerouac "stopped challenging himself" around age thirty or thirty-one. "I like to drink, too, but what fun is there in sitting around and drinking all the time?" he asked.

In fact, Keith has the simplest and greatest workout of all time. For the past twenty years, he has gone over to the baseball field at Laredo Junior College, where he runs an easy mile to limber up, then completes a dozen hundred yard sprints, and goes back home. You can see the imprint of his feet across the outfield grass, he has done this so many times; and in so doing, he has maintained the sturdy physique of his thirty-year-old self.

The woman points the way to a large, empty concrete locker room, and I change into my trunks and don my watch and goggles and wade into the pool. After the blast furnace heat of the day, the water is cool, blue, and pleasant. For nearly an hour, I swim laps up and down and emerge, dripping wet, onto the concrete feeling like I have received a gift from the Perezes.

"How was it?" the man asks.

"Beautiful. After ten hours in the car, you made my day."

The man shades his eyes, gazing over the dimpled surface of the pool. Beyond the fence, Keith has returned and is changing his shirt and socks and rummaging in the trunk of the car. "You guys work out every day?" the man asks.

"Try to. My buddy just got off a river in California. We're heading for his place in Laredo and then to Mexico City."

Holding a long-handled squeegee, the man takes a few steps toward the fence, still looking over at Keith. "That sounds like fun," he says, in a soft, wistful tone. He glances back at his wife, who has exited the snack bar and is standing forty or fifty feet away, not quite close enough to hear us, though she is frowning at him.

"That would probably kill me," the man says. "Have fun, though. Have a safe trip."

5

Two guys in a pickup stop in the middle of the two-lane and get out to look at a rattlesnake on the side of the road. We're on the first high ground west of the Mississippi, the Edwards Plateau, which rises until it meets the foothills of the Rockies. "The U.S. changes a lot when you go west to east," Keith says, who drives around the country all summer, every summer. "If you go north to south, you can drive over a thousand miles and still see the same country."

On the outskirts of San Angelo, we pass "Wild William's Used Cars," a half-dozen battered Caddys and Impalas inside a hurricane fence and surrounding an ordinary cinder-block house and dirt yard. "It appears that various economic and social factors have combined to tame ol' William," I say to Bongo.

Crossing Kickapoo Creek in the early morning, Bongo notes that the temperature is still below eighty degrees on a day headed past a hundred. In the dusty town of Eden, Texas, we turn onto Route 83, past the "Parish Wool and Mohair WHSE" that rises up large and black from the flat empty ground. Huge ranches line the highway, "The 4W," "Ruffin Ranch," with iron gates and long dirt roads leading to farmhouses and outbuildings so distant they're hidden by the curve of the earth. Two buzzards picking at a road kill go flapping off with giant black wings. For some reason, this inspires Keith to tell me about Scotty Hayes of Beverly, Mass., who makes love to his girl "four times a year." Hayesey is self-employed as a landscaper, and they have sex when his quarterly tax payments are due.

When Keith moved to Beverly, Mass., in the early '80s, the Pitcher family owned a large wooded parcel of land across the street from their home. Situated in a clearing was the foundation of an old carriage house, which Keith piled over with twigs, pine boughs, and sheets of plastic to make a crude shelter. He lived in what Pitch called the troll house for several months, working for Hayesey and writing letters to his girl by candlelight.

I visited Keith a few times that summer and especially recall Pitch's annual croquet and Wiffle ball tournament, "the Martini Open," which was played in a clearing beside the troll house. Inside Bongo's lean-to was a photograph of a lovely dark-eyed girl who looked like the Ava Gardner of Latin America. Keith had met this young beauty during one of his frequent trips to Bolivia, in a place called Cochabamba. It was a doomed intercontinental love affair, fraught with desperate letters back and forth and the sneaking suspicion that the girl was actually a high-priced prostitute looking to score a green card into the U.S.

In *On the Road*, when Sal/Jack met Terry/Bea, the "Mexican girl," on that Bakersfield, California, bus, he fell in love at first glance but then doubted his own instincts, believing for a while that she was trying to hustle him, while Terry, in her "simple and funny little mind," thought Sal might be a pimp. Driving along the Edwards Plateau, Keith and I rhapsodize on his old troll house, the Martini Open, and the goofy little alpine hat that Pitch liked to wear during his croquet matches. Occasionally, in the years after their romance ended, Keith would receive a letter from the Bolivian girl claiming that he had fathered a son with her. "OK—send me a picture," Bongo would write back. She never did.

6

We cross under I-10, which goes from Jacksonville, Florida, to Los Angeles, the same road Surfer and I were highballing over just a few weeks ago. A long iron bridge traverses the clear, rocky band of the Llano River, which lies far beneath us. The marked speed limit here is eighty mph, the highest in the land, and soon we're passing through the coveted hill country of south central Texas. Groves of mesquite, live oak, and mountain cedar are scattered across rolling grasslands as far as the eye can see and perhaps as far as the mind can imagine. An orange-and-black butterfly is swept up and over the windshield as we pass beneath it, making it appear like a Nabokovian taxidermy specimen, pinned flat by the crosscurrents of wind and magnified through the lens of the windshield.

Keith says the fenced-in ranches around here make money selling hunting licenses. Sportsmen come in from San Antonio and Houston to hunt the wild deer or, for an outrageously high fee, the "exotics" that are stocked by the ranchers: mountain lion and big horn sheep and antelope and maybe even gazelle and cheetah. "Why don't they put some fish in a barrel and let 'em shoot those?" I ask.

We're driving between forested hills covered in live oak. Deep ravines create small mountains out of these hills, with the River Frio off to the east, curving between stands of bald cypress, pecan trees, and other deciduous varieties. "Don't Mess with Texas" signs begin to appear on the side of the road, warning of a $2,000 fine for littering. It's close to a hundred degrees, and with no air-conditioning in the Mazda, I'm broiling in the plastic seat.

Departing from the county highway, Keith finds a toy inner tube on the bank of the River Frio where it overflows the road in Leakey, Texas. Going waist-deep in the cold, clear water, I pull off my T-shirt, jump on the tube, fall off, and get back on just in time to run a little hundred-yard rapid while Bongo hoots from the embankment. The current flows over a few jagged boulders where I whack my ass pretty good. Arching halfway out of the tube to clear the shallow bottom, I hit a nice ribbon of current and go rushing beneath the tangled branches of the live oaks bordering the river.

Cool and refreshed, I change clothes on the side of the road, and Keith finds a little German restaurant back in Leakey called Nena's Café.

"Somewhere along the line the redundant bratwurst will be handed to me," I say to Keith, following him inside.

The small dining room is subdued and Germanic. Five customers are scattered across half a dozen tables, and the proprietor, standing with his hands spread on the counter and a slight hunch to his posture, is a bearded and bespectacled gent in his early sixties. The faint sound of a Bavarian dirge can be heard, and two silent Mexican women are in the space behind the owner, preparing the food. The proprietor takes our order, bowing slightly. "Very good," he says, like a mysterious figure in a Stanley Kubrick film.

Back outside, we sit in the shade of a good-size live oak, at a table covered with a red-and-white-checked tablecloth. There's a mild aromatic breeze, and large white clouds are scudding overhead. Without a word passing between us for nearly half an hour, Bongo and I sit across the table from each other, scribbling in our notebooks. Once, when Geoff Pitcher was living in Cambridge, Mass., with his girlfriend, we all went out to the Can-Tab lounge on Mass. Ave. where Little Joe Cook and the Thrillers were playing. Even back then, Joe Cook was pretty old, a short and stubby fellow in a shiny dinner jacket, with pomaded hair and a falsetto. He played the Can-Tab for more than twenty-five years, singing his one big hit from the early sixties, "Peanuts."

After a night of wild dancing and drinking, Keith and I crashed on the floor in Pitch's living room. When Geoff stumbled out of his bedroom the next morning, he found the two of us, awake and alert at opposite ends of the apartment, writing in our journals.

"You're like a couple of CIA agents," said Pitch, heating up the water for his coffee.

7

Lay a piece of tracing paper with the route of my journeys over Kerouac's map from 1947 to 1949, and it would be crooked and imperfect but fitting at all the right places. After lunch we pass through

Uvalde, the big stucco homes set back from the road and framed with giant shade trees. Downtown, there's a transformed movie theater, with "God's House" on the marquee in big red letters. Pretty girls in sundresses are walking on Main Street, which is under construction, picking their way along to the drugstore, the beauty salon, and the 5 and 10.

Out of the hill country now, into the low dry plain of south Texas. The shoulder of the road is dominated by Tamilapas thorn scrub, a low, spiky bush with yellow flowers, but only an occasional mesquite tree breaks up the empty distances beyond the highway. We've been talking about Mexico and what lies ahead. "Your whole life, society is telling you, 'you can't,' 'you shouldn't,' 'don't,'" says Bongo. "But nobody's gonna tell you that down there. Mexico is like that Vegas ad." He laughs and shakes his head. "What happens in Mexico stays in fucking Mexico, that's for sure."

On the road to Crystal City, we pass a small prison with aluminum Quonset huts, a square of barbed-wire fence, and a thirty-foot guard tower staffed by a man wearing a Stetson and toting a rifle. I silently consider the string of bad decisions each of the inmates must have made, and then, thinking aloud, I wonder what those kinds of mistakes would lead to in a place like Mexico.

"You don't want to find out," says Bongo.

Nearing the Mexican border, Keith dips into his tin of cut tobacco, spitting into a plastic bottle. Fifty miles from Laredo we see our first checkpoint, Border Patrol agents stopping cars on the northbound side of Route 83. "There's no real border anymore, not like there used to be when Kerouac and Cassady came through," says Bongo. "There's 'the zone.' They stop you thirty to fifty miles out on each side of the line, and they keep stopping you until you get past them all." Bongo pauses over his tobacco. "If you do."

8

At a truck stop forty miles outside of Laredo, where gas is more than half a buck lower than the national average, we chat with a Mexican American Union Pacific railroad cop about hoboes riding the rails. He's a tall, pot-bellied, wavy-haired man wearing sunglasses.

"They been here, some of them, since the forties, fifties, and sixties," he says. "We just run them off the property. Sometimes we ride them out to the bus station and get them a ticket, but they almost always come back. They don't know anything else. It's like telling a dog not to eat a hamburger that's lying on the ground."

In *On the Road*, Kerouac said that Laredo was a "sinister town," the bottom of America where all the heaviest villains had sunk. At noon, the downtown streets are thronging with teenage Mexican girls in black halter tops and snug jeans. Salsa music is blasting from the shops, and the sun is hot enough to melt a plastic cup lying in the gutter. Keith lives in a second floor walk-up in a small stone house just a few blocks from downtown. Outside his front door is a tiled deck with a roof overhead; that's where I'm sitting as I write this, with a strong, sultry breeze blowing and the sound of a Mexican ballad coming from a house two doors down. I'm sketching my impressions as I go along, as quickly and unconsciously as possible, following Kerouac's advice that each chapter should be like a line of verse in an epic poem. While he was figuring out how to construct *On the Road* from his various rough drafts and false starts, Kerouac wrote in his journal that each brief chapter should be an "illuminative point," like in a dream.

Keith's apartment on Iturbide Street is a narrow, spartan place with a small unplugged refrigerator, an old television for watching ball games, and a very basic-looking computer. The furnishings are spare, and there are piles of books, his journals and photo albums, and a few hanging photographs of rafting trips—Bongo piloting himself solo down wild stretches of river, where he's happiest and most at home. In many respects, his apartment is similar to my place back in northern Mass.; writers and book wranglers must confine themselves to tiny spaces in order for their imaginations to roam free. Plus, the rents are killing us.

After dropping off our stuff and turning on Bongo's appliances, we head out for dinner at Mariachi Express on San Bernardo Street, a breezy joint decorated in pastels with neon green pipes running across the orange walls and the rotating X's of ceiling fans whirring overhead. The smell of *frijoles* and grilling meat wafts out from the kitchen, and the blare of a *telenovela* comes from the TV mounted on the far wall. In answer to my queries, a Mexican kid wearing a hairnet mumbles out the description of an *enchilada suiza*, and Keith waves his hand and says to me, "Just order it."

Bongo is especially quiet after such a long day, but over the enchiladas and iced tea, he tells me about his childhood friend Tony Meyers, a civil engineer who builds subdivisions in California. Together, he and Tony mountain-biked the first leg of his epic journey down the Rio Grande. And a couple of years ago, Tony named a street in a development near Sacramento after Keith. "It's a dead end, of course," says Bongo.

At dusk, Keith pays $3 U.S. to traverse the long raised span of the International Bridge separating Laredo from Nuevo Laredo in Mexico. Hoping to save time in the morning, we're going over to purchase tourist visas and register Bongo's car. The Mexican customs officials are off to one side, and they ignore us; moments later, we're over the bridge and into Nuevo Laredo. With its crumbling cinder-block buildings, beckoning café girls, and legless beggars, it looks, as Kerouac himself noted, "surprisingly like Mexico."

Bongo and I drive a half-mile to a large white air-conditioned building called the "Hall of Mexican Justice" to fill out paperwork for the car and acquire our visas, which are good for six months. A friendly but tired old man gives me a form, sends me to the pay window where I fork over $23, and then I return to the old man and he stamps my visa.

"*Gracias*," I say, and he smiles, revealing a large gap where his two front teeth should be.

An attractive girl in a tight white blouse enters Bongo's car registration into her computer, then hands it back. He pays her the equivalent of $29.70 with his credit card. A gaggle of beautiful dark-eyed women are looming behind the glass, and Keith's efforts in clearing the car are smooth and swift, thanks to his fluent Spanish. All of it takes fifteen minutes, when we were expecting to wait in line for a couple of hours, even now, on a Sunday evening. My latest experience of Mexico—after sixteen years away—is of a drive-through wonderland staffed by gorgeous women.

On our return, it's too hot for me in the apartment, so after Bongo calls it a night, I take my bedroll—consisting of a padded quilt, Keith's old mummy bag, and a wadded-up jacket and pair of shorts—onto the cool tiles of the veranda. Crickets are singing in the garden, and the shadow of Bongo's live oak tree, cast down by the nearby street light, shimmers and dances over the sleeping bag. I position myself beside the wrought-iron railing, with a view of the Big Dipper above the housetops in the northern sky. It's well past midnight, and there's music playing from the next street, mingled with a chorus of gleeful voices.

Occasionally, a hot rod guns past on Iturbide Street, which sets off the neighbor's dog. His barking is loud and coarse, and I give up on sleeping for a while, rubbing a little mosquito repellent behind my ears and knees. It's uncomfortable inside the mummy bag so I lie on top in my boxer shorts, enjoying the open air.

To pass the time, I try to say an Our Father or a Hail Mary for everyone I can think of, starting with Keith's daughter, then Keith, his ex-wife, Pitch, Hayesey, Boushel, my son, Liam, Jeff Ness, my neighbors; my sisters and brothers and brother-in-law and sister-in-law and nieces and nephews; the lady from West Virginia who lost her daughter and suffers from cancer; and Surfer and Piercey and Frank Baker and all of those guys.

I'm trying to work my way down the roster of my soccer team at Acadia but lose consciousness somewhere after our fullback, Phil Moxom, a dairy farmer from Antigonish who sold me a hundred pounds of beef every September, in various cuts, all of it wrapped in butcher paper and carefully marked, at just a dollar a pound.

9

In the rising heat of 7 a.m., I take Keith's mountain bike for a ride, first down to the end of Iturbide and north alongside the rail yards. A giant yellow-brick warehouse sits at the end of the street, Jose E. Mayormeyer y Hijos, and I wonder what Mexican American Dreiser-esque tragedy has hit Senor Mayormeyor and his children (since it comes to all great families, in spades). Beyond the warehouse is the Union Pacific freight station, with its graceful mansard roof and a long, low overhang supported by wooden pillars.

Hundreds of rail cars are lined up on the sidings, waiting to be filled or unloaded. It's another workday in Texas, the brakemen arriving with their lunch pails amid cries of *Buenos dias!* and *Como esta?* Whistles are blowing, great diesel engines starting up with a roar, and suddenly I'm struck by the vast energy of this daily Herculean undertaking: sneakers, coal, produce, shale, hay, cotton, auto parts; all the matériel of the Americas collected at the border and shipped everywhere, to everyone.

A small, happy dog begins following me. Two and then three other dogs join him, and before I've covered another block, I have a canine posse. The six dogs in attendance are well-fed house pets, and when a mangy stray with a mottled coat appears just ahead on the sidewalk, it smells and then sees the other dogs and veers off, slinking beside the ratty fence. Apparently, this mutt is not a "player" on the local dog scene.

I pass a ramshackle house with a tall wooden fence decorated with old metal Coca-Cola advertisements and stickers and decals for defunct tobacco companies, motor oil, spearmint chewing gum, and other sundries. A sign on the gate advertises "Victor Guevara, Notary Public and Tax Advice." By the looks of the place, Senor Guevara needs a little financial guidance his ownself.

After I ride out to the Laredo water tower and back and take a quick shower, Bongo and I head into town to buy something called "Mexican in-surance" from Johnson's Insurance Company, established in 1949 by Tommy Johnson. On the wall is a picture of a balding man smoking a cigar in his office in the El Rey Hotel. (These days, they're located behind iron grillwork in the lobby of a Burger King.) The current Mr. Johnson is an easygoing fellow in a Ban-Lon shirt who admits he hasn't been to Mexico for quite awhile. After a little give and take, it's $65 for four days' worth of accident insurance for Bongo's car.

"Do you realize that those rates would mean five thousand dollars a year?" asks Keith, on our way out.

"Yeah, but four days is how long they think we're gonna last in Mexico," I tell him.

Behind the plate-glass window at "Casa de Cambio" in downtown Laredo, 100 dollars quickly becomes 1,080 pesos. We roll over Bridge #1 at 11 a.m., right where "Kerouac and Cassady crossed," Bongo says. The old red-and-white Mexican Customs building is still here, with a yellow gate across the exit and a last tiny pavilion marked "Vigilancia" for the last smiling cop, who waves to us when we drive by. When Kerouac and Cassady reached the border, they could smell "a billion tortillas frying and smoking in the night." Kerouac had never been to Mexico and was amazed at the grinning border officials and the desultory way they poked through their baggage. He had a great affinity for what he called the "fellaheen" people of the world, which included the dark and brooding folks of both Mexico and the Middle East, and he couldn't wait to dig them in their entirety. On the other hand, I've visited contemporary Mexico and have been forewarned about the drug cartels and the ruthless way they do business. Never one to exaggerate, Keith has told me horrifying stories about former students of his, guys he coached in baseball, junior college kids, who got mixed up in the cartels trying to make a fast buck and ended up being murdered: shot execution-style, asphyxiated, beheaded, you name it. It's much worse now than when I was last here to play rugby in the '90s, and as we roll into Nuevo Laredo, I wonder what we'll find in "the magic land at the end of the road."

Now we're inching along, stoplight to stoplight on the road to Monterrey. Keith says the nightclub and bar business in Nuevo Laredo has all but shut down because of the violence perpetrated by the drug cartels, which run just about everything and operate brazenly in the midst of Mexico's general culture. "It's not astronomical by American standards," says Bongo of the local murder rate. "But they do it in broad daylight. Bang-bang-bang. Old-fashioned shoot-outs."

The nicest structure in town is a giant cemetery behind pink stucco walls, occupied by a thousand statues of Jesus to three-fourths scale, standing over the vaults with outstretched arms. A small personalized Christ for the myriad lost souls of Nuevo Laredo, and our mad journey deep into the country begins with a dirge as a funeral procession goes winding around an interior road.

Keith speculates that the black-clad mourners are grieving over another drug cartel victim. "A pound of very good marijuana is a hundred dollars over here," he says. "But when they make a bust on the U.S. side, they value that pound at a thousand bucks. It used to be five hundred, but if they get lucky and stumble over a bunch of smugglers, it sounds more impressive to say you seized two million worth of pot than one million."

One thing's for sure, the junkyards of Nuevo Laredo are legion. Just beyond a sign that says "*Yonke*" in huge crooked black letters are more ruined cars than Queens's earnest automobile boneyards ever thought of; cars without title or name, imponderable hulks that once ferried the skeletons of men, women, and children long buried under the stone statues of diminutive Jesus, their ashtrays filled with the dust of hands that held the dust of cigarette ash years upon years ago. Mexico seems like nothing more than the tired, overwrought junkyard of America, protected for all eternity by the Lamb of God.

As I ride along the dusty highway, it strikes me that I could produce a pretty comprehensive documentary film of my trips across the U.S. by compiling all the surveillance videos I've wandered into. Parking lots, hotel lobbies, restaurant waiting areas, ATMs, highway off-ramps, and street corners have become the new Hollywood studios of America, generating innumerable cinematic epics of "la comedie humaine" by the hour. (This is the fulfillment of Ken Kesey's prophesy during the Merry Prankster's journey across America that one day we'll all be stars in a great movie that depicts each and every person's tiniest thought and movement.) Somewhere among the uniformed personnel monitoring all this footage is the next Erich Von Stroheim, the next Bertolt Brecht, a dime-store auteur who will mold this raw material into a heartbreaking film that will resolve once and for all what we're doing to one another on this planet.

Not so *Me-hi-co*. When you cross the border here, you fall off the grid. Even in Nuevo Laredo, so close to the American side, there's the sense that your most grievous sins will be ignored rather than forgiven. It's hard to describe exactly, but it's like a place with no adult supervision. Rolling onto the plain that lies beyond the last crumbling house, an old tune by Tom T. Hall is playing in my head: "Faster horses, younger women, older whiskey, and more money." Bongo was right: what happens in Mexico stays in Mexico.

10

Twenty-six kilometers into Mexico we hit the first government checkpoint and are waved in by a portly, cheerless sergeant wearing fatigues and shiny boots. On the other side, heading toward the U.S., every vehicle is being crawled over and inspected by men in full combat gear and automatic weapons. A shiny black "ATI Policia" van is parked nearby.

While we're waiting for the soldiers to approach, I ask Bongo if they're looking mostly for drugs or just contraband in general.

"If you're smuggling drugs, you have to be part of the organization," says Keith in a low voice. "The cartel calls the shots. No freelancing whatsoever."

Before I can ask what happens to freelancers, the sergeant arrives at the window and looks inside. He reeks of aftershave and sweat, and his lustrous black hair seems a bit unkempt for a military man. His gaze is quite unfriendly, and though we're guilty of nothing, this man's power over us borders on the absolute. But sitting calmly in the driver's seat, Bongo has that Gary Cooper reliability and stillness, with a lot going on behind his eyes. He says good morning in Spanish, and the sergeant nods, then straightens up and walks away from the car.

"*Pasale*," he says, and Bongo zooms off.

There's a cloudless blue sky overhead, with low ranchlands stretching away to the horizon on either side. The smoothly paved toll road and the "Libre" road are side by side at this juncture. Right now, we're cruising along on the freeway, and saving the $20 toll is beginning to look like a smart move. It's called the "Carretera Nacional," the bumpy and winding national highway, and Bongo speculates that Cassady and Kerouac selected it as their route because it sounded grand and official. Like everything else in "official" Mexico, however, it's slow and filled with obstacles, as we'll soon find out.

After an hour of driving, we're approaching the Sierra Madre range, which lies off to the east, and enter the town of Sabinas Hidalgo at noon. With pedestrians everywhere, alongside with burros and chickens and an occasional stray horse, Bongo slows down to five miles per hour. Leather-skinned cowboys in straw hats are tipping back in old wooden chairs beneath the palm trees. Concrete buildings painted in bright colors lie close to the road on both sides: Pollo Coco, Casino Mirage, Banco Azteca. Myriad taco stands crowd the alleyways, the smoke rising from their wood fires and starving dogs hanging around. Rickety kiosks hung with baskets and cheap pottery. Comb salesmen, gum vendors, scrawny kids hawking maps and pencils and toiletries. In the glare of the noon light, there are half a dozen bars with swinging doors, the cool gray darkness beckoning from within.

Strange, spindly cacti appear as the Sierras loom closer. Soon we're ascending Mexico 85, a winding road that climbs up through the mountain passes, higher and higher, and choking on the diesel exhaust of the slow-moving trucks that precede us. Here and there, lighted Plexiglas boxes containing little plaster saints dot the road-side, memorials to those unlucky drivers who gambled on the many blind turns and lost. I'm sure these electric monuments reminded Kerouac of the similarly garish but haunting Stations of the Cross at Notre Dame de Lourdes Grotto in Lowell.

Our cooler is filled with bottled water, green tea, sports drinks, and, rolling around somewhere beneath the ice, a few cold cans of Tecate beer. It's blazing hot, and I'm halfway over the seat, rummaging around in there, when three armored vehicles pass us going in the other direction. Soldiers in camouflage are milling about on top, pointing their .50-caliber machine guns. Bongo notes that they're not fighting the war in Iraq or Afghanistan: "They're fighting the war in Nueva Leon," the state we're in right now. But it's hard to say who's winning and who's losing, even who it is they're fighting.

Looming above Monterrey is Cerro de la Silla—literally, "chair hill"—and I pause long enough to make a drawing of it in my note-book, the slopes below the peak dotted with tiny concrete homes. In *On the Road*, Sal/Jack looked up at this same formation and called it a "wild saddle." He compared the approach to Monterrey to the outskirts of Denver, with the lines of smoking factories and shifty hipsters loitering in doorways and whores calling from the open windows. Just like Sal, I want to stop and check out Monterrey, but Keith is like Cassady: he drives like a fiend and never rests.

As we enter the city, it's obvious that Mexico is the undisputed world champion of Mickey Mouse construction. Working at Latin American speed, crews are building some kind of raised tramline through the center of Monterrey, and traffic is completely fouled up. It's ninety-eight degrees, and there are guys wearing straw cowboy hats and sweeping the dust everywhere. Mexico has hundreds of thousands of these apparently semi-official street cleaners, and one can only imagine the paltriness of their collective income and the incredibly old and sad government clerks who process their sporadic pay checks.

Outside of Monterrey, there's a weird statue of John Lennon dressed all in white, strolling along the stone wall surrounding a rock 'n' roll memorial park of some kind. There's a great psychedelic guitar jutting up from behind the wall, and the whole enterprise reminds me of that giant, surreal portrait of the singer-songwriter Paul Simon that guards Lower Manhattan. Beginning, I suppose, with figures like Elvis Presley and James Dean, somehow we've made deities of our pop stars and expect them to deliver us.

Bongo says that every year, he and his best friend Tony get together and watch *Paint Your Wagon*, an old movie starring Lee Marvin and Clint Eastwood about two gold prospectors who share a wife. It's both a Western and a musical, featuring songs by these famous tough guys in their thin, cracking voices. Then I tell Bongo a story about my father's kid brother, Uncle Johnny, who used to travel often between Boston, New York, Phoenix, and LA for work. Back in the 1970s, first-class airline accommodations included a smoking section, and on a flight to Arizona out of LaGuardia, a man with prematurely white hair greeted my uncle. He looked like an old circus bear, moth-eaten and ragged, dressed in beat-up khaki pants and an old gray sweatshirt. "Do you like scotch?" asked the man, introducing himself as Lee.

Uncle Johnny responded that he did, but before he could say that he usually didn't drink it at nine o'clock on Monday morning, a bottle and two glasses appeared and the transcontinental cocktail party was under way.

When the two men deplaned in Arizona, my uncle, who's not much of a film buff, had a new best friend. Only when he returned home to New Hampshire a few days later and told my Aunt Jackie whom he had met on the airplane did Uncle Johnny realize that he'd been drinking single malt with Lee Marvin.

One of my favorite movies is *The Professionals*, starring Lee Marvin, Burt Lancaster, Robert Ryan, and former NFL player Woody Strode. In this flick, a Texas millionaire played by Ralph Bellamy hires four hard-boiled adventurers to travel deep into Mexico to rescue his beautiful young wife, who's been kidnapped by a diehard revolutionary named Raza. Lee Marvin's and Burt Lancaster's characters supposedly once fought alongside Pancho Villa and are familiar with both the territory and the mercurial Raza, portrayed by Jack Palance.

In a great early scene, Lee Marvin is invited onto Ralph Bellamy's private railroad car to discuss the terms of his employment. A skeptical cowhand points to an old sepia-toned daguerreotype hanging on the wall that's purported to contain the images of a much younger Lee Marvin, standing alongside Raza and the estimable Pancho Villa. "Your hair was darker then," says the cowboy.

Marvin barely glances up. "My heart was lighter then," he says.

11

Approaching Montemorelos, we pass a sign in Spanish that says "Change Lanes Opportunely." Beyond is a gigantic landfill with an elaborate, fortresslike gate, weather-beaten and scarred by the years, a forgotten kingdom of trash and "*yonke.*" Another sign says "Don't Light a Fire on the Pavement," and Bongo notes that local roads are marked with a myriad of such polite, inexplicable directives. Also, a number of sway-backed horses graze on the side of the highway, unattended. Besides being a land of junk and wing-it construction, Mexico is a haven for orphaned horseflesh. Whereas horse thieves were once hanged like murderers, now horses wander around unwanted and unseen by the main body of the populace.

Lunch is chicken, frijoles, rice, and tortillas at a roadside bodega in Linares. We're waited on by the proprietor, a stout, gray-haired man with a pencil mustache (Kerouac called a similar-looking gentleman the "father of antique life on earth"). On the television is a dating show with "*quatro hombres y ocho mujeres*" (four men and eight women), with the selections based on the participants' horoscopes. The women are rouged and powdered, in clinging dresses, although they're not what I would consider TV stars. But the proprietor's son, a young fellow in his twenties, and a soft drink company employee who's making a delivery, pause beneath the TV to leer at these women, chattering to each other in rapid-fire Spanish.

Keith asks the two men where the game show takes place. The proprietor's son replies, and Keith and the other man laugh. Sopping up beans and hot sauce with a tortilla, Bongo looks over at me: "He says they're in Los Angeles and all the men on the show will get laid, if they don't get deported first."

On the other side of Linares, we cross back into Tamaulipas, the state we began in. To the west is a large mountain range, dressed in long green folds with up-thrusting, phallic peaks. They've torn up the road to repave it, and a truck is ascending the grade with two men perched on the tailgate, spraying with a hose to keep the dust down. Especially here, on the way to Victoria, you could fill a good-size auditorium with all the road kill that has been knocked to the shoulder, half of them furry beasts I've never seen before.

In the slanted afternoon light there's a long golden plain to the west and then the blue, humped-up mountains. Roaring past the towns of El Sauz, El Galindino, Santa Juana, and Nuevo Padillo; past the peanut and orange juice salesmen in their ragged jeans standing right on the lane lines of the highway, the great-grandsons and grand-nephews of the ragged juice and nut peddlers of 1949.

For a long empty stretch of roadway Bongo doesn't say a word, and neither do I. Two middle-aged guys in a small car with no air-conditioning driving two thousand subtropical miles in five days is not most people's idea of a vacation. And Keith can go hours without making a sign that he knows I'm there, dipping his tobacco and staring out the windshield. But I don't think it's strange and make no mention of it, because we've known each other for thirty years— long enough, as Kerouac once said, to have no preconceptions whatsoever in our minds.

12

We drive into Victoria in late afternoon, a booming metropolis that probably bears little resemblance to the sun-baked village that Kerouac, Cassady, and the nearly forgotten Frank Jeffries/Stan Shephard entered in 1949, spending the day in the local whorehouse. Guided by "Victor," a young Mexican lad who sold them huge joints of marijuana and acted as laid-back pimp, the heroes of *On the Road* danced to wild mambo records all afternoon and into the night, taking turns with various "gurls" in the little rooms out back. So typical of Kerouac: he had sex with one of the prostitutes but fell totally and silently in love with a sullen dark-eyed girl who was bringing them drinks and sweeping up. As he did with certain women his entire life, Kerouac idealized the girl and the "unimpeachable dignity" that had left her broke and friendless, even in a whorehouse; he spent the night watching her from across the room but never approached.

In downtown Victoria, large color posters of a man named Arturo Diez hang from every other utility pole; he's running for political office, and with his extraordinary white teeth and perfect auburn hair, Senor Diez bears a striking resemblance to NFL quarterback Tom Brady. Many of the buildings are new; the plague of American chain stores has infected Central Mexico, and we're bombarded with giant throbbing signs for McDonald's, Burger King, Holiday Inn, Wal-Mart, and the Home Depot. Apparently, there's no rest *from* the wicked, even in the land of the Tricolores.

In the exact center of the city is a rectangular park where groups of young women in black halter tops and jeans stroll arm in arm, and two teams of shirtless youths are playing a joyous game of basketball despite the oppressive heat. Hawkers are waving newspapers, and a woman in a bright yellow dress is selling colored lumps of shaved ice from a pushcart on the sidewalk. The kinetic energy of Mexican commerce is driving the hoopsters, hawkers, peddlers, hustlers, and touts of the city; even the gray-haired gents smoking cigarettes on the iron benches look on the scene with restless eyes.

On the outskirts of town, Bongo finds the perfect place to stay: a grand, rambling hotel compound jutting up from behind an adobe wall. As we turn into the entrance, there's the unexpected sight of a middle-aged lady taking a dump on the shoulder of the road. Two matronly accomplices stand beside her, throwing up their crossed arms to block the view of passersby.

The hotel includes a roped gate and guard shack, the winding pebbled driveway, a free-standing lobby with three carpeted stairs, and a grinning bellman followed by a grave-looking maître d'hôtel with a debonair cocked eyebrow. We are scrutinized, sized up, briefly debated, and then admitted.

Beyond the dry fountain is a swimming pool, a six-foot brass cage containing a green macaw, a party pavilion with a tented wooden roof and cosseted windows, and five or six *dormotorios*, buildings that contain the narrow, ornately decorated rooms, some of them in disrepair. The entire compound looks like it had been abandoned for years and then reinhabited. The tennis courts are weedy and overgrown, several outbuildings are deserted, and the chatter of hammers and carpenters whistling to one another comes floating out from various locations.

After an hour's swim in the pool, I join Keith outside the room for a Tecate. He has reconnoitered the entire campus and reports that there's a local watering hole in easy walking distance. We cross an empty field and pass by a group of men hacking at the foliage outside the walls with machetes. Apparently, there's not a single electric weed whacker in Mexico.

El Triangulo is a tall, flimsy aluminum building with a dirt parking lot and two local swells manning the corrugated iron door. Inside, the triangular room is lined with plastic chairs and round plastic tables; a 1970s-era disco ball is rotating over the empty dance floor, and a small bar with a thatched roof occupies the corner to our left as we enter. The air-conditioning is turned up high, and the place is nearly empty.

A Mexican ballad is blaring from the jukebox. As soon as she spots us, the only visible female in El Triangulo gets up quickly from her seat at the bar and dances over the concrete floor to us. She's a chubby young woman in a short denim skirt, red halter top, and red headband pushing back her wavy brown hair, which falls to the middle of her back. Watching the girl undulate toward us, I say to Keith, "The best thing about this trip is that you speak the lingo and—"

He finishes the thought: "—the worst thing is that I speak the lingo."

Soon the three of us are seated at a table overlooking the dance floor, and Bongo is talking with the girl in his mellifluous Spanish, obtaining the lay of the land within El Triangulo. Her name is Rosario, and she works six nights a week at the bar. Although my first thought was "prostitute," in actuality, Rosario is a taxi dancer; she sits and talks with the customers, dances with them, even drinks with them.

When Bongo orders a trio of *Victorias* from one of the swells who has sauntered over, our beers are twelve ounces and cost 150 pesos—approximately $1.50. Rosario's bottle of *cerveza es poquito*—only six ounces—costs the same. Five pesos are given to the bar man, and ten are handed discreetly to Rosario.

Within half an hour, thanks to Keith's fluency and my contributions of pidgin Spanish, we learn that Rosario is thirty years old and a native of Victoria. She's also a single mother of an eight-year-old girl who's starting to rebel and whose father doesn't pay child support or have anything to do with his kid.

Hard on these revelations, the three of us trade facts and fables about our children. As best I can, I try to follow the thread of what Keith is saying, studying the bones of his face in the shifting light of the disco ball. Some of it is making fun of me: how weak my Spanish is and how fussy I am, since I don't smoke or eat red meat. Rosario thinks this is hilarious, pulling up the top of her blouse and slapping my knee.

"You're a sour bastard in English, but you're the life of the fucking party in Spanish," I say to Bongo, shouting to be heard over the music. "Yeah," he says, smoking a cigarette that Rosario has given him.

Then the talk grows serious, and I can tell that Keith is speaking about his daughter. Pitched beneath the driving thrum of the music, his tone is slow and hypnotic; he touches his cheek and says she was *rubio*, blond. Motioning to his brow, Keith says that his little girl had dark, deep *oyes*, the eyes of a beautiful saint. Much of what Keith says beyond that is lost on me, but I get the message. So does Rosario.

Her eyes well up, and she wipes her face with a napkin. A local trio has come in and set up their instruments on the small stage across the way, and following a brief sound check, the singer launches into their first number. It's a slow melancholy ballad, and the front man croons each of the verses in a liquid tone, like there's a river of molten metal pouring from the stage onto the dance floor.

Looking at me, Rosario shakes her head and says something I can't make out. Then, in the dark and glittering cavern of El Triangulo, she wraps her arms around herself in a sort of pantomime and rocks all our troubled children to sleep.

13

The next day we cross the Tropic of Cancer in late morning and stop for lunch at a tiny clapboard restaurant decorated with Carta Blanca signs. Inside the screenless doors and windows a man in a cowboy hat waits patiently on the business side of a half-door dividing us from the kitchen and his unseen wife. Packages of dried fruits and nuts and potato chips are hanging from the walls, beside pictures of the Blessed Virgin and a photograph of the straw-hatted forebears of the current proprietor. In the courtyard beyond the tilted open rear door, a rooster crows repeatedly.

Two orders of scrambled eggs with onions and tomatoes, frijoles, tortillas, and juice costs the equivalent of seven dollars. "Just substitute toast for tortillas, and these are 1965 prices back in Methuen," I say to Bongo, digging into the steaming platter.

The wholesome breakfast fortifies us for a heart-pounding ride into the mountains. We ascend past a sign that says "Caution: Cloud Zone" and mount higher and higher on a winding road. Descending a series of tight switchbacks, Bongo drives with one hand, videotaping the sheer drop-offs and rocky walls with the other. "That's my Cassady impression," he says. "I never got a speeding ticket, I don't like to talk, and I hate speed. But I can drive with him in the mountains."

We twist down out of the sierra, a green vista to the east with the round, forested knobs rising from the valley floor. Keith goes bombing around the hairpin corners, accelerating into the impossible turns just as I believe he's going to slow down. But I don't show an ounce of fear or anxiety, I just keep writing in my notebook as we descend, faster and faster. If we're going to crash into a banana truck or plunge over the abyss that lies just inches from the bumper, then fuck it, I'm going to die with a pencil in my hand, recording what I see.

Into Felipe Angelos with cardboard shacks lining the road, and emaciated local cowboys selling mysterious brown nectar in slender bottles hanging about their necks on little brown cords. A white-spotted horse grazes among the weeds, and evenly spaced banana trees loom over the road. In the Mexico portion of *On the Road*, Kerouac writes of a mysterious phosphorescent horse that appears in the midst of the jungle. Sal watched as the riderless horse, whinnying softly, trotted straight toward Dean, who was sleeping in the middle of the road. The horse stepped right over him, and when Dean woke up, he reported having dreamed of a ghostly white horse.

El Guayabo is next, with its carefully swept yards; two lovely young *chicas* are sitting on a stone bench with an aluminum awning over it, and a man in a straw hat leads a burro on a rope up an embankment. In El Ojital, giant himosa trees form an arch over the two-lane, plunging us into deep, dark shadows. Outside of town, pretty much in the middle of nowhere, a pedestrian walkway goes up and over the road; there isn't another car in sight, and this seems like a luxury that could've been saved for a busier stretch of the Carretera Nacional.

Small cattle farms and poor villages appear in succession, with roofless cinder-block outbuildings and collapsing fences. It's cloudy this morning, cooler, long fields of sugar cane demarcated by irrigation ditches. A bunch of shirtless men are dismantling a sad-looking carnival, and one of them, a wiry fellow with gray hair, reminds me of a guy from Concord, New Hampshire, who played rugby there back in the 1970s. His name was Billy Blue, and he was a marrying fool. His third or fourth wife was an exotic dancer of sorts, and the night after they got married, Billy was supposed to embark on a rugby tour to Ireland. His new wife forbade him from leaving the house, and after supper, Billy excused himself, taking the evening newspaper upstairs to the bathroom. Once inside, he slid open the window, threw his kit bag into the yard, shimmied down the waterspout, and hurried to an agreed-on location where some of the lads were waiting. Thus, Billy Blue went to Ireland and was divorced upon his return.

Billy died of cancer a couple of years ago. Watching his doppelganger climb the rigging of a Ferris wheel, I have to laugh, shake my head, and salute him. You bring your own history to the road.

14

In Ocampo, we discover a progressive citizen using a battery-powered weed whacker; he must be the envy of his machete-wielding neighbors. At a military checkpoint that appears suddenly in the road, a young corporal in fatigues stops our car. There's an armored vehicle blocking the way, its .50-caliber machine gun pointed straight at our windshield and half a dozen soldiers standing there with nasty-looking automatic weapons.

Keith tells the squared-away corporal that he's a professor of "*Ingles en la universidad*" and that I am "*escritor*" in the midst of "*escrite un libro*" about Mexico. While remaining silent, I assume the demeanor of a serious writer, affirming Bongo's declaration.

The corporal removes his sunglasses for a moment and bends down to get a better look at me. It's like paying to see the geek in the circus. After a moment, he smiles and says something to his confederates, and they wave us around the machine gun and through the checkpoint.

"He probably thought we were gay," says Bongo, gesturing toward the postcard of Kerouac and Cassady, each with an arm slung over the other man's shoulder. It's been there all week, and we'd kind of forgotten about it. "The Mexican army are not big supporters of homosexuality, despite the fact that they probably have their share of it," Keith says.

"Making them representative of the world at large," I say, putting the postcard into the glove box. "Nothing against the local gay populace, but I don't want to visit a Mexican prison on their behalf."

Juan de dios Villarreal is an industrial area with a couple of small manufacturing plants, a propane station of considerable size, and two or three small factories under construction, along with several gas stations. Then we pass a shaded area, and I see two boys washing clothes in a brook that's lying at the bottom of a ditch. The suds from the washing have spread downstream, and a white gossamer froth is heading into the construction area, where it will no doubt mingle with various other chemical compounds.

"There's no Environmental Protection Agency in the Third World," I say.

Just then the engine light blinks on the dashboard, and Bongo says, "It could be an air leak, or an oil problem." He stops the car and gets out and opens the hood and begins poking around. "Air is okay," he says, checking the hoses and then removing the dipstick from the reservoir. "An oil problem would be bad. No parts, no service. I've only seen one other Mazda since we came into the country, and it had American plates."

The oil pressure seems all right, and we continue on. It begins raining for the first time all week, which offers a break from the heat. We pass a working quarry, with a huge Satanic gash in the valley's rock wall and the sound of infernal engines. After the storm abates we drive into a low valley, cloud banks sitting off to the east, dark and treacherous, with a view to the ridgeline that stretches over ten miles. At the fertile nadir of these bottomlands, we pass into the state of San Luis Potosi.

Hospital General de Zona #6 is a big, smooth, light-orange building in the midst of the urban sprawl of Valles. One of the traffic lights turns green, and instantly someone toots his horn. "There must be one Massachusetts driver here," I say. Teenage schoolgirls in uniform stand waiting at a bus stop. "Watch out for Neal," I call out the window, and they let out a collective giggle.

From here, it's 457 kilometers to "El Jefe," Mexico City, the federal district. We cross a long suspension bridge over a river at 1:30 p.m. The river is fifty yards wide, dotted with canoes and pickup trucks ranging along the banks. A short while later, we pass a large, grand hacienda behind a flower-entwined iron fence, with two women approaching beneath the black plumes of their umbrellas. On the side of the road, men are walking home in straw hats, carrying machetes.

Looking back at the long curve of the river valley, with the ten million–peso views from the fifty-peso tin shacks, we marvel at the cloud forest far below. The mountains grow taller here, patches of cultivation rising as high as a couple of thousand feet on the opposite valley wall, with dense gloomy mists filling the pass in between.

"I have friends who tell me 'Come down here at age sixty, buy a *palace* for a hundred thousand dollars, and within a month you'll be fucking the seventeen-year-old Indian girl who's cleaning your floors,'" says Bongo, his sentiments reminding me of Neal Cassady. After his trips with Ken Kesey petered out in the mid-1960s, Cassady retreated to Mexico on several occasions and was found dead beside the railroad tracks outside San Miguel de Allende, a few days shy of his forty-third birthday.

We go traveling through an arch of ficus trees with the first six feet of the trunks painted white. It looks like the trees are wearing spats, and I ask Keith if they're painted with some kind of botanical medicine to keep the insects from ruining them.

Bongo giggles and shakes his head. "It's so you don't run into them when you're cocked," he says.

15

Winding our way through a tiny, cramped village halfway up the mountain pass is like going back in time. Old women dressed in black are carrying bundles of firewood and saying the rosary as they plod along. On a bend in the jungle road, we encounter a huge yellow crucifix forty feet tall. It's a Dadaist plaster Christ with chiseled abs and bloody tears and a placard that reads: "Senor de la Cruz." Kerouac was driving when they passed through here, alongside shepherds in flowing robes and Indian women carrying bundles of flax; he woke up Cassady so he could "see the golden world where Jesus came from."

Driving on past, it strikes me that back home, a lot of people imagine Christ as a meek and scrawny longhair who got pushed around by the Romans. But when you consider where and how he lived—traveling on foot across a scorched and hostile landscape, eating whatever came to hand, enduring the harangues of a ruthless, godless oppressor—my perception of Christ matches that of the locals. "Senor de la Cruz" was like a Nazarene triathlete: strong in body and mind; fierce, gritty, and determined to run his course. And when he turned himself over to Pilate, it was an act of *will*; a choice, and not a form of submission. His bona fides as the Son of God are without question. As a man, there's no doubt that he was one tough hombre.

• • •

Our little detour takes us up and over a rutted dirt road lined with broken-down tin shacks and toothless Indians. "This looks like Guatemala," says Bongo in Tzepolaco, the land of the skinny dogs. Around the next corner, there's an incongruous turkey by the roadside, apparently hiding in Tepetzintla from the Pilgrims. Then we head downward into the steepest and greenest valley yet, like the vales of Scotland, only this is Tamazunchale.

Mexico is under construction; everyone is building and rehabilitating everywhere, and everything is a mess. The sound of hammers and mallets and the *chop-chop* of machetes rises from the hollows of the jungles and from the unseen back rooms of the most horrible run-down shacks. Roadside shrines are also ubiquitous, more elaborate and overtly religious than the highway memorials you see back home. These are little adobe structures the size of a very small doghouse, painted canary yellow or azure or teal and containing stations of the cross and mass cards and votive candles.

Mosquitoes swarm over the road, and we pass a guy on a motorcycle with the dark hair, wide flat mustache, and handsome features of my late running buddy, Jeff Ness. *Pretty buggy up here.* Bongo follows the motorcycle through the town of Vega Carga, where several men are repairing cars in the middle of the street and an array of hanging baskets are for sale.

We stop at a roadside joint to eat, sitting at a plastic table draped with red and yellow tablecloths inside an open garage. Below us, on the cliff side, is a larger, open-air dining room with a thatched roof overgrown with tropical foliage. The sound of a loud television can be heard, and the waiter and the barmaid are standing beneath it, discussing the show. A girl about eleven years old brings a little basket of chips and salsa to the table, averting her gaze when I thank her. She departs shyly, and I'm reminded of Kerouac's fascination with a little local girl who had the "eyes of the Virgin Mother."

Two men arrive in a pickup, drinking cans of Modelo and looking around the place. After they sit down, Keith excuses himself and goes over to chat with them about the road up ahead. One of the men does all the talking, while the larger, surly-looking fellow drinks his beer and stares out the open end of the garage. On his return, Bongo tells me that the beer drinkers don't think much of our choice of routes to El Jefe. The "highway" is slow and treacherous, and the one talkative gent has suggested doubling back a hundred miles to the toll road. Then Bongo says, "Guys of that age are pretty reserved, because they've been to the States and been treated like shit. The quiet one worked in Boston."

Keith glances across at me with a knowing look and then sets himself over his meal; Boston is one of the most parochial and provincial towns in America. Certainly, a non-English-speaking Mexican laborer would have about as much clout and cachet there as the invisible man, and I'm fairly certain that the Modelo drinker spent a lot of unhappy days in some crowded apartment in Somerville or Dorchester.

After lunch, we follow a garbage truck up the mountain with a kid hanging off the back, ringing a cowbell. At the apex of the pass, amid the creeping tendrils of fog, is a sign for El Purgatorio. There are just four or five shacks comprising Purgatory and not a soul in sight. An hour before dark, Bongo explains that he never drives at night because of the lax Mexican attitude toward driving under the influence. "Those guys in the restaurant probably drive drunk as well as they do sober," he says. "It's the Indians I worry about, and I'm always thinking about it, even now."

Keith takes the Mazda rocketing down the pass in a long slalom, like a two-man bobsled. Halfway to the bottom is a strange moun-tainside village that time forgot, with the houses piled nearly on top of one another and hanging off the cliff side like some weird Arab town. A little shack overlooking the road in Santa Maria has a fenced-in garden flowering with a type of tangerine-hued rose I've never seen before. A lost lamb wanders by the side of the road, and half a dozen cows are standing sideways in incredibly vertical pastures. The clouds are so thick below us that they obliterate towns and screen off the valley floor.

Santa Ana is filled with little concrete homes that look like bombed-out bunkers. A sign advertising the Internet sits on top of a seedy café made from cinder blocks without any mortar. "It looks like Beirut in '78," I say as Bongo peers at the road ahead. There's a single wire running from the top of the building out into the fog of the valley. "It's the only Internet connection that's maintained by a three-legged chipmunk running around one of those little wheels," I say.

Bushes are whipping against the side of the car as Keith hugs the outer curve. We're right inside a cloud, with less than ten feet of visibil-ity. Pink orchids strung along a vine are hanging from trees overhead. We pass five teenagers standing in tableau at a bus stop, four young hombres and a beautiful light-haired girl in tight-fitting jeans and a lavender blouse. They look like they've been posed against such a grungy backdrop for a magazine ad.

Seeing a group of attractive young people on the side of the road naturally leads Bongo and me to discussions of Kerouac and his entourage of mostly young, male, often good-looking hipsters. This cross-continental group of poets, posers, and partygoers constituted what Allen Ginsberg once referred to as "the boy gang," a fluid and flexible mélange of memorable characters, quite suitable to a writer's purpose. A guy I know said he attended a party just a few years ago where an aged Norman Mailer, God rest his soul, claimed to have had sex with Jack Kerouac in the 1950s and that he, Mailer, was "the top." But that tall tale had more to do with Kerouac's star being on the rise and Mailer, the consummate self-promoter, attempting to hitch his wagon to it. In Peter Manso's oral biography *Mailer: His Life and Times*, Allen Ginsberg describes an awkward meeting between Kerouac and Mailer in 1958, and how Kerouac thought Mailer, who had recently published *The White Negro*, was really just a square, an "intellectual fool" trying to steal his thunder. The two men shared a girlfriend in those days, and in a letter to Ginsberg written on October 28, 1958, Kerouac said, "Fuck Norman Mailer. . . . Why wasn't he a hipster when it counted?"

In the back of our minds, Keith and I both know we're heading toward the place where Neal Cassady died, and like a petulant and reckless older brother, he'd done things to his life and his talent that have continued to bother us over the years. Since Kerouac loved his friends very much ("I hoard them forever") but presented them with an unerring eye, as a reader you feel like you know them and are pulling for them to do the right thing—when you know they probably won't. Cassady, in particular, gets under your skin: so much charm on the surface, yet he was the kind of fellow a guy with any brains would never trust.

"Neal Cassady was a paid entertainer," I say. "Kerouac knew what he was getting when he signed on with Cassady. He was getting his book."

"Then Kerouac just ossified. He sat down at a kitchen table to drink and stayed there for fifteen years," says Bongo. "In a way, that's even sadder than Cassady."

"Yeah, 'cause Kerouac didn't go down swinging," I say.

16

In the Las Marimoles National Park, Bongo is following a sinister tractor-trailer down through unusual pine forests at dusk. Mists and rain squalls envelope the road when it begins to climb again, higher and higher, until Keith stops at a vista, and we get out of the car to look at the canyon floor eight thousand feet below. The elevation is greater here than at Copper Canyon in Chihuahua, greater than the Grand Canyon. There's a flimsy black-and-white guardrail over the precipice, which drops straight down over two thousand feet before billowing out in jungle folds and thick, soupy mists.

Jumping back in the Mazda, Keith steers the car ever upward, toward the Indian mystery town of Ixmiquilipan. He's been iron-manning the wheel for twelve hours, up and over the steepest mountain passes this side of the Chile-Argentina border. That's where the plane crashed containing the rugby players in 1972; I've flown over those same passes with the Florida Select side rugby team, and it's a bumpy ride. And I've driven over in a bus, drinking the local wine with Surfer and old Florida rugby pals Carlos Ballbe and Conrad Merry.

Half an hour before dark, we enter a new territory, with red cliffs and better roads, shadows deepening to gloom in the lee of the rock faces and the smoke of a thousand supper fires rising into the heavens. We've been following the same dust-smeared truck for two hundred kilometers, and when we reach the vast broken edge of the plateau at Zimipan and turn off, the driver blasts his air horn in farewell, and the sound, like the roar of a primordial beast, echoes over the land.

On the outskirts of Zimipan is a strange hotel comprised of stucco modules sponge-painted a deep orange color and connected to one another by tiny garages hung with blue plastic tarps. It looks like Disney World's gulag or some kind of Reichian pods, and Bongo explains that the curtains are meant to hide the license plates of the cars inside.

As we pull into the driveway, the manager emerges from the office, accompanied by his little daughter, to explain that it's a "couples hotel."

He points to the sign at the entrance that advertises five hours for 150 pesos, and Keith begins to laugh, his voice carrying out across the high desert that lies beyond the complex. Apparently, we have found the "no-tell motel" of the Latin world, where subtlety is considered frivolous, and people come to fuck in peace.

Still giggling, Bongo claps the man on the back and works out a deal for two pods, overnight, which comes to about forty dollars. After grabbing a beer from the cooler, I bid Keith good night and enter my room. It has a tiled floor, low lighting, a tiny bathroom with a shower, and a large, flat, hard bed that dominates the room. The walls ooze with the vestiges of desperate middle-aged sex and teenage lust. It's a utilitarian Latin American love nest, and there's nothing for me to do but finish the Tecate, brush my teeth, and turn off the wall-mounted lamp.

Then I dream of every woman I am tangled up with or eyeing from afar, in a haunting kaleidoscope of girls' lips and breasts and flashing teeth, a haunted love chamber dream. But the star of all these is a girl named Dash, a glamorous and poetic blonde whom I met five years ago in a bookstore, tried hard to forget about (we were both involved with someone else), and then suddenly ran into on a Boston street a few days before I left on this trip. It's what Kerouac would call her "unimpeachable dignity" that has somehow kept me away from her; the idea that if I have Dash, I'll have solved the mystery of my life while not being sure why I deserve that. Dash has floated through my nighttime reveries since then, but never like this, so close and real and tender; she snuggles against me, kisses my neck, and whispers something that I can't quite make out. . . .

17

Very early in the morning I wake up in the pod and take a shower and go outside into the darkness. Keith's light comes on as I pass by, and I walk down and sit on the berm at the far end of the lot and witness the dawn shaping out the raw hills and then the birth of the mountains looming beyond. It's cool here in the early morning. The light rising on this landscape hasn't changed in a million years; the pods of the motel arrayed behind me are as ephemeral and temporary as egg cartons, and looking out at the vista, I can feel the great weight of the Sierras pressing down on the arid Mexican plain.

Far off in the valley, a cock crows several times, and then a barking dog fills the space in between. Warming in the early sunlight, I'm reminded of Rob Boushel's "Springsteen theory," which Keith related the day before. In his scientific mind, Boushel has hypothesized that the reason Bruce Springsteen hasn't written anything in the past twenty years to match the gritty emotion of his first few albums is because he's achieved so much success and the creature comforts that attend it.

"What's he going to sing about?" asked Bongo when he told me the story, imitating Springsteen's raspy voice: "*O, the goddamn maid left the towels on the bathroom floor. . . . Come down to the bathroom, and make sure the bathroom is clean. . . .*"

Kerouac made something real and true and good from his childhood wonder and from his early horrors (first among them, the death of his brother, Gerard); then his teenage athletic exploits and desire, as a shy, French-speaking kid, to fit into the social compartments of Lowell; and finely wrought artifacts of American literature were crafted out of the ramblings and religiosity of his early adulthood. Then he stalled: *Big Sur* and *Vanity of Duluoz* are really books about his failure to continue writing books. Like Bongo said, he sat at his kitchen table with a bottle of liquor and watched himself hardening up like a fossil with his portly Franco American "Memere" and third wife, Stella, perched over either shoulder like cartoon vultures.

Thus far, I've avoided the booze, any semblance of financial success, and the creeping despair of middle age. Coming here is antidote to all that; every so often, stuffing your gear in a small bag and jumping in a car will keep your bank balance manageable and your mind focused on the next curve in the road. Although he couldn't outrun his own gloomy thoughts, it strikes me as more than a bit ironic that several generations of balls-to-the-wall adventurers owe a great debt to Jack Kerouac and his work.

In the stunning light of morning, the mountainsides are covered with various types of cacti as we drop onto the plain. I ride shotgun beside Keith, sketching one type of cactus after another into my notebook, which seems like good discipline. Oblivious to all this, Bongo is like a Mexican rally driver, gassing into the tight curves, leaning, sweating, a touch of the brakes on the switchbacks, and then more acceleration, pressing me back into the seat and sending a flood of adrenaline into my chest. He's racing our deadline of noon to Mexico City, at which point we'll have to turn and race back to Laredo. Eat your heart out, Neal Cassady.

The valleys here are wider, more spacious, crisscrossed by burro trails, with the villages placed miles apart and visible on the arroyo. At Guerretara, beside a *comidas* stand, little more than a picnic table and a wood-burning stove beneath a tarp advertising Carta Blanca beer, is a little girl with a stunted arm and a shortened leg. She's about five years old, dressed in a white smock and pale yellow leggings, clutching a grass doll. She looks at me with baleful eyes, and I feel a surge of guilt that I don't have time to stop and talk to her, though I don't know what I would say to alleviate her suffering.

Then we pass through a town that's like the Latin American Lowell, with auto body shops and small restaurants and pharmacies and car washes and dusty tire stores and funky little haberdasheries jumbled all together, the broad-paned sidewalks populated by cocky, well-dressed teenagers. When my son was nine years old, we would pass a broken-windowed factory building on our way to watch the Lowell Spinners Single-A baseball team. "Who lives there?" I'd ask, and my son would always reply with a question: "The ghost of Jack Kerouac?" and I'd say, "That's right."

18

It's much cooler here, 150 miles from El Jefe. Yesterday, coming out of the mountains, I sweated through two shirts, and riding in the car with the windows open was like sitting on a blast furnace. Along this same stretch, Kerouac noted that his and Cassady's and Frank Jeffries's clothes had turned black with the crushed bodies of thousands of mosquitoes and their own dried blood. Merchants appear on the side of the road selling brightly painted glazed pots, and the radio stations play slick pop songs with sexy female vocals and rock and roll harmonies. We're nearing the great ancient & modern city of the mountain plain.

Bongo passes a family in a battered, rusty pickup: straw-hatted Dad all serious at the wheel, Mama in her modest shawl, the four children riding in the bed with a well-groomed pair of sheep. Our first Mexican traffic jam is created by a cop in a blue jumpsuit directing traffic against the light—same as back home. He allows trucks to cut in at funny angles, snarling the line of vehicles all the way back to a broken-down carnival out on the desert flats.

Suburbia has clusters of nice homes and lawns and gas stations and convenience stores. Prowl cars sit in the median, watching for speeders. We stop at a roadside place where a slender young man is roasting chickens atop a brick barbecue. Inside, a trio of ladies tends to large silver pots cooking over a gas fire, and a young woman in a light blue baseball cap arrives at the table with several wooden bowls of hot sauce, chopped onions, rice, and tortillas. We're served a limp green vegetable that looks like the tentacles of an octopus. I believe it to be tamales until Keith informs me that it's boiled cactus. It has a pungent odor, tasting kind of sweet and sour with dry, rough threads running through it; "plenty of fiber," says Bongo. Next, the soup is delivered to the table. Large yellow chicken claws with half the leg bones still attached jut from the wooden bowls. Imagine this back home: Sugarcoated Cactus Flakes with chicken-feet soup.

After the meal, we settle the tab and head out through the doorless entrance into the parking lot. A mustachioed older fellow wearing a white dress shirt and brown polyester pants has joined the young man at the brazier. The man smiles and nods as we go by and then approaches, saying that he has "*un pregunta*," a question, for Keith.

Much talk ensues. After several minutes of discussion, Bongo goes around and opens the trunk of the car, removes his journal from his bag, opens it, and allows the man to write a series of numbers onto a blank page, gesticulating and explaining something to Keith at the same time. The son remains with me on the other side of the car, watching his dad with the tender, intent respect I've seen everywhere in Mexico, where the patriarch is the undisputed king. The son watches and listens, knowing that he'll be the boss one day.

Gradually, I acquire the gist of the conversation. The older fellow is proposing that Keith enter into a business arrangement with him, a perfect stranger, whereby Keith will purchase a very expensive piece of agricultural machinery in Texas and drive it over the border at Nuevo Laredo, allowing the man to take possession of it. This will save the man a lot of money, and he's willing to pay Bongo a substantial fee, which is not discussed in much detail. He also says that Keith will need a truck with sturdy axles to transport "la machina."

The man has written down the serial numbers of the machine and his telephone number. Then Bongo detaches a piece of the notebook paper, jots down his name and number, and gives it to the man. They shake hands, Bongo replaces his journal in the trunk and then closes it, and we all say our good-byes.

The homely restaurant and the man and his son disappear behind us in a cloud of dust. "He asked a total stranger to buy him a ten-thousand-dollar piece of equipment, hire a crane to lift it, lash it to a truck, and get it through customs," says Bongo, dipping into a tin and pinching up some tobacco. How that part of the task will be accomplished is not mentioned.

But Keith is the consummate Latin American politician, and I note that back in Boston I would not waste any time in telling such a street-corner entrepreneur to go jump in a lake. "Down here, you listen to what he has to say, be polite, and then ignore it," Bongo says.

19

At noon we drop toward the last bit of the continental bowl, and there's Mexico City thirty kilometers off, hazed over by a bluish fog and pushed into the bottom folds of the mountains. We motor toward the outskirts of town: cars going everywhere on eight-lane roads, horns beeping, square white ambulances screaming past; men in the street hawking newspapers, peanuts, packages of flatbreads, and candy; marimba music blaring from storefronts, straw-hatted cowboys on rusted bicycles, and long-legged women flashing by in high-heels.

Mexico! Trucks filled with bales of hay, or with sheep, or goats; shiny delivery vans advertising "Boing" or "Bimbo." A man beneath a tarp strung up on poles is chopping young coconuts in half with a machete and sending his customers away drinking the coconut water from a straw.

Mexico! A crazy self-appointed traffic director wearing an orange shirt and waving an orange rag dominates the first big intersection. He opens little holes in the constant stream of cars, whistling in a sharp low tone, the gap just big enough for a particular vehicle to shoot through. He's the soot-tooted maestro of El Jefe highways, and he helps us twice in the span of five minutes as Bongo decides that the nearby pyramids are not on our crowded agenda and backtracks over the same streets.

I'm sweating in my seat, twisting around and around, sticking my head out the window, mopping my face with my shirt, and generally rubbernecking in every direction. At one frantic intersection, I give a woman who's collecting for charity a few pesos, and Bongo asks her for directions back to the highway. "I think the car has just about had it," says Keith, his eye on the oil gauge.

A guy driving a van pulls up to a street vendor in the midst of heavy traffic and buys just one cigarette, and the vendor lights it for him. Wild, fucked-up Mexico! We won't even have one crazy night here because I have to get home for Liam's birthday, but I convince Keith to stop for a moment and run over to a street vendor and buy a hand-tooled leather saddlebag for Dash, who, I'm beginning to understand, has galloped past me again like an outlaw, setting my heart on fire. Broken stone walls line the outskirts of the city; huge gaps continue for a quarter of a mile, then pieces of the wall jump up again. It's all that's left of the great fortress that once repelled all invaders, and young urban slackers lounge on its ramparts, smoking cigarettes bummed from local hustlers.

The statue of a great liberator on his horse towers above the busy street scene, waving good-bye to us with his sword. He's wearing a tight waistcoat and wide trousers, and Keith says his name is Miguel Hidalgo, the Father who fathered the country. A father to two illegitimate daughters, Hidalgo was a Roman Catholic priest, a humanitarian, and an opportunist; his classmates called him *el zorro*, the fox.

"I came here thirty-two years ago and swore I'd never drive in this city again," says Bongo. "I should know better."

Bongo and I weave through a stretch of oral hygiene vendors: one fellow in his early twenties selling sugarless gum, a young boy in a red shirt peddling toothbrushes, then an Indian woman in a knitted shawl with fruit and more gum. There's a giant lifelike portrait of the Doors' Jim Morrison painted on a concrete wall: "This is the End." Surfer and I once visited his grave at Père Lachaise cemetery in Paris, watched over by a pair of well-tailored gendarmes and joined by hip-looking pilgrims from all over, including a young Norwegian woman who cried bitterly until her sandal-wearing boyfriend led her away.

Junkyards are everywhere, filled with wrecked Mexican buses, taxis, tractors, halved chicken trucks, and a Mayan pyramid of abandoned tires. Then a flatbed loaded with manure pulls up alongside us, Mexico City's last shitty truck, and Bongo announces that we've driven 1,993 miles since Denver.

20

"It feels like we're in a rocket ship," I say, when we enter the wide, flat toll road, going seventy miles an hour. "Or a time machine," Bongo says.

Temperatures are in the eighties, and it's sunny and dry. We have a long talk about Neal Cassady being "essentially a male prostitute," says Bongo, often reduced to gay hustling when he wasn't sponging off Kerouac or Kesey or Ginsberg. In *On the Road: The Original Scroll*, which I am reading thoroughly on this trip, there's an unexpurgated scene where Cassady, trying to extract some travel money from a closeted homosexual in a Sacramento hotel room, flips over the middle-aged man and gives him a "monstrous huge banging" while Kerouac hides in the bathroom. The fact that Cassady was left to his own devices at a very young age and spent time in prison has been glossed over in many accounts, but Kerouac doesn't hold back in this frightening passage. Now that we're heading back to Laredo, Bongo has calculated that we have just enough time to visit San Miguel de Allende, where Cassady died on February 4, 1968.

Traveling through low, lush agricultural valleys arrayed below the piedmont, Bongo notes that we've visited eight of Mexico's thirty-one states in less than four days. In the village of Cerritos we pass a large mission-style church behind pink stone walls, with two donkeys grazing out front and an old man in a tattered vest grilling shucked ears of corn on a brazier. There's something authentic and solitary about him, loitering in the shade of the holy walls surrounding the church with its gigantic wooden cross. He's the Old Man of the Piedmont.

A flash thunderstorm roars in from the mountains, pelting us with rain while daggers of lightning glisten in the northern sky. With the wiper blades thumping back and forth, we enter San Miguel de Allende. The narrow cobblestone streets are wet with the rain, dropping down toward the center of town past long unbroken stone walls that are actually a series of connected stucco buildings with small, gated entrances and barred windows, which reminds me of Pamplona in Spain. The market squares are filled with sculpted trees and shrubs, black metal fountains, and raked-over gravel walks. Large stone churches adorn every block of this continental city, interspersed with elegant little open-air restaurants, diners sitting just out of the rain at crowded, linen-covered tables.

Streamers are stretched across the roadway, and little white lights on strings cascade down from the eaves of three-story buildings. Men on scooters. Hooting buses. It's the town where Superman died, and now I feel sorry for him, all that energy and enthusiasm burned down to a nub in San Miguel de Allende, an anonymous American, dead on the railroad tracks.

"Is this a good place to die?" Bongo asks before answering his own question. "As good as any."

Here on a rainy street corner, while Bongo hunts for a place to leave the car for a while, I'm reminded of his call to that Los Angeles radio show so many years ago. It was after midnight and Carolyn Cassady was on the other end of the phone, about to make her one-and-only pronouncement to an eighteen-year-old Keith Bowden regarding what kind of man her late husband had been. Bongo said that when he asked her what Neal Cassady had done between his years on the road with Jack Kerouac and on the bus with Ken Kesey: "She was very short with me. She said he was working on the railroad, and raising his family."

At that moment, a beautiful young European woman in tight jeans steps out of a taxi in front of me, lean, dark-haired, with lustrous golden skin and high cheekbones. Our eyes meet. My pants tighten at the crotch, and there on the corner in the city where he expired, I think of Neal Cassady, always on the make, always hustling, gurls gurls gurls, and for once and for ever I understand and forgive him and all that he did in this world of men and women.

21

We spend the night a few miles beyond San Lois Potosi, and in the cool morning air, I practice yoga mudra, while in Zen counterbalance, Bongo clips his fingernails onto a slip of paper. Normally, Keith would defer to me as his guest in every aspect, but in the past few days he's made most of the decisions, given that he identifies so strongly with Latin people and admires their culture. For my part, I've felt at home in different parts of the world at different times and see this trip as part of maintaining the elasticity of my life by stretching past the boundary of home, moving out farther than expected, then rebounding back, keeping my line loose and ready.

When we pack up the car for the last leg of the journey, Bongo says that he dreamed Hayesey had become "the Kurtz of northeastern Mexico," residing in an ornate mansion waited on by retinues of eager locals.

"I asked him if he could set me up, you know, with girls, et cetera," says Bongo. "He said, 'Anything you want, kid.'"

We cross back over the Tropic of Cancer in the morning light, flying along now on this smooth desert road. At 6' 1" and 210 pounds, Keith is big on hydration, drinking two liters of water or more each morning, then a coffee in mid-afternoon, more water, and beers in the evening. We take a piss break every hundred miles or so, unzipping on the shoulder of the road in the land without shame. For breakfast, Bongo stops in the village of Matehuala at a three-booth open-air café where a lovely young girl makes us two platters of *huevos con frijoles y tortillas y agua mineral* while the radio plays a lonesome ballad from inside the tiny kitchenette.

While the meal is cooking, I'm busy reading *On the Road: The Original Scroll* again. The only real version for me is the scroll now, just one of the many versions of the book, I realize, but the manuscript that Jack banged out fast before the dried-up editors of New York anesthetized him and then sanitized and cauterized his book. (I can dig it!) In a way, it represents a part of what he always meant to do with his great life's work, "The Dulouz Legend," connecting all his true-story novels into one final, definitive epic by 'inserting his "pantheon of uniform names."

In the 1950s and '60s, Kerouac fought continuously with the Manhattan denizens who were bringing out his books. While editors like Malcolm Cowley and Don Allen were drawn to the manic energy and marketability of Kerouac's work, their literary ideals were rooted in an earlier time, and they often insisted on changes that Kerouac refused to make. In a 1957 letter to Don Allen, Kerouac wrote, "I can't possibly go on as a responsible prose artist . . . if I let editors take my sentences." Kerouac was reacting to what he considered the editorial "castration" of his book *The Subterraneans*, to be published right after *On the Road*. Incensed by attempts to impose the "house style" on his work, Kerouac believed that riddling the manuscript with excess punctuation robbed it of "the rush of lowdown confession that embarrasses no one but me." Although financially insecure at the time, Kerouac offered payment to return his manuscript to its original condition.

His relationship with Malcolm Cowley was even more tumultuous. Born in 1898, Cowley acted as literary adviser to Viking Press from 1948 to '85, and was acquainted with Ernest Hemingway and William Faulkner. He was influential as a poet, critic, and editor, and his flip-flopping on Kerouac's work must have been confounding and, finally, infuriating to the writer and his agent, Sterling Lord. In 1955, Cowley offered to write a foreword to *On the Road* so other Viking editors would take it seriously. He also helped Kerouac place a story with Anabelle Porter at *New World Writing*, his first legitimate publication since *The Town and the City* several years earlier. But before the 1950s were over, Cowley was routinely turning down Kerouac's new manuscripts and wrote to the best-selling author that *Desolation Angels* "wasn't the sort of book" that Viking "or probably any other publisher could persuade people to read." In an internal report, Cowley referred sarcastically to Kerouac's attempts to record the totality of his experience as the "interminable Dulouz Saga."

But Kerouac knew what he was doing. Responding to a generation of New York editors, he wrote to Viking's Tom Guinzburg in 1962: "My business is not to write like in the 1920s but to make a new literature, which I've done." Not long before he died in 1969, Kerouac prophesized "just wait and see what the Astronauts of the Year 2000 . . . will be reading on Venus and Mars ('t'won't be James Michener.)"

22

The desert heat is up past ninety degrees and rising as we rejoin Mexico 85, the national highway, on the other side of Monterrey, making a big fifteen hundred–mile loop around northern and central Mexico in just four days. I'm down to 150 pesos and rationing my last *agua mineral* and "Bimbo" bran and fruit bar when we reach the final military checkpoint, ten miles from Laredo. Approaching the barriers, Bongo tells me to turn over the photograph of Kerouac and Cassady that I've returned to the dashboard.

"It's funny that those guys still have the juice, counterculturally speaking," I say, regarding the photo for a moment.

Four soldiers with sophisticated-looking automatic weapons wave us to the shoulder of the road. We're spirited out of the Mazda by a wiry young private with a pencil mustache, and an old Warren Zevon song begins playing in my head ("Send lawyers, guns and money/The shit has hit the fan"). Immediately, the young soldier begins looking under and behind the seats, in the glove box, the cooler, my backpack, and the trunk, while asking Keith a series of terse questions. At the same time, a quartet of lean young commandos, positioned strategically around the car, move in closer, futuristic weapons in hand.

This is the first time during the entire trip that I feel like something bad is about to happen. We're on the apron of the road, away from the other motorists, and Keith's interrogator isn't looking at him or me as he methodically searches the car. There's something decidedly cold in his manner that supersedes our complete innocence of any wrongdoing, and I have a creeping sense of dread that we're being appraised by one of the drug cartels, not the Mexican government.

Suddenly, the mood changes. The private asks Keith, in hurried Spanish, for an impromptu English lesson. I know this because Bongo, speaking slowly and enunciating each syllable, replies to the soldier's query by saying, "Check . . . your . . . car."

The soldier is busy sifting through my dirty socks and then my notebooks and loose pencils, repeating softly to himself, "Check . . . your . . . car. Check . . . your . . . car."

In a moment he comes up smiling and gestures for me to get in the front seat. "Thank chew," he says.

Back in the car, Keith giggles. "You're welcome," he says as we drive off. "I should have charged him. I'm a professional. I get $380 a day to do that."

23

The line on the bridge over to Laredo is long and crowded, and the sun beats down on us through the windshield.

When Keith and I finally get to the front, a very thorough, ball-breaking U.S. Customs agent asks Bongo and I how we know each other and where we've been and why. Keith explains briefly, and the agent calls in another officer with a trained dog, who leads the shepherd around the car, tapping the exterior panels, one by one, and saying, "Find it. Find it," over and over.

But there's nothing to find, and after we get our IDs back, Bongo and I are in Texas. It's a sunny ninety-nine degrees, the downtown streets empty and quiet at mid-afternoon. Over at the Laredo Wal-Mart, I buy a couple of baseball T-shirts for my son and two young nephews, and then Keith and I go out for quesadillas, wash his car, and return to his house. On the front porch he brings up two cans of Tecate dripping from the cooler, and we sit in the dappled shade of the live oak tree and think our separate thoughts about what we've seen and experienced over the past few days.

Bongo has driven 2,720 miles in a week's time and goes to bed early. I unfurl my bedroll on the cool tiles and lie in my boxer shorts, sipping from the can of beer and trying to catch a breeze. Next door, a family arrives home sometime around nine o'clock, and I can hear children in the yard, their voices excited and silvery against the coming dusk, as one of them retrieves a ball from the car and they begin playing catch. One time, the ball rises higher than Bongo's porch, and I see it there, spinning like a planet against the violet horizon.

Just about every adolescent, coming into his strength and hardening his or her will, experiences that moment when they realize life is going to change. When I was a kid of thirteen or fourteen, I remember going into the backyard with a baseball and my glove. I threw the ball as high as I could, straight up, waiting underneath as it soared into the sky, higher than I'd ever thrown a ball before. There was that exact point where the baseball reached the zenith of its flight and hung there for an instant, turning and turning against the radiant blue sky.

Every journey has that same moment, where the traveler reaches the apex of his trajectory and starts coming back down. It kind of makes me sad that I don't know when I'll see Bongo again, but Kerouac wrote in his journal that we must love and be reverent toward one another, "till the day when we are all angels looking back." By midnight the squares of Laredo are mostly quiet, except for the cicadas along Iturbide Street, and I hit the top of my flight path and drift off to sleep.

24

When Bongo and I arrive at the Greyhound station early the next morning, the clerk sells the last ticket to San Antonio to the man directly in front of me, and we race across town to buy a ticket for the "Mexican bus." They don't take credit cards, and in his final act of generosity, Bongo throws a fifty-dollar bill over the hood of his car, and I say, "Thanks, man," and go running for the bus door, which is just closing.

At the twenty-eight-mile mark, just as Keith predicted, there's a "border zone" checkpoint. The bus is pulled to one side, and a U.S. Customs official wearing a green uniform and a straw cowboy hat and carrying a firearm enters the bus and goes down the aisle, looking closely at everyone's identification. When the customs officer takes my Massachusetts license, he stops for a moment and looks at me over his gold-rimmed spectacles.

"U.S. citizen, sir?" he asks.

"Yes."

Apparently, I'm the only one among the twenty-nine passengers this morning. In less than five minutes, the sweep is concluded; dogs have been led around the bus to sniff at the luggage compartments, and one of the officers runs a mirror on an aluminum pole beneath the chassis all the way around. When we are on our way again, celebratory salsa music plays over the sound system, and the men and women and several children on board all breathe a sigh of relief and sit back.

The woman in the row across from me is carrying a special black case with air holes in it. After we've been riding for over an hour, she takes out a little perforated Tupperware container and entertains two children from up and across the aisle with what looks like a hermit crab that she had stowed in there. Holding her hand palm up, the woman stares at the children with shining eyes as the creature dances forward on its many legs. Maybe it's some kind of Mexican scorpion, and it's a wonder to me that the straw-hatted Customs agent missed it. The woman might be carrying an entire zoo of live specimens and nobody cares, except for the seven-year-old boy in the row ahead of me, now holding the crab-spider and wheezing with delight.

PART FOUR

CALIFORNIA

1

When someone asks me what it's like to write a book, I tell the inquisitor to imagine a block of ice as large as the room we're sitting in. Lodged in the center of the ice block is a rare and precious diamond. The writer is then handed a toothpick and told to extract the small glittering gem from the ice.

At first glance, the task seems hopeless. Certainly, if the writer attacks the block of ice in a frenzy, the toothpick will shatter, leaving a small, damp stub between the thumb and forefinger. Patience is the key, for if the writer returns to the task every day, painstakingly scratching at the block with the point of the toothpick, worrying the same spot for as long as he can stand it, eventually a tiny fissure will appear in the ice. Finally, acted on by time, heat, and energy, great segments of the block will crumble and fall away until, in the end, the diamond of his story has been revealed.

To write this particular book, I must travel to the places where the diamond is located. Right now, I'm stuck just outside Manchester, New Hampshire, on a crowded, mid-winter flight to San Francisco in a jet with a balky generator; we're still waiting on the tarmac for the airport mechanic to visit the plane from wherever he's presently occupied. Every trip is bogged down with paperwork and procedures, and the road out is often blocked by the lassitude of the hired man.

Flying now, over the bristly brown-and-white hide of the country, twenty-five thousand feet below. I'm listening to Johnny Cash sing "Folsom Prison Blues" over my headset. It was recorded live, and my head is filled with all those jailbirds hooting at the plucky guitar solos, which freed their spirits. By noon, I can see the rugged topographic folds of the Rocky Mountains below, the snowed-over massifs tricked out with shadows. Soon we're traveling over the vast

156

broken piecrust of the Grand Canyon, with Joni Mitchell singing about ruined love affairs and drinking in old hotels.

Coming out of Vegas after another long delay, there's no doubt in my mind that Kerouac would've embraced every technological advance at my disposal—which is another reason I'm not engaged in the sort of "Civil War re-enactment" that David Amram warned me about. The penny postcards that Kerouac wrote to his mother from the road were like primitive text messages, and the long impassioned letters he penned to Neal Cassady and Allen Ginsberg and John Clellon Holmes (with "yr" instead of "your," "hiway" for "highway," and other cool abbrevs) from bus stations and rail yards were the undiscovered and un-thought-of "e-mails" of the 1940s.

Kerouac's version of the mp3 player was music emanating from car radios and juke joints, bits and pieces of the American song catalogue sampled on the fly. And by typing the "scroll version" of *On the Road* on those taped-together sheets of paper, Kerouac anticipated the ease of word processing by more than three decades. For forty-seven years he spent just about every waking moment "downloading" everything he felt and thought and saw, wasting no time in "linking" it all together and "uploading" this vast catalogue of material into his journals and books. Certainly, John L. Kerouac would have loved the go-go gadgets of today's world.

2

It's a raw January afternoon in San Francisco, a cold mist blowing off the harbor and soaking everything in sight. I'm usually quite organized when I travel, with every necessary item arranged economically in my day pack: wallet, cell phone, mp3 player, phone charger, boarding passes, car keys for when I return home, etc. But at the counter of the woebegone hotel where I'm staying, I realize that I've forgotten my ATM card on the console of the Impala (I used it for gas to the airport at five a.m. and never returned it to my wallet). And when I climb the stairs to my room on the fourth floor (elevator broken), I further discover that I've left my phone and mp3 chargers back at home and about $45 in protein powder and green packets on the plane that I flew into San Francisco. On top of that, the heater in my room isn't working and neither is the phone when I attempt to call the front desk.

I go out for a walk, and pretty soon I'm sitting in a little noodle house at the corner of Broadway and Polk Street. Darkness is falling, along with the rain that's pebbling up on the cars outside and shining on the pavement. A Mass. state trooper I know is working a surveillance back in Roxbury and calls to shoot the breeze; Mario says it's raining in Boston, too. After hanging up, I take stock of my bona fides. With my buddy Chris Pierce not due into town for a couple of days, all I have is sixty-two dollars in cash and a nearly maxed-out credit card.

After dinner, the intersection of Broadway and Polk is teeming with pedestrians, trucks, taxis, buses, and agile little foreign cars that go puttering up Broadway. The garish neon signs and marquees above the businesses are swirled together and reflected in psychedelic trails on the wet pavement, a sight congruous with the city's fantastic history.

Hurrying out of the rain, I enter the Real Food Company, est. 1969 and located at the corner of Polk and Vallejo. While I stroll among the brightly lit aisles of organic avocados, prickly pear, long brown rice, Vega powders, and natural peanut butter, my cell phone startles me. It's Lieutenant John Goodwin of the Revere Police, checking in to see what I'm doing.

"Still alive?" he asks. When I tell him exactly where I am, Goodwin says, "Let me guess. You got some peanuts, some wacky fuckin' powders and shit like that, and some magic fruit. You put one of these magic fruits up your rectum, and you get all the fuckin' vitamins and nutrients you need for like a week."

I look down at my basket. "I got peanut butter, six packets of Vega powders, and I'm not putting any of the fruit I got anywhere near the place you're suggesting," I reply, talking low when a white-haired woman passes by me in the aisle with her German shepherd.

Goodwin laughs, telling me to be careful. At the checkout, I arrange everything in my backpack and head down Vallejo to a place called Big Swingin' Cycles. I've arrived in the nick of time; one of the wool hat–wearing clerks is dragging the metal grate across the entrance when I approach. After letting me in, he and Brian, the affable brown-haired owner of the shop, set me up with a rental and a good bike map for $50. Since tomorrow, Wednesday, is a "ride day," and they don't bother opening the shop till 2 p.m., I can take the bike and return it Thursday morning and pay then; it's a good deal. Brian and I chat for a while about John Steinbeck, and then we shake hands and I go into the darkness of Van Ness Avenue and ride down the hill on a full stomach, not worried about money or anything else.

3

I wake up in my unheated room at 4:30 a.m. It's dark and cold outside, and I warm up the room by running the hot water in the sink and the shower; then, using a bar of hand soap, I wash my underwear and socks in the basin, wring them out over the tub, and hang them on the rack. For a few minutes I run the hair dryer over them; I'm traveling light, and I'll need these clothes again when I return from my bike ride.

Dressed in cycling pants and a fleece top, I go outside for a moment to check the weather. There's a giant palm tree growing up from the courtyard, its long gray crown of leaves hanging limp and dead. Beside the tree is an illuminated swimming pool, dimpled by a light rain. Swinging my arms to stay warm, I go back inside and lock the door.

Kerouac told the novelist John Clellon Holmes to light a candle when he began writing and to blow it out when he was finished. I have the stub of a candle in my backpack, and in the tiny halo of light from it I tear off a piece of hotel stationery from the little plastic rack and address it to Dash, the secret heroine of these journeys. We've been bones-jumpy about each other from the start, and have an incredible brain congress (gestalt) that allows us to communicate without speaking. But just like in a Graham Greene novel,

I haven't talked to her since the day after Christmas, and barred by new, frustrating circumstances, I have no idea if we'll ever see each other again.

Kerouac once noted in his journal that he wrote his letters to Neal Cassady "as though it were my last night on earth." For a long time the only sound in the room is the scratching of my pencil as I tell Dash everything I couldn't bring myself to say when we were together. Then I fold the paper in half, retract the lead of the pencil, and extinguish the candle.

Piercey *is* a fucking genius. With my ankle just about disintegrating from all the insults I have perpetrated upon it over the years, he told me to ride bicycles whenever I can, and he was right. In the soft gray womb of early morning, I make four peanut butter sandwiches, mix some Vega powders in a bottle of apple juice, and load all that and the map into my pack, shoulder the bike down the stairs, and descend Van Ness Avenue toward the bay.

A right turn onto North Point and I'm gliding past clusters of men in orange vests working on the road, and then bus stop after bus stop, one lovely blonde at each corner, each one a doppelganger to Dash, perplexed about being late and referring to her slender wrist-watch. Apartment buildings and cafés go flashing by, and then the shiny glass façade of the Marriott, the doorman in a striped, nautical-looking shirt, keening on his whistle to signal a cab for two serious men in raincoats and neckties. I laugh when the great edifice of Petco appears in the mist—Bongo was right!—like a fortress guarding all the dog food at the end of time.

At the conclusion of North Point, where Kerouac trudged around with a copy of Jack London in his coat pocket, I reach the Embarcadero, which follows the peninsula of the city all the way around to the Presidio. Reaching in my pocket, I discover that I've dropped my letter to Dash and turn the bike around and pedal furiously up the slope of North Point. Two hundred yards along, in the middle of the bus lane, I spot its folded half on the pavement and sweep it up like a relay racer and turn back toward Fisherman's Wharf.

Seals are honking in the fog and the gulls wheel overhead, laughing in Yiddish like Borscht Belt comedians. As I ride past the unopened stands and clam shacks, their umbrellas folded upward like tulips, I remember coming here with Uncle Johnny when I was fifteen, my first big trip, from L.A. to San Fran to Salt Lake City and on to Chicago and Detroit and finally back home to Massachusetts in his brand-new Monte Carlo. Uncle Johnny smoked Parliaments incessantly as we walked around Fisherman's Wharf, looking at the giant orange crabs hanging over the steamers and eating hot dogs and pretzels. Then we jumped in his car and drove straight across the continent with the windows rolled down and Jimi Hendrix and the Mamas and the Papas and Otis Redding on the car stereo.

Riding along Fort Point with the ocean to my right, the pink and salmon and light blue houses along the beachfront remind me of places I've seen in New Orleans. I cruise down one of the long cement piers toward the gloomy shape of Alcatraz rising from the mist, which looks close enough to touch. A large number of Chinese American high school boys and girls are running out to the end of the pier and back in their Phys. Ed. uniforms. When they get to the furthermost point, each one is handed a paper chit by the star of the class, a slender Asian kid who's also clad in the purple-and-gray "Athletics" T-shirt and shorts. I reach out for one, and he shakes his head and grins.

Back in Fort Point, I'm joined by other runners and bikers and walkers, stringing their Pomeranians and poodles along and listening to their headsets. Cutting across a marshy field, I spot a sign that reads: "No Volleyball north of this sign until 6 PM." I laugh out loud, recalling Surfer's complaint that today's America has "too many rules."

San Francisco is a cruel little bitch of a city, and just climbing the switchbacks from Fort Point puts an ache in my throat and makes the Achilles tendon in my fucked-up ankle feel like it's going to pop loose. I'm listening to Neil Young on my mp3 player, and near the apex of the second long hill, I stand up in the toe clips, churning the pedals.

Halfway up the serpentine approach to the Golden Gate Bridge, my phone buzzes and I wait till I reach the next plateau to stop and check it. It was Piercey, and breathing in great gulps of the raw air with my heart hammering in my chest, I listen to his message: "Listen, man, bad news. Tanya is having some trouble at work and it's all fucked up and I'm not coming out there—"

Just like Kerouac, I don't like to drive and have no money to rent a car anyway, unless Piercey shows up. Besides that, I only have about forty dollars left and, hands shaking, I pick out Chris's number on the keypad. He answers right away: "Hey, I'm sorry, man, but I can't get away right now . . ." Piercey laughs. "Ha! Ha! I'm just kidding, man. I'm in Chicago at O'Neill's bar waiting for my flight. I'll be there eleven o'clock tonight, just you wait . . ."

"You're a fuckin' idiot, Piercey," I shout into the phone. "San Francisco is *kickin'*, dude. You're gonna fuckin' love it."

Above the trees the mist clears out for a moment, and I can see the giant orange superstructure of the bridge jutting out of the bay.

The Golden Gate Bridge isn't golden at all but kind of a shit orange color in the gloom. It rises dramatically from the landscape, stretches high above the San Francisco bay for half a mile, and then disappears into the fog of Marin County on the far bank. As I ride up the empty bike lane in the sharp, freezing wind, Tom Waits sings over my headset: "Go ahead and call the cops/you don't meet nice girls in coffee shops."

At the very tip-ass top of the span, I stop for a moment with the early commuters roaring past and reach into where I've secured the letter to Dash in my backpack and read it again:

Dear Dash,

I love you as much in San Francisco as I did in Brooklyn, Denver, Flomaton, Gulfsport, Algiers, Colorado Springs, Dalhart, Texas; Laredo, Monterrey, Victoria, El Jefe, San Miguel de Allende and San Antone. It's a mysterious love and everything about it is a mystery, except for the lovely planes of your face when you're riding beside me in the car, the blonde dip of your hair over one eye like a secret Greta Garbo, and the taste of your mouth and your breasts with the snow flakes dropping onto the lake and secret fishermen coming up the embankment with giant trout they've caught through the ice. I'm afraid the very idea of your face, your hair, your mouth, your breasts and the tight pressure of your body against mine is not going to change as I move southward and it grows warmer here. . . .

Then I slowly tear the paper into bits and open my hand above the railing and watch the little flakes sift down toward the roiling black water. Some kind of updraft intercepts them, and quickly the bits of letter are swept away, disappearing beneath the underside of the bridge.

I watch for a few long seconds, but all evidence of the letter is gone, and I zip up my jacket and buckle the straps on my pack and ride off, feeling tiny and helpless and alone in the vicious wind off the bay.

4

Pumping my legs, I go up a steep corkscrew road to the top of a bluff and then descend with the wind in my ears into the sleepy waterfront village of Sausalito. Very few people are on the street, and most of the quaint little businesses remain closed at this hour. Sitting outdoors at a green, faux marble table beside Café Trieste, I eat the first of my peanut butter sandwiches and watch the rain dripping from the awning. Before me is the main coast road, Bridgeway, which runs through the center of town, a collection of antique shops, trendy bistros, and marinas filled with shrink-wrapped sailboats and yachts. In the postholiday doldrums, most of the vacation homes ranged over the hills are buttoned up for winter, and the sailboats on either side of the café are tucked into their berths with the canvas taken in and masts folded to the decks. A long black limousine with a hatted driver cruises slowly along Bridgeway, the windows tinted dark and impervious to the scrutiny of passersby. The driver sees me and tips his hat with a gloved hand; the prince of Marin County is passing through.

Kerouac came through here on the way to visit his old friend from prep school, Henry Cru, called Remi Boncoeur in the 1957

version of *On the Road*. An aspiring bon vivant who occasionally
scored at the racetrack but spent most of the time wandering around
his shack in an old army cap and boxer shorts, Cru had left a note
on his door that Kerouac should climb in through the window if
no one was home. When his old pal from the Horace Mann School
followed these instructions to the letter, Cru reacted with glee, roaring
with laughter at Kerouac's observation that "there must be a lot of
Italians in Sausalito."

At the far end of the beach, a collection of ornate houseboats is
listing on the ebb tide; expensive float planes are tethered to several of the boats, for the purpose of bohemian getaways. Riding
along the bike path into Mill Valley, I pass a bulldog of a man—
red face, pug nose, black watch cap, and black sweats—walking
two proud English bulldogs. On a park bench beside a soccer field
is a tiny child's doll, abandoned and naked but for a little white
shift that is sewn into its plastic legs. Estuarial tributaries and tidal
pools lie just off the path; a small black-and-white aquatic bird
floats placidly along just a few feet from where I pass, until it turns
up its rear end and dives, never surfacing, I suppose, until I'm out
of sight.

The Golden Gate Bridge and the town of Sausalito disappear
into the murky distances, and I begin a long, slow climb into the
hills that lasts for a couple of hours. On Vasco Court, a jackrab-
bit the size of a beagle zooms across the road in front of me and
lopes uphill into the weeds. At a dead end beside the Scott Valley
Swimming and Tennis Club (*Members and Guests Only*), I stop for
lunch: peanut butter and peach preserves on whole-wheat pita; two
organic fig bars, and a crisp green apple. It's a meal fit for the prince
of Marin County, and I do not regret my lack of membership in the
Scott Valley Swimming and Tennis Club.

Doubling back after a long day of exploring the hills, I ride
into Marin City shortly before dusk. Kerouac lived here for several weeks during his first trip to the West Coast. A giant, ugly
shopping mall dominates the flats, and long lines of prefab
houses—not much nicer than Henry Cru's shack—are tiered on
the steep valley walls. A number of luxury cars drive past and then

a sleek black Mercedes, its driver puffing on a big cigar. For some reason, the looming edifice of the mall and this cigar-smoking fat cat make me feel sad, and I head back downhill toward Sausalito. During Kerouac's stay in Marin City, Henry Cru encouraged him to write a Hollywood screenplay that would make them both rich, but all Kerouac could come up with was a "gloomy tale about New York" that was so depressing, Cru never even finished reading it.

Fifteen minutes later, I ride straight into Peter Pan Donuts for a hot cup of chai. It's about forty degrees and damp, with the chilly wet fog settling back in. The chai burns my tongue but helps keep the dampness at bay. Inside the shop, the little Chinese woman behind the counter motions outside. "Not cold? The wind, for you?"

I raise the Styrofoam cup. "Not now."

Sitting at one of the wire grille tables on the sidewalk, I watch the pedestrians go by, huddled in their scarves and winter jackets. A tall man in a dark blue overcoat is walking toward me. His hair is turning gray along the edges, he's wearing a blue-and-white-striped dress shirt over his substantial paunch and a bright red "power" tie. The man is in his early sixties, distinguished and determined, and looking at him I suddenly ask myself the question that always occurs to me when I spot a person who's oblivious to the delights of the world around him: *What was he like as a boy?*

Back through town and up the thigh-burning corkscrew of Bridge-way and back over the Golden Gate. Reaching the apex of the span, I glance over the railing where I tossed the letter a few hours ago. The waves are choppy and black, and I'm reminded of Kerouac's remark that he tried "everything in the books to make a girl" when he was in San Francisco but had no luck. It got so bad he even fantasized about robbing a jewelry store and using the haul to run off to Nevada with Cru's girlfriend, Diane. It's dark and raw in mid-afternoon, and although I've been alone in more remote places than this, I feel a strange longing for Dash and frustration over the impossibility of our situation. Like Kerouac, I can't seem to fall in love with the right girl at the right time, and I'm reminded of Henri Cru's motto: "You can't teach the old maestro a new tune."

5

On Polk Street at 6 p.m., I spot a Chinese seamstress dozing beside her sewing machine in the window of a tailor shop and glide silently past, trying not to wake her. After dinner at a clean, sparsely furnished Cambodian place, I stop for a cold one at the Royal Oak. I'm the only person in the joint, but the barmaid tells me to pay up immediately on opening my bottle of Magic Hat. When I say I want to start a tab, the haughty brunette shakes her head. "That's just how we do things," she says, and I give her the six bucks. (*Six bucks!*)

The Royal Oak, at the corner of Polk and Vallejo, is billed as San Francisco's first fern bar, a dark, leafy saloon with blood-red walls that looks like a Parisian whorehouse, circa 1895. I finish my beer and am about to leave when the barmaid comes back in from smoking a cigarette. Her name is Dixie, and she's a little friendlier now, saying that she just got back from visiting her family in Alabama and needs to tone down her partying. "They used to let us drink while we were working, but not anymore," she says. "Thank God."

A tall, easygoing guy who looks like a basketball player comes into the bar and orders a Guinness. Turns out that he's Kevin Dempsey, a 6' 7" forward who played on a national championship team at UCLA back in the mid-nineties. Today he's a chef at a major San Francisco hotel, and he and Dixie and I start talking, and Dempsey buys us all a shot of Jägermeister. A few other customers have arrived, and when Dixie sashays past in her high-heeled boots and tight jeans, Dempsey says, "Man, she's pretty cute. I'm going to start coming in here more often."

Because of the absurd local rents, Dempsey still lives with his ex-girl friend in a tiny apartment down the street, an arrangement that helps financially but cuts into his social life. "I wonder if Dixie has her own place . . ."

Dempsey reminds me of Big Slim Hazard, a former Louisiana State University football player and Jack Dempsey look-alike whom Kerouac talked about in *On the Road*. A tough son of a bitch but affable and generous with his money, Big Slim eased along through life, hailing everyone from his great height and splurging on drinks. Kerouac worked with him on the tugboats in New York but lost track of his old friend until he ran into Mississippi Gene on that flatbed truck; Kerouac was delighted to find out that of all the tramps crisscrossing the country, the two Southern gents had been hobos together.

Before long, Kevin Dempsey and I are downing Negra Modelos, and he keeps offering to buy me shots. He's also busy explaining that his basketball career was shortened, despite his forty-two-inch vertical leap and his 4.4 forty-yard dash, because he was diagnosed with Sherman's disease when he was a sophomore at UCLA. The disks in his spine are degenerating, and eventually he'll need to have a metal rod inserted to keep him from falling over.

"They said I could take a medical 'red shirt' and stop playing but keep my scholarship," Dempsey says, turning up his beer. "But I kept playing, and it fucking hurts like hell."

I have a couple of hours to kill before Piercey arrives, so Dempsey and I leave the Royal Oak and walk down to Shanghai Kelly's, a narrow, dank corridor of a bar that reminds me of Sullivan's Tap over near Boston Garden. (The bartender is a dark-haired guy with crooked teeth from Norwell, Mass. "Everybody's from Boston, or wishes they were," he says.) "It is what it is," says Dempsey, of his condition, which robbed him of a chance to play pro ball and is ruining his posture. "I'm not going to stop enjoying life," he says, going outside for a cigarette.

After two pints of Guinness, we run back to the Royal Oak to have another beer with Dixie. The bar is more crowded now, and a young swell in a shiny leather jacket tries to strike up a conversation. He asks me about my cell phone, which is a relic. I look down at it, while the guy natters on about his technological wizardry. My phone is about as relevant to this monologue as a tin can attached to a piece of string or a discarded piece of copper wire in Alexander Graham Bell's basement. San Francisco is the bastion of gay male supremacy, and the guy is speaking more hurriedly as he realizes I'm not tuned in to his frequency. Kerouac had a lot of gay friends, including Allen Ginsberg and his longtime companion, Peter Orlovsky, and a tolerance for all sorts of people that was remarkable in his era, yet, as chronicled in *On the Road*, he was so unnerved by his loneliness in San Francisco that he scared away a "queer" who approached him by brandishing a gun.

Right on cue, Piercey walks into the Royal Oak at ten minutes past eleven, carrying his giant backpack and wearing a huge grin on his face. "What's up, dog?" asks Piercey, lifting me in the air like a rag doll. I only played rugby with Piercey once, in a summer tournament in Acton, Mass., five years ago, but that's all I needed to see. We've been brothers ever since.

The weight of his pack towering above him threatens to knock us to the floor. Chris Pierce is a crew-cutted rock of a guy, bespectacled, with square shoulders and an exuberant manner. A former two-sport athlete at Ithaca College in New York, he's the captain of my old rugby club, Amoskeag RFC of Manchester, New Hampshire, which has just been named one of the top fifteen clubs in the U.S. Piercey is an aggressive, optimistic fellow, and the tenor of the trip has changed dramatically with his arrival.

Dempsey buys Piercey a drink, and then Dixie sets up shots of tequila and says they're on the house. We bang the tumblers down on the bar and shake hands all around and say goodnight. Swaying down the street with his enormous backpack, Piercey is soon engaged in a discussion with two yokels standing in front of another bar. I double back, thinking that Piercey met these guys in the cab from the airport. A drunken bond trader with premature gray hair is talking about hitting the strip joints. The other guy is a college football player from Millinocket, Maine, a hulking fellow who just arrived two days ago; he's engaged to a local girl.

"What's your mix?" asks the bond trader, scrutinizing Piercey.

"Half Pomeranian, and half German Shepherd," I say.

Piercey laughs. "You see a little Chinese in there? A little Asian?" he asks the guy, winking at me. "I'm Slovenian, brother. Slo-venian."

"Where's Slovenia?" says the bond trader. "They got strip joints there?"

Piercey laughs and bumps the guy aside. The football player is wearing a dark blue University of Maine baseball cap and three days' worth of stubble. He smiles at the bond trader's antics as the three of us turn and watch him stagger across Polk Street, waving at the traffic. "I was in Maine day before yesterday. It was freezing there," the kid says. "Getting married in three weeks. Anything that happens is fine by me."

6

In the morning Chris and I pick up the car near Joseph Conrad Park, a small triangular plot of grass where I found Dash's letter yesterday. Within half a minute, Piercey endears himself to the teenage girl behind the Hertz counter when she complains of knee pain. The girl says she injured her knee a year ago, when she fell during a cheerleading practice. While her boss, a middle-aged Latina, watches with mild skepticism, Chris seats the girl on the counter and examines her swollen knee. She groans when Piercey rotates her knee back and forth, and he kneads the outside of the joint with his fingertips and asks her a few gentle questions.

Piercey demonstrates a therapeutic exercise called the "quad set," tightening the quadriceps muscle isometrically for ten seconds, then resting for a few seconds. He tells the girl to repeat this activity five times a day after the swelling comes down.

The guy who picked us up at the hotel, a sullen Mexican dude in his thirties, is looking sideways at Piercey's instruction, suspicious of his motives. But the girl looks relieved, and after we sign the paperwork for the car and retrieve the key from the manager, the girl stands on her tiptoes to hug Piercey, and his face turns crimson along his hairline. "Thank you so much," she says.

"Take care of yourself," Piercey says.

7

We decide to fuel up at Nick's Tacos on Polk Street, a large, gaudy ballroom of a place, featuring long crimson drapes and a dozen cheap chandeliers with hanging glass beads. Everywhere in San Francisco looks like a whorehouse.

The tacos are little cornmeal plumes stuffed with fresh guacamole, pinto beans, dusky salsa, and Jack cheese, a delicious crunchy mixture of hot and cold. We're sitting at a raised table with a crushed red velveteen banquette, like we're on the dais of visiting itinerant dignitaries. Norah Jones is singing from the overhead speakers, and a variety of hipsters and cyclists are grinding away at their burritos and enchiladas to the left and right of us.

During lunch, Piercey is flipping through the scroll version of *On the Road*, and he stabs at the page, invoking Neal Cassady's famous mantra: "'We know time.' What do you think Cassady meant by that?"

I wave my finger in the air, rotating it like I'm mixing up the gases in the atmosphere. "This. All this. What you see," I reply.

Piercey shrugs, returning to his tacos and the book. "We . . . know . . . time," he says like a schoolboy memorizing his lessons.

"A lot of chicks wear boots around here," I say as a leggy blonde sways past over the blood-red tiles.

In the mist and drizzle, we cruise out of the city on the Embarcadero with Piercey at the wheel. Orange cable cars are passing beneath a row of giant palm trees in the shadow of the Oakland Bay Bridge, while James Blunt sings "So Long, Jimmy" to the beat of the wipers. We're listening to the same CD that was playing at Nick's; Piercey liked it so much, he ran down the street and bought a copy just before our meter ran out.

We cut across the peninsula on Route 280 and hit the coast highway in Pacifica. Trailer-size prefab homes and self-storage places crowd the highway, and just a quarter mile beyond is the heaving gray-green surf of the Pacific Ocean. On Miramar Beach, the waves are three and four feet tall, and surfers in wetsuits are cutting through backyards with their colorful boards tucked under their arms.

At Pescadero, we park the car along the beach and go hopping over the sandstone rocks, then up and over the cliffs, the empty beach stretching away for a mile in every direction. The fog and rolling foam blur the line between surf and sand, and harbor seals are barking in the distance. The sea is cold, threatening, and beautiful here, growling at our feet.

Standing on the bluff, Piercey talks about the weekend in 1993 when he and Tanya went to Rochester, New York, for a summer anatomy class. The pretty blonde coed was his lab partner then, not his wife like she is now, or even his girlfriend, and after a day spent dissecting a well-muscled male cadaver and a very large woman, they climbed to the roof of a frat house at the University of Rochester.

Sipping his beer, Piercey asked her if they were going together, if they were a couple. (It was the "Summer of Tanya," Piercey says, when he set out to win her heart. "Late nights in the lab dissecting cadavers, oh yeah!")

She thought he was cocky and resisted him for months, but there on the frat house roof, Tanya bent her head, looking at him with hands clasped over her knees, and said, "Yeah, we're a couple," and Piercey threw his beer into the yard, pumping his fist at the risen moon.

8

Ten miles outside of Monterrey, Highway 1 is nearly empty, drenched in fog and tendrils of mist. We're driving through the long, flat planes of the artichoke farms, brown, newly plowed fields alternating with vibrant green patches of cultivation. At an open-air stand, Piercey stops and we buy avocados and tangerines. It was not far from here that Kerouac met and fell in love with the blue-eyed Mexican girl he calls Terry in *On the Road*. After the first blush of their attraction and a couple of nights spent in a hotel room, the lovers enjoyed a brief affair that mimicked the sort of domestic life that Sal insisted he was looking for; Terry had a little boy named Johnny, and the three of them set up housekeeping together.

Renting a tent on a wooden platform for a dollar a day, they picked cotton beneath the unforgiving sun and drank in the roadhouses at night, never worrying about "mañana," which was a word so beautiful that Kerouac thought it must have meant "heaven."

Here in the open-air fruit stand, two squat brown-faced laborers, bundled up in parkas and hooded sweatshirts, are watching a Spanish-language show on a small television mounted on the wall, and one of them gets up wearily and mans the cash register. For some reason, I get the urge to sit in his rickety lawn chair and watch the *telenovelas* with the other guy, but I've barely taken a seat when Piercey whistles me to the car, and we take off in a cloud of dust.

Back on the highway, Piercey calls his wife. "Hi, monkey," he says. ("I'm Pierce monkey, Tanya is Mamma monkey, and Kaya is Baby monkey," he has told me. "We're a family of monkeys.") "It's me, Piercey," he says.

While Chris talks to the monkeys, actually breaking out into loud chimpanzee utterances when Tanya puts their daughter on the phone, my phone rings for the first time in three days. It's Dash, and her broken-china voice instantly grips my heart.

"Hi," she says as Piercey makes outrageous monkey noises. "I have a question. Tell me why I should read the classics. Why everyone should read them."

This is a continuation of a late-night discussion that was interrupted some weeks ago, and before I launch into an abbreviated version of my four-hour commercial lecture, I blurt out, "I wrote you a love letter yesterday, but it's at the bottom of San Francisco Bay."

9

Twenty-six miles from Big Sur, we're winding along the coast road with a fifty-foot drop out the passenger-side window and the slate-colored waves pouring over the rocks below. Cows are grazing in verdant pastures arranged just above the gray swells of the sea. Into Big Sur as the sun is going down; gas is $4.25 a gallon at the River

Inn Motel, and I whisper to Piercey, "I feel as though I'm being violated by the oil concerns."

Piercey hangs up the nozzle, saying, "My ass hurts."

At the Pfeiffer Big Sur State Park, Chris and I set up his tiny dome-shaped tent in the fading light. Surrounding our campsite are several redwoods that arch overhead, blocking out the sky, and the remnants of some giant trees that have been lopped off that I call "Stump Henge." A light rain has started up again, and gloomy afternoon shadows are deepening in the space between the trees. This is where Kerouac holed up in 1962, occupying a small cabin a few miles up the road, tired of being sought after by fans, sodden with drink, and desperate to return to his earlier strength and creativity. But people wouldn't leave him alone, and the old demons came back and wore him out.

Piercey's tent is raised by an ingenious latticework of interlocking poles that link together in minutes. Just beyond the screen of trees a mountain rises into the fog, looming above the valley that is traversed by a fast-moving green river. There are perhaps three or four occupied campsites among the eighty-one available, and the quiet here is ancient and pervasive, filtering down through the monolithic trees.

The entire campsite and surrounding deadwood have been soaked thoroughly by the rain that has been falling all week. After setting up, we drive back out to get something to eat. The restaurant inside the Big Sur Lodge is empty, and we take a wooden table near the fireplace, where embers are throwing a reddened light against the beaten copper wall. "You've only been in California, like, twenty-four hours, and you're carrying on like you've been here forever," I say to Piercey, who has navigated around the entire lodge, talking to the Mexican janitors and short order cook and the woman in the gift shop.

"Yeah, but we know time," Piercey says, looking over the menu.

During the meal Piercey gets up, chats again with the woman in the gift shop, and returns to the table with a postcard in his hand. It depicts a good-size man with a white beard standing beside a wizened Chinese fellow against a backdrop of strange mountains.

"There's a poetry reading down the street," says Piercey, shoving his empty plate aside. "We need to go."

10

The Henry Miller Memorial Library, where the author lived from 1944 to 1962, is a small, well-maintained cabin set back from Highway 1 and demarcated by a clearing among the redwoods. Miller wrote Kerouac a letter from here in 1958, praising his novel *The Dharma Bums* and guessing that Ti Jean "must have written a million words before." A string of white Christmas lights outlines the low peak of the roof, and in the clammy darkness Piercey and I follow a meandering path from the parking lot toward the cabin. A large double door has been flung open, and a small gathering of silhouetted figures is seated in the main room, which is flickering with candlelight.

The evening's program has just begun, and Piercey and I tiptoe onto the porch and hover in the entranceway, our eyes growing accustomed to the dimness. Inside, the poet and translator Bill Porter, aka "Red Pine," is standing before an audience of twenty or twenty-five ruddy outdoor types, superannuated hippies, apple-cheeked septuagenarians, and a local avocado farmer or two, dressed in old ski parkas, car coats, and rubber sheep-shearing boots.

These colorful-looking folks occupy a crescent of metal folding chairs, and when we settle onto the porch, boards creaking, a young woman in a peasant dress rises from her chair near the door. She has an infant slung over her shoulder in a gauzy swatch of fabric, with the baby kicking its legs and mewling. Suddenly, the woman pops one of her breasts loose and heads outside. While feeding the child, she flashes a beatific smile and motions for me to sit down.

The interior of Miller's cabin smells of patchouli and candle wax. Red Pine is a short, substantial, white-bearded fellow, in sturdy shoes and corduroy pants, a moth-eaten sweater, and brass-rimmed spectacles. He's reading from a book of Zen poems, first in tuneful Chinese, followed by his English translations. Glancing around the room, I notice that many of his listeners are cradling the very same book or a similar volume, their tattered dust jackets featuring a picture of Red Pine wearing traditional Chinese garments and carrying a wooden staff. I look at Piercey, and he looks at me; Bill Porter's peace-loving zealots have dominion here.

As Porter reads, I'm thrust back in time, just a month and a half earlier, when Dash and I attended an uncannily similar event at the John Greenleaf Whittier farmhouse in Haverhill, Massachusetts, where the Quaker poet and abolitionist was born in 1809. It was the Saturday after Thanksgiving, and an early snow had fallen, dressing out the fir trees and covering the old Whittier farm with a thin white blanket interrupted by curlicues of hay. The chilly, high-ceilinged room contained a double row of wooden benches, and a group of Whittier devotees were huddled in their L. L. Bean coats and duck boots, many with their eyes closed, reciting sotto voce the lines from one of the master's poems ("As night drew on, and, from the crest/of wooded knolls that ridged the west/the sun, a snow-blown traveler, sank/from sight beneath the smothering bank") being read aloud by a woman from the local Whittier society. Dash was snuggled up next to me on the last bench, nodding at the scene and hugging my arm with her mittened hands. In between readings, a gray-haired gentleman, who wore a silk scarf and laughed like a villain in a B movie, announced that refreshments would be served afterward. At that, Dash put her lips to my ear and whispered, "Oh, cookies!" and I stifled a guffaw.

Here at Big Sur, Miller's cabin is filled with the exact same people—only with different names and histories—and that memory cleaves me like a sword, sending a flood of light into my chest. Meanwhile, Red Pine has arrived at the heart of things, reconvening his audience after a brief intermission to crack open his translation of Shih-wu, known as Stonehouse, a fourteenth-century Zen monk and hermit.

Four or five naps a day
Still don't exhaust all my time

Declaiming these lines, Porter, the old Zen detective himself, is poised before a shelf stocked with Henry Miller's books; additional volumes are suspended by monofilament above our heads, like the dissertations of Damocles. Photographs of the bald-headed Miller, smoking his pipe or lounging in Paris with other expatriates, decorate the planks of the cabin. There's even a picture of Kerouac, his old neighbor from up the canyon, and below it a tiny shelf that holds a few of Ti Jean's books. Several years ago, I attended a reading and discussion in Lowell with the late Robert Creeley, a member of the Black Mountain poets and an old friend of Kerouac's. One of the last, dwindling voices of his generation, Creeley said he felt like one of those Confederate veterans who was left marching in the Memorial Day parades of his youth. A bearded, bespectacled man in a rumpled gray suit and patterned necktie, Creeley talked for a short time in a quiet voice, and there was a sense that this man who had given his life to poetry would be silent soon. He said of Kerouac's work: "to see him as a gifted natural or amateur is absurd. He wasn't simply writing a journal, he was writing the evidence that manifested a life."

I haven't written a poem in quite some time, but the ghosts of Creeley and Kerouac and Stonehouse compel me, and I grope around for the pencil and notebook I've stowed beneath my chair.

Shelves of books
Candles burning in nooks
And crammed into
Folding chairs are grannies
And grammarians and
Unitarians listening
To Chinese songs

Mr. Porter, in his jovial beard, notes that translating verse is not like "dancing with my feet on top of yours." It's a complex endeavor, more intuition than science, and I can tell that he *feels* his way toward the possible meaning of a poem, rather than merely thinking about it. He's a humble fellow, making it clear that his versions of Stonehouse's poems are not the last word on the subject. As a matter of fact, there's something elusive about the work of the Zen master, a slipperiness that has not been reduced by the sixty-five-year-old Red Pine's long apprenticeship to them.

"The poem on the page gives you the feeling that there's something *under* the poem," Porter says.

In a Zen poem there's something "not there" that somehow must not be there in the translation as well, and that's exactly how I feel about retracing Kerouac's journeys and ruminating on his book. Between these crazy trips, I've been back home in Methuen working out, teaching, coaching Liam's hockey team, and appearing at bookstores and libraries to talk about my new novel, *City in Amber.* Instead of writing that book in chapters of traditional length and scope, I constructed what I call "panels," longer, more in-depth, and fairly self-contained sections. Each panel is like its own small book, delving deeply into the history of Lawrence, Mass., in particular eras and detailing various events therein.

I came up with this notion while thinking about Japanese pagodas, with their translucent rice paper walls. Each of these panels features the depiction of a scene; for example, Mt. Fuji against a star-filled night sky; a cherry orchard spanning a range of low hills; the quaint buildings and quiet streets of a small rural town. In the end, a three-dimensional effect is created by sliding one panel in front of the other: the grandeur of Mt. Fuji, framed by cherry blossoms in the middle distance and foreshadowed by the present-tense happenings of a little town.

In this way, Kerouac's *On the Road* looms over everything I'm doing here like the great, white-tipped bulk of a mountain. As I slide the panel of my experiences over the template of Kerouac's great narrative drawing, I can see more clearly the track of my footprints across the sands of North America. And I can hear the bop rhythms of Ti Jean's horn: *wahk-pah; paw, paw, wahk; pah, wahk, paw; wahk, wahk, paw-paw* in the light mountain air of Colorado and against the pounding waves of Big Sur.

Inside Miller's cabin, the wicks are burning low and the chill has become more pervasive, creeping in from the shrouded meadow. Red Pine thumbs the pages of the book, deciding on a final poem, then, with a dazzling glint of his eyeglasses, he changes his mind and flips to another section. After singing in Chinese, he reads his translation:

For a piece of jade, you can own a whole cliff
But gold won't buy you a lifetime of freedom

11

Dawn lightens the canvas of the tent. Overnight, temperatures have dropped below thirty degrees, and there's hoarfrost on the picnic table and spread in a hieroglyphic over the hood of the car. I emerge from the tent, shake out my limbs, and go over and study the frost like I'm reading one of Stonehouse's poems.

The ghost of a moon is out for breakfast and inside the iron ring, the fire has been reduced to ashes. Above our camp, the shrouded mountain of the night before has clarified itself, the bulk of its slope looming over the campground. Immediately, I begin sketching it in my journal, naming it "the Mountain We Missed." An unseen bird calls *oop-ugwahh, oop-ugwahh*, and in the dim softness of morning, fallen redwood limbs are lying about like weapons discarded in a battle of the titans.

Piercey ties on his sneakers and thrusts a woolen hat over his steaming dome and heads out for a run around the campground. My ankle prevents me from joining him, and starting up the car, I hunt around for a pencil and begin chronicling *everything* I can think of while the battery charges itself and heat begins circulating around my legs. Last night, we had a hell of a time starting the fire with very little expendable paper, wet kindling, and our $7 bundle of wood. Piercey kept the car headlights trained on the campsite, and when we were about to give up on the fire, I walked over to start the Honda and the battery was dead.

"The night is taking a turn," said Piercey, shaking his head.

We assiduously fanned the tiny bed of coals until one of the larger, dry hunks of wood caught fire, and we were able to start a blaze in the fire pit. Then I announced to Piercey that I would say a prayer to Saint Charles Borromeo, the former cardinal of Milan, who was canonized in 1610. My parish priest, Father Paul McManus, introduced me to Borromeo as the patron saint of cutting through red tape and de-obfuscation. As part of this abbreviated commercial lecture, I told Piercey that when Kerouac was a boy, the nuns believed his nine-year-old brother Gerard was a saint because of the heavenly visions he reported from his deathbed, and thereafter Kerouac prayed to various saints his entire life. At Big Sur, I got behind the wheel of the Honda in the chilly darkness and inserted the key: "Dear St. Charles Borromeo, help me to start the car, as a glory to our Lord Jesus Christ, Amen."

Turning the ignition, I delighted at the roaring engine; the red, white, and orange lights of the dashboard came on, and the late Keith Whitley began singing from the radio.

Piercey let out a whoop. "Who was that guy? Saint Charles, who?"

"B-o-r-r-o-m-e-o. Saint Charles Borromeo."

Piercey nodded, poking at the coals with a stick. "Charlie is clutch," he said.

In the firelight, we chatted about the road up ahead, and I told Piercey a few stories from the annals of our rugby club, passing the torch to a new generation. When the embers died, we crawled inside the tent, jammed our clothes into the stuff sacks for pillows, and zipped ourselves into the mummy bags that Piercey had carried all the way from New Hampshire. Then Piercey reached up and turned off the lamp, swiftly and gracefully, the vanished nimbus of light still clinging to his silhouette like the aura of a medieval saint.

When I had inserted myself completely into the bag, it rose only as high as my chest; my head and shoulders were thrust outside, in the frosty air.

"Whose bag is this?" I asked Piercey in the darkness.

"Tanya's."

"I'm glad you're not married to a fat chick, Piercey, but your wife is freakin' tiny."

Our shoulders touched each other's and the outside edges of the tent; it was a snug fit. "I feel like I'm sitting at the kids' table on Thanksgiving," I said.

Piercey dug around in his pack and handed me a woolen ski hat; I put it on and immediately felt warm and toasty. Chirrups and crackling twigs invaded the silence, and Piercey told a last bedtime story about camping with Tanya on the edge of the Mendenhall Glacier in Juneau, Alaska, before we turned up the hoods and went to sleep.

12

We hit the Pacific Coast Highway as the sun comes up over the mountain, the first bright day we've had so far. We're so high up, the clouds are below us here, obscuring the vast Pacific and pouring against the cliffs like a ghostly gray ocean. Descending into the cloudbank, the road dips and twists along the cliff, which drops three or four hundred feet to rocks below, where a legion of seals is hooting in chorus.

Just like Keith and I did in Mexico, we ride straight into the cloud forest behind two slow-moving tractor-trailers. The sky is turning greenish-blue, aqua, and then cerulean as the haze is burned off. Down into the Pacific Valley, almost at sea level, and the visibility is less than fifty feet. Trees appear out of the gloom, and Piercey navigates down the slope into rolling green-gold fields as we approach San Luis Obispo.

We stop in Cambria for gas, which is very expensive and the worst part of road-bound travel these days. "Piercey, if they have the *New York Times*, get me one," I call after him when he goes inside to pay for the gas.

He stops, turns dramatically, and holds up a paper from the entranceway of the country store. "L.A.," he says.

"Buy it."

When he returns with the newspaper and bottles of green tea and chewing gum, bending over the wheel in an exaggerated manner, Piercey says, "I'm going to go left here, and as we drive through town . . . we're going to look at different things."

Piercey spots his bank and offers to cash a check for me. In the parking lot at the Bank of America, a gray-haired man in a sports shirt is having trouble starting his brand-new BMW. Hustling over there, Piercey offers to give the man a jump if he has cables.

"It's the computer, not the battery," says the man, shaking his head. "I have another car, and whenever I let this one sit, the computer acts up on me."

After Piercey emerges from the bank and hands me a wad of cash, he says I should tell the guy about St. Charles Borromeo. So I go over.

"I'm a Catholic, too," the man says, turning the engine over and over.

But he won't utter the prayer and keeps grinding away at his dead connection. "Try it. It works," I say, walking back to the Honda. When I shut the door behind me, Piercey raises an eyebrow, but I shake my head. "Doubting automotive Thomas," I say.

Coming out of town at the far end, Piercey insists that we must take a right turn to get back on the highway going south. "Go left," I tell him, but he doesn't listen. After a short drive, we encounter the traffic light where we turned originally and Piercey negotiates a tight U-turn in front of a sign that says "No U-turn."

"Back home, you keep the ocean on your left if you're going south," he says. "That's what screwed me up."

13

Wide blue skies have appeared above Steinbeck's undulating hills. Soon we're entering the clean-swept streets of Cayucos, the sidewalks empty, no one around, just a man and a woman walking on the cold, sun-splashed beach. It's a short drive to San Luis Obispo, a neatly arranged college town in the Pacific Coast foothills. Inside a little Mexican joint called Tio Albertos, two short order cooks are behind a glass enclosure, and a middle-aged woman is helming the cash register tucked against a sponge-painted orange wall. I'm reading an article about jazz musician Chet Baker in the *Los Angeles Times*. Baker was one of the leading practitioners of "West Coast cool jazz" and a favorite of Kerouac and the Beats. He could answer a question just by saying, "Yeah," that communicated oceans of loss, longing, indifference, venality, carnality, and poetic suffering, and he could play the trumpet and sing like the vain and tortured son of the devil himself. Outside on Higuera Street, a beat-up Saab passes by with a bumper sticker that says, "My President is Lee Marvin" alongside a picture of the white-haired actor. If Lee Marvin is president, I nominate my hard-charging uncle Johnny for secretary of defense.

Piercey and I go back to the car and drive through town. Located on the southern edge of the business district, Wally's Bike Shop is between Benjamin Franklin's Sandwich Shop, Aladdin's Bail Bonds, and a trailer park. It's a refurbished auto repair shop with bikes hanging from eyebolts in the ceiling and racks filled with replacement pedals and state-of-the-art helmets and jazzy water bottles. Wally is a small, brown-faced Guatemalan dude, hunkered over a vise while threading new aluminum spokes onto a wheel. Cheerful and soft-spoken, he explains that very few bike shops in San Luis Obispo offer rentals, due to the high cost of liability insurance.

But Wally is an accommodating fellow, and after a moment's reflection, he tells Piercey that he'll loan us a couple of used bikes and we can "settle up later."

Out at the car I pack a small bag with the bike map, an extra sweatshirt, a notebook, pencils, tangerines, a lemon, and my water bottle. After two days in foggy San Francisco and a cold night on Big Sur, the weather here is sixty degrees, the sun climbing over the large, bald hills above Cal Polytech. On reentering the shop, I discover that Piercey has secured a nifty blue cruiser for himself and a ridiculous girl's model for me, with a bell and a basket.

"Wally's karma's gonna get you," I say as Piercey laughs. "It's gonna knock you off your feet."

Downtown is crowded with cafés and bakeries and lingerie shops, tree-lined sidewalks teeming with pedestrians, and a maddening number of traffic lights and short, steep hills. Riding ahead of me, Piercey loses his chain from the sprocket, dismounts to fix it, and a few minutes later, the shifting mechanism pops off the right handlebar and rolls beneath a parked car.

"This bike *sucks*," says Piercey as I thumb the little bell on my handlebars and ride past him.

Piercey soon catches up and passes me, his giant legs churning. Up a long trio of hills we go, rising above the city, the neat little houses diminishing behind us. The winter sun is filling the entire valley, and I'm nearing my maximum heart rate, lungs heaving and an ache in my throat as I struggle with the clumsy bike.

Finally, we reach the low stone marker denoting California Polytechnic Institute and go rolling across the upper edge of the campus.

One last giant hill looms above, while below and behind me is the verdant green spread of college athletic fields, then the tidy arrangement of homes and San Luis Obispo's downtown beyond.

High on the crest above the city, I'm sitting for a few minutes on the green wooden bench of the rodeo grandstand at Cal Polytech writing in my notebook. Just below are the tubular iron fences of the paddock and then the combed dirt of the ring itself. Beyond the grounds are agricultural fields; orchards of stunted fruit trees, their ID tags floating about on the breeze; and the large beige structure of the veterinary clinic and outbuildings. In this part of the country and this same breezy kind of weather, Sal Paradise went out to the local cemetery, climbed a tree, and sang "Blue Skies."

In a lot adjacent to the grandstand is a collection of horse trailers and pickups; beside one of them a young, denim-clad Californian cleans the shoes of his horse, while his blond girlfriend, hands clasped over her knees, watches him from the lip of the trailer. (Dash is everywhere, it seems.) The sweet stink of manure blows across the entire campus, gagging me for a moment.

From the top of a hill above the rodeo grounds, Piercey waves and shouts halloo. He's standing beside his bike on a stretch of dirt road. Next to him is a tall bulky fellow dressed in black and wearing a Stetson. He's facing Piercey, and after a brief conversation, the man turns on his booted heel and Chris follows after him, pushing the bicycle.

When I arrive at the man's pickup truck, which is parked on a little cutoff alongside the upper pasture, I learn that Piercey has a flat tire. The man, large and sunburned with tousled blond hair, has offered to drive Chris to a nearby bike shop for a repair. I shake hands with Piercey and agree to meet him at Wally's at four o'clock, if I don't get to the other bike shop in time.

Halfway down Charro Street from Cal Polytech, I stop for a few minutes at the Old Mission Church, which was founded by Father Junipero Serra, a Franciscan, in 1794. I'm sitting in the courtyard on a bench beneath a latticework of withered grapevines, basking in the late afternoon sun. There are yucca plants and long-leafed palm trees and sycamores here; three iron bells, cast in 1818, are hanging from a wooden frame. The walls of the old mission, painted white, are thick and solid. I wonder how many prayers have gone up from this place: fervent entreaties for wealth, sanctuary, healing, revenge, benediction, deliverance, and fertility; for easement of sorrows, relief from oppression, from physical suffering, from the anguish of loss.

Great military leaders, bedizened generals gloating in triumph, have ridden into this very courtyard on horseback, accompanied by their grenadiers and cavalrymen, asking God for His blessings and humility. And in this quiet place, the breeze hissing among the treetops, I wonder if Christ our Lord did or can or would answer all these prayers, or if His gift to us all is merely listening to them.

14

For more than an hour, Piercey and I conduct our separate investigations into the people and the mood of San Luis Obispo. When we rendezvous at Wally's precisely at four o'clock, the proprietor, who's dismantling an Italian racing bike, waves off any mention of payment for the bicycles. "It was just a ride, man," Wally says. "No problem."

Piercey says that the tire on his ride went flat a second time after he got it repaired at the other bike shop. He was downtown near a natural food restaurant and found a mountain bike with an air pump chained to a telephone pole. He waited ten minutes for the owner to appear and then decided to use the pump to put air in his flat tire. After a few more minutes of waiting so he could thank the person who had assisted him, Chris snapped the pump back into place on the other bike and rode off.

"It's some kind of new doctrine," says Piercey. "People helping each other out without having to know about it."

"Absentee Good Samaritanism," I say.

While we chat with Wally and refill our water bottles, I pick up a heavy cylindrical package from the counter. It's approximately ten inches long, two and a half inches in diameter, weighing about a pound and wrapped in brown paper.

"What's this?" I ask Wally.

He explains that it's pure Guatemalan chocolate, made with organic cocoa beans and prepared by his sister-in-law, who, even if she works like a maniac, can produce only about two hundred pounds a month, since the process is so detailed. A pound of the chocolate, which is shaped into compacted disks about three-quarters thick, is twenty dollars.

Piercey and I buy a sleeve and split one of the cakes, discussing with Wally the two bullet wounds he received during the civil war in Guatemala; he shows us the scar on his left hand where shell fragments were removed. The injuries allowed him to come to the U.S. under a grant of political asylum.

After taking turns using the facilities, Piercey and I wash up, shake hands with Wally, and go around to the rear of the shop and repack the car; the sun is going down over Cal Polytech, and our departure is imminent. "There's something in that so-called chocolate," says Piercey, smiling broadly. "I'm high right now."

On Kerouac's first trip to the West Coast, he was amazed by the quality of the "tea" and would head straight for "Negrotown" and try to buy some weed. Munching on my half of the disk, I say, "You're out of your mind." But Piercey wags a finger at me. "Look at your eyes," he says. "You're flying on that stuff."

He slams the trunk shut, comes around to open up the driver's side, hops in, shuts his door, and buckles the seat belt in one smooth movement and then lets out a whoop. "We're tripping on Guatemalan chocolate and heading for L.A.," Piercey says.

15

From San Luis Obispo to the outskirts of Los Angeles takes us more than four hours, creeping along the coast highway in the dark. Traffic is light, and, just as Kerouac and Cassady did on their trips, Piercey and I discuss each of our lives in detail, even going back to childhood to explain who we really are. Approaching the exit to Mulholland Drive, Piercey reaches his old buddy, Dustin Miller, on the phone; he played second base on their high school baseball team and Piercey played shortstop; they're tight, and anticipating a joyful reunion after not seeing each other in almost two years. My old rugby teammate, Frank Baker, who played for our club in New Hampshire a few years before Piercey arrived on the scene, is an editor for the Associated Press and lives in Long Beach not far from where Dustin lives. Both guys are expecting us, and it's clear that Piercey and I must figure out the most efficient arrangement when he hangs up the phone.

"We've got an hour, so let's get this right on the table," I say. "You want to hang out with Dusty, and I want to see Frank and [his wife] Brandee. But we have to be comfortable and do things that don't hurt anybody's feelings, given that we're used to consulting each other on everything and coming to perfect agreement about avocados for breakfast and whether to drink Magic Hat or Sierra Nevada and all that good shit." I've never met Dustin before, and his wife is eight months pregnant. "So let's think about this, Piercey."

"Yeah, I'm thinking about it, and I think you should stay with me at Dustin's house."

I haven't seen Frank and Brandee since Frank and I played in a rugby tournament in Fort Lauderdale almost three years ago, and I also know I'll be comfortable at their house. "Maybe Dustin—or Dustin's wife—doesn't really want another houseguest but just won't tell you," I say.

Piercey insists it's all right, and we pass the bright sterile towers of Los Angeles muddled in our own thoughts and finally, around ten p.m., drive into Long Beach. Dustin and his wife live in a neat walk-up apartment behind a cluster of graceful palm trees on Yimona.

After a journey of 706 miles, we knock on the door, and Dustin's wife answers; he's out at the grocery store. Jessica Miller is a lovely, petite brunette, dressed in black jeans and a long cardigan sweater. The bulge of her stomach is hard and round and obvious, and Piercey kneels in front of her and kisses it, placing his hands on its upper half.

"I can hear him," says Piercey, his ear pressed against Jessica's abdomen. "The little feller."

We sit in the tidy living room, waiting for Dustin to return; I'm struggling to stay awake in my chair. When the man of the house arrives, a lanky, ginger-haired fellow in jeans and a baseball cap, he and Piercey sit beside each other on the couch, an arm around the other's shoulder, drinking a beer. It's like the reunion of Kerouac and Henri Cru. In the meantime, Frank has called and we've decided to split up'; Piercey will stay here and I'll spend the night across town at the Bakers'.

Piercey and Dustin take me over to Val Verde, and Frank is waiting in his driveway, tall, sturdy, and gap-toothed, with mobile features and white-blond hair. There are handshakes all around. Piercey fetches my backpack from the trunk, joking how my shit is scattered all over the car and extrapolating on his pivotal role in overcoming my forgotten ATM card, phone charger, mp3 charger, and sleeping bag.

"You're a fucking mess," he says, crushing me in a bear hug.

Brandee waves to me from the doorstep, looking fresh and beautiful in the golden light from the living room, beckoning me inside. Piercey and Dustin and I say our good nights, and with his arm clasped around my shoulder, Frank says, "Great to see you, Aroo," as he leads me toward the lighted entranceway of his home. (Frank and I refer to each other as "Aroo," just as Kerouac and one of his pals called each other "Yo.") It's great to see him, too, my old teammate, but I'm sad to be leaving Piercey.

16

Frank and Brandee's home is an elegantly appointed ranch decorated with colorful, vaguely Cubist paintings by her great-uncle. There's a tiled entranceway, hardwood floors, marble counters, and a comfortable guest room arrayed in light greens and earthy browns. The large, four-poster bed, draped with a thick down comforter, is a luxury after the cold night I spent sleeping on the ground at Big Sur.

I've arrived just in time for a party that Frank and Brandee are throwing the next day. In *On the Road*, Kerouac wrote about Mr. Snow of Marin City, Henry Cru's black neighbor who had the greatest laugh in the world. Brandee's friend, Grace, a beautiful Filipino girl who works with Brandee at a local hospital, could give Mr. Snow a run for his money. (There's just something about California that evokes ridiculous amounts of laughter.) Grace is helping Brandee get ready for the big night; the two women in a fury of prowess are busy chopping fruit for the homemade sangria, baking enchiladas, hanging up balloons, and spreading confetti over every flat surface. ("I'm going to be picking this stuff out of my jockey shorts for a week," says Frank.)

At the slightest provocation, Grace throws her head back and launches into something that sounds like *hoo—hoo—hooo—wah— ha—ha—haa—ha—hoo—hoo—whoo—hoo—hee—hee—hee*, which makes me laugh and sends a surge of benevolent chemicals through my bloodstream. Then Frank laughs and Brandee laughs, and we're all stumbling among the confetti-strewn coffeetables and countertops in an endorphin high that trumps any rush that comes prepackaged or prefabricated and is healthy, too.

I wish to record Grace's mirth for my mp3 player; whenever gloom overtakes me, I can listen to the laughing OR nurse of Los Angeles County and get over things. If you bottled Grace's laughter, no one would ever have to buy one of those overpriced sports drinks again, because, after our fit in the kitchen, I go into Frank's garage and bang the weights around for an hour and never feel tired.

The next evening, at Frank and Brandee's social gathering, I get the strange feeling that I'm watching a movie of myself attending a party. Going on this trip has shocked me out of my comfortable local circuit of teaching, gym, post office, Liam's school, hockey rink, and grocery store; sending me on a shuddering loop over Russian Hill, the Golden Gate Bridge, redwood forests, and shrouded canyons, down to Long Beach and through a living room decorated with art and filled with doctors and nurses munching on enchiladas and talking about the abject humiliation of colonoscopies. Now it's almost time to go back, haunted by the tendrils of mist creeping down the ravines of Big Sur, and jump onto that roller coaster of church and school and rink and restaurant.

As the colorful jumbled roar of the party continues, I pad down the hallway with Lex the cat following me, open my door, let Lex in, close it quietly, and spend a few minutes reading *Big Sur*.

Pursuing these journeys has made me wonder what happened to Jack Kerouac; why his talent drove him, ultimately, to despair, and what interior demons ravaged him. In the San Francisco gloom, in the dark redwood forest at Pfeiffer, and up on the ridgeline in Marin City, I've felt closer to Kerouac the person than anywhere else, more connected to what he must've been like, trundling down North Point in his old U.S. Navy raincoat, carrying a huge rucksack loaded with his sleeping bag, the battered cook kit and utensils, and his old railroad watch.

When Piercey left last night to see other friends and have new adventures in Los Angeles County, I understood what Kerouac must have felt like when he departed Henri Cru's shack in Marin City, or when he walked away from Terry on the farm outside Selma. We all have our own roads in life, and even our great friends and our great loves, and even our boon companions, by their very nature and the nature of things generally, will only accompany us for a short while.

17

Right around midnight the doorbell rings, and Piercey strolls into the party wearing his giant backpack, with camping gear hanging off the sides on bungee cords and his laptop computer in a saddlebag around his waist.

"Let's do it," he says, laughing at me.

In the midst of the chicken wing–munching neurologists and wine-guzzling general practitioners, Piercey is an incongruous sight, dressed in his stained T-shirt and khaki shorts, that mangy fleece vest, goofy grin, and his Slovenian eyes, mistaken for the local Chinese. I look up from the sunken living room holding a chicken wing like a baton, and I'm oh so happy that Piercey has arrived.

"I'm afraid you'll have to wait in the garage till the festivities are over," I tell him. "This is a high-end party."

Piercey has attention deficit and hyperactivity disorder, and I'm certain that Neal Cassady had it, too—undiagnosed, mistaken for a Benzedrine habit and fascination with the myriad teeming details of life on the move. But Chris Pierce has a wife and a daughter and a business and a fierce devotion to them all, and through force of will has taught himself to concentrate and achieve things he wouldn't otherwise be able to do.

Right now, he's going around the living room with that ungainly pack nearly knocking vases and glass figurines to the floor, admiring the eight or nine large bright paintings that are hung on the walls. There's a blue-gray arrangement of shapes that reminds me of Georges Braques and two red plains divided by a black line in the spirit of Piet Mondrian, and others that look like they were started by Jean Miro and finished by Henri Matisse, but all completely honest and original in their own right.

Piercey goes humping across the living room with the big pack shouldered high, stepping over hassocks and outthrust legs and little trays of hors d'ouvres sitting on the carpet. He's peering at Brandee's great-uncle's paintings like he's an appraiser from Sotheby's, and without a hint of self-consciousness, he says, "I can dig it," and "Nice!" and "Sweet brush strokes." Piercey means every word he says, and I just love the guy.

The living room empties for a big dart tournament, and Piercey and I sit across from each other and watch football highlights on the television, chatting quietly about the trip. Then Piercey gets called out to the dart game, and through the open slider I can see the lit embers of cigarettes as Brandee and Grace are swimming deep in the vat of sangria; Grace lets out one of her feminine belly laughs and with *whoo—hoo—hoo—ha—ha—hee* echoing through the house I clear my dishes and rinse them in the sink, then go down the hallway to my room with Lex padding along behind me. Lex turns right into the guest bathroom, and I turn left, close the door, undress, say my prayers, and in less than five minutes, I'm asleep.

PART FIVE

COLORADO

1

Although Graham Avenue in Brooklyn looks much the same as it did a year ago, the sidewalk populated by neo punks in snug black jeans and studded collars, lovely, ethereal young women pushing ergonomic strollers designed to reduce lower-back strain, and a guy walking a dog that has the body of a yellow lab and the head of Bob Hope, Najeeb Shaheen has vacated the premises of his old falafel shop, leaving something called the Odara Restaurant in his wake. He has disappeared like the honeybees.

Outside it's ninety degrees and humid, same as last summer when I was here. The ouds have been removed from the pale yellow walls, and Bob Dylan's wailing harmonica has been replaced by a muffled basso profundo voice, obscured by the roar of an air conditioner, which sounds like Orson Welles reading from the United States Tax Code. The only decorations remaining from the Najeeb era are the "First Aid for Choking" schematic and a copper samovar and teacups on a small, round, fabric-draped table over by the windows.

Taking down a rosewater lemonade from the cooler, I chat with the Odara's sole employee, a wizened short-order cook with a closely trimmed beard, half glasses, and scant gray-black hair covered by a weightless paper cap.

My energetic Lebanese friend "has gone to California," says the counterman. "Going out to the desert. Going to the beach." The man shrugs. "Who knows if he's ever coming back?"

This is the last great leg of my trip, from Boston to New York by train early this morning; New York to Chicago via Greyhound bus tonight, where I'll meet up with Surfer and head westward, then on to Denver and the end of the road. Three months after major reconstructive surgery, my left ankle runs straight and true, but my left calf is like a bag of jelly, and I still have a pronounced hitch in

192

my get-along. Lingering at the Odara allows me to rest up for all the standing and walking I'll have to do this afternoon and tonight.

Over the next hour, I put together the mosaic of Najeeb's story. Restless, enterprising, and fancy free, he remains in some kind of loose partnership with the invisible owners of the Odara. His West Coast trip is the beginning of a new chapter in his life, the Lebanese Johnny Appleseed, strumming his hand-painted oud as he strides over the American continent toward the bathwater of the Pacific. Najeeb and his brother, Simon, who lives in Pennsylvania, are also running an immersion school for Middle Eastern musicians, three weeks' intensive study, where expatriates learn to sing and play traditional Arab music, the tambourines and guitars and ululating voices from the land of the solitary cedar. His brother provides the music, Najeeb cooks up a traditional feast each afternoon, and they all sing late into the evenings.

"I remember you," says the counterman, who looks like Charles Bukowski. "You used to come in here all the time. You were a good friend of his."

Perusing the stiff new laminated menu, I spy an item called "Najeeb's Marinated Chicken," $5.50. "Yes," I say. "Najeeb counseled me to avoid white girls. They all want to be men. He suggested I limit myself to blacks and Latinas, as he does."

The counterman laughs as he slings the mujaddara. "That's Najeeb," he says.

Najeeb has a friend in California who's a multimillionaire and bought him a car. "Twenty thousand dollars," says the counterman. "It's sitting in the garage for whenever he wants to use it." But Najeeb's absence has had a chilling effect on business at the restaurant, the cook says. "Women loved him. Young, old. They would come in for two, three weeks after he left. 'Najeeb here? Najeeb here?'"

As I gaze out through the front windows, the Oak Café, Law Offices of Daniel Castoria, and EnZ, PC Inc., across the street all have the illusion of permanence, but one phone call from a distraught relation in South Dakota or Ohio and these storefronts will fall vacant, their proprietors whisked away to new circumstances. So it was when Kerouac performed his wizardry up the street in Ozone

Park, and so it is within the minimally decorated, box-filled condominium I call home, and so it forever shall be.

"That's eleven-fifty for the chow," says the counterman, ringing me in, "and a hundred bucks for the conversation."

I laugh, toss a couple extra bills down on my littered table, and go out through the front door. If the road teaches us anything, it's that the great cities on the horizon, the solid-seeming towers that warp and waver in shafts of golden sunlight as we approach, all these are, in the reckoning of Walt Whitman, the original beatnik, "maya—illusion."

2

The Port Authority Bus Terminal on 42nd Street is a major waystation for America's underclass, of which I am a card-carrying member. As the glittering neon lights come on over the Royal and the Empire, citizens from every impoverished nation in the world enter the glass-and-granite beehive of the Authority: tall, grave Somalis; Turkish men wearing light blue soccer jerseys; shambling Indian women in orange, teal, or azure saris; and slender Haitian dudes smoking their hand-rolled cigarillos.

While I'm standing here killing time, a transit cop with a shaved head walks up and kicks the foot of a middle-aged black man trying to catch a nap on the front steps at rush hour. Instantly, the man rises to his feet and scuttles away as the cop follows after him. With uncanny precision, the cop taps another man on the shoulder who's sitting at the far end of the stairway among half a dozen other beat-looking characters. This fellow also moves off like he's been touched with a cattle prod. Apparently, there's a pecking order among the nation's have-nots.

By 8:30 p.m., I'm in the bowels of the Port Authority, waiting in line for the 10:15 bus to Chicago, watching every tiny detail through "the keyhole of my eye." The fellaheen people of the world, as Kerouac called the poor and working poor and who were often brown-skinned and dark-eyed, are a patient lot—like the shepherds with their crooks, standing outside that crude mud hut, waiting for Christ to be born. There's nowhere to sit, and those of us waiting at Gate 70 have been standing in the dense, smoky heat for more than two hours—most of that time spent listening to a heavyset woman with frizzy hair singing along with Cat Stevens on her disc player. Even Yousef Islam, the former "Cat" himself, would've told her to shut up after the ninth or tenth off-key rendition of "Morning Has Broken."

Casual friends and acquaintances back in Methuen, on learning of this project, figured I'd take a few little pleasure trips, come home, write up my notes, and that would be it. When I visited Mexico, a lot of people assumed I'd be staying in a resort at Cabo San Lucas, just like they do when they're in Mexico. If I was headed into Manhattan, for instance, they'd ask me if I'd be attending a Broadway show or sampling the marjoram-scented grilled quail at the Russian Tea Room. When I replied that on this particular leg, I'd be taking a Greyhound bus to Chicago, they pulled their children away like I was a crazy person. *Why the hell would anyone want to take a bus to Chicago?* Just for the hell of it, I answered.

The dirtiest secret about middle-class suburban life is that it's no safer than other varieties of life. Having a perfectly manicured wife and/or lawn won't prevent cancer, or a sudden, precipitous drop in the market. Kerouac knew that only too well: his brother, Gerard, died at age nine, knocking Ti Jean's entire universe for a loop. Of course, hitchhiking and staying in fleabag motels and driving all night are exciting when you're young. The world is rife with possibilities, and you're seeing it for the first time. But doing all of this at my age is about endurance. It's about measuring yourself and seeing if your early idealism, your "beginner's mind," as Kerouac called it, has held up over time.

Just ahead of me in line at the Port Authority is a small, pudgy Mexican with a wispy beard. After an hour's silence, we strike up a conversation. He's a truck driver from Cleveland who picks up RVs there and drives them to Brooklyn and then takes the bus back to Ohio. Originally from Guadalajara, he recently bought a nice little place in his hometown for ten thousand dollars. He goes down every year from Thanksgiving to March and then returns to Cleveland and starts working again.

Making small talk, I tell the truck driver that I was in Mexico last August. "Lots of pretty girls there," I say.

"I don't like girls," says the truck driver, staring at me. "I'm a gay dude."

"That's cool," I say, looking straight into his eyes. "Good for you, man."

I hold the man's gaze, and finally he turns away. After another long silence, broken only by departure announcements over the loudspeaker, the Mexican dude turns to me and asks, "You married?"

"I have a girlfriend."

The guy looks at me closely and then smiles. "That's cool," he says.

At 10 p.m., the whole sorry lot of us climb onto a special charter that says "Chicago" on the rotating sign above the windshield. Behind me somewhere is a woman hacking away like a coal miner; it sounds like she has whooping cough. When a Japanese fellow climbs aboard wearing a paper surgical mask over his nose and mouth, I have a brief, apocalyptic vision based on Japanese disaster movies and wonder if I've gotten on the wrong bus.

We emerge from beneath the Port Authority onto 42nd Street and are soon on a stretch of elevated highway heading past the city and then westward. Looking out at the tottering skyscrapers of Manhattan outlined by golden light, I'm reminded of a passage from Tennyson: "For my purpose holds/to sail beyond the sunset, and the baths/of all the western stars, until I die."

I'm sitting in the second row beside a tall, smug thirty-something Russian on his way to meet his wife in Cleveland. Rushing through the dark in Pennsylvania, he expounds on his theory that organized religion is for "uneducated people" (although the Christian faith itself has "value," he'll admit). My traveling companion believes that the Romans, usually tolerant of local politicians and preachers in the management of the empire, considered Christ some sort of fakir or magician, an offense punishable by death. His "miracles" were just illusions meant to fool the crowd, swaying their minds toward insurrection through cheap parlor tricks, which the Romans took a dim view of. In this fellow's opinion, Christ was an entertainer, a sort of Galilean Houdini.

After a couple of hours spent pontificating on the "Spear of Destiny" and other mysterious relics, my new friend goes silent, and I fall into a nodding, intermittent sleep, ghosting past Harrisburg and Wilkes Barre and over a forested, starlit pass into Ohio. In my sleep, I can hear the woman coughing, sending its echo deep into my subconscious.

I'm haunted by weird little dream snippets: a sad-faced Christ doing card tricks and pulling loaves and fishes from a top hat. We reach Cleveland in the rawness of dawn, bleary-eyed, stumbling from the bus into the Greyhound terminal. The floor is cleaner here, and after shedding the Russian agnostic, the gay Mexican truck driver, and the tone-deaf Cat Stevens fan, we sink onto the tiles, forming a queue in front of Gate 50.

3

Our new driver, Ken, is a sturdy black dude with a military bearing and take-charge attitude. Soon he has us all back on the bus, crossing into the flatlands of Ohio. Ken picks up the loudspeaker as we depart: "Remain seated at all times. No smoking, alcohol, or drugs, including in the restrooms. CDs and radios require headphones. Nobody wants to listen to your music. Turn your cell phones on vibrate. I run a tight boat. Everyone complies, and we get into Chi-town early." Ken signs off, then abruptly picks up the microphone again and says, "Thanks for going Greyhound."

After a few hours alone on the road, we make our next-to-last stop in mid-morning. Toledo, Ohio, is one of those staid, respectable, mid-American cities that looks like it was all built in the same week in 1900: a raft of three-story buildings in cream-colored brick, the streets lined with abandoned cars and closed-up shops on a mild Saturday morning.

After eighteen hours of listening to that woman hack and sputter, we arrive in downtown Chicago at 3 p.m. local time. I spend a fruitless half hour trying to get information on city buses, then jump in a $9 cab for Lincoln Park. Four stories of brick trimmed with limestone, the Arlington House International Hostel is a lofty, leafy enclave just a few blocks from Lake Michigan. My room is narrow and spare, with two worn-out single beds, chair, veneer dresser, and large warped mirror. Down the hall, the gent's is tiled in white, with four showers and half a dozen stalls, resembling the bathroom in a World War I–era barracks, Siegfried Sassoon territory.

Three blocks away, Clark Street is bustling with Irish pubs, dry cleaners, bike shops, sushi joints, and dozens of pretty women in bikinis topped with little terrycloth sarongs, exiting the beaches with the harbinger of bad weather riding in from the north. It's incongruous but pleasant to see them on a busy city street, in their designer sunglasses and hair pulled back.

Sitting at one of the curbside tables outside Sultan's Market, I have to hang on to my dinner when the wind howls down the canyon of brick buildings so intensely it rips the falafel out of my hand and blows half of the tabouli into the gutter. Passersby and a handful of other diners barely seem to notice, and I suddenly recall Chicago's nickname and laugh as my plate flies off the table onto the sidewalk.

Afterward, I meander the dense, closely packed aisles of the Lincoln Park Supermarket, choosing a bar of soap (I haven't showered for thirty-six hours), some cut-up fruit, and several bottles of green tea and sparkling water. Toting my purchases a couple of blocks, I ride the creaking elevator up to my room and stare blankly out the window like a man in a poem by T. S. Eliot. After my long night and day on the bus, the chunks of papaya and watermelon and cantaloupe are cold and sweet, and I eat them slowly as church bells toll from the next street over and a thunderstorm pelts the concrete just below me.

No one knows I'm here except for Surfer, and he won't arrive until tomorrow afternoon. It feels like I'm on the lam, hiding out in some west side Chicago flat with my violin case and fedora, tipping the edge of the blind to keep an eye on the street. But nobody is pursuing me, no one but the ghost of Dash, looming over the dim prophetic mirrors of the Great Lakes like some feminine colossus, one leg in Massachusetts and the other blocking my route to Denver, where I once lived and where I believed I could be free.

I haven't seen Dash since late fall of last year. It was an unseasonably warm day but cold and fragile along the edges of the pond, as ephemeral as the Whiffenpoof song. Leaning against me, she was as warm as blood and her skin white like marble.

Like Kerouac and Bukowski, I've always had luck with women, most of it bad. I lost my virginity to the first girl I ever really loved (as every young man should), a gorgeous little brunette with a petite but voluptuous body, large brown eyes, and the sort of wry intelligence I've been attracted to ever since. In my time, I've dated cheerleaders, flight attendants, doctors, swimsuit models, and the Rose of Tralee; the prettiest girl in my high school, Elaine Foderaro, and the most sought-after coed in college, Marni Fullerton. I've had—as my uncle Jack used to say of his own colorful exploits—my share of lovely women and a bit of someone else's. But I never met anyone like Dash.

After so much trouble in both our lives, I thought things were about to happen for Dash and me in a big way. Then *wham*, her past arrived on my doorstep like a bad subpoena. There was a French guy she knew some years ago, and they made promises to each other, although she thought he was dead or married, or worse. Sure, I'd heard about him, but he was no more dangerous than any other two-dimensional figure from the past was to either of us.

Then, like some accursed St. Tropez Lazarus he shows up, ostensibly so they could straighten out what they had once meant to each other. I wasn't going to sit home waiting for that to happen, and I also had this dumb idea that things didn't work out for us because of my limp.

With my son, Liam, visiting his grandmother in Connecticut, I decided to pack a bag and hit the road again. As it turned out, Surfer was in Champaign, Illinois, visiting Giz's family, so we made plans to meet up in Chicago. I've never been away from Liam for more than a week since he was born, usually for a rugby tournament or a magazine assignment in some remote location. Being the father of a teenager is never easy, but sharing custody and contributing only half the parenting for a child you love with your entire heart is nerve-wracking sometimes. Going on these trips makes me look forward to the time when Liam is old enough to hit the road with me, and we can see the world together.

But Surfer is family, too. My mother suffered a miscarriage two years after I was born; the baby was a boy and would be the exact same age as Surfer is now, if he'd lived. I have two fine brothers, James Jr. and Patrick, and two loving sisters, Jodie and Jill. But Surfer has always been my blood brother of the trail and the rugby field, and it'll be good to get moving again. Anyway, he already knows that every story about the road is really just a story about a girl.

4

After a restless night, I'm sitting on a low concrete wall next to a bed of pink, purple, and white flowers, reading and writing in my notebook. A swarm of little gnats is hovering over me; birds fluttering in the lower reaches of the sky; spores floating past and little dandelion angels on the wing. There's a breeze pushing the crown of the trees back and forth along West Arlington Place; it sounds like they're haunted by voices.

The smell of frying bacon is wafting in from North Halsted; I can also make out vast amounts of lake water and fresh, clean oxygen from the trees and flowering plants. Here in the early morning, Korean girls are coming in and out of the hostel; Palestinians, Slavs, English kids with cockney accents, even an aspiring Playboy bunny checks in, a tall shapely lass holding an embroidered pillow with the white bunny ears. Then bells start ringing and I push off, looking for the church.

Saint Vincent de Paul Catholic Church, established in 1875, is located at the corner of Sheffield and Webster streets on the edge of the DePaul University campus. It's a massive gray stone edifice, seven stories tall, with a large, round stained-glass window on its front and scaffolding set up here and there for renovations that are taking place. Next door, trimmed out with a beautiful plush lawn and shrubs and plots of lilies, is a formidable-looking rectory and administration building. Near the corner of the lot, a five-foot statue of Father Robert Brennan stands beneath a shade tree, clutching an infant to his chest and brooding on gloomy apostolic thoughts. While I'm examining it, the pure white rabbit of God hops by in the grass.

The el rattles past at 7:45 a.m., and it's time to go in for mass. Inside, organ music fills the great vault of the cathedral, and shafts of colored light stream in through the main window, throwing golds and blues and reds across the vast open spaces. The altar is two stories high, made of intricately carved marble, and a baptismal font the size of an aboveground swimming pool dominates the center aisle. The nave of the church reeks of incense and candle wax as I dip my fingers in the holy water, bless myself, and take a seat in one of the carved wooden pews up front.

The priest is a large, white-haired fellow in crimson vestments, and after a reading from Saint Paul ("I have competed well; I have finished the race; I have kept the faith"), his homily is rife with tales of the early martyrs being put to the sword, burned alive, hung upside down, and eaten by lions. He also notes that for centuries, every Roman Catholic Church was built over a bone fragment or some other relic from one of the martyrs. We as a church—as a people—have a bloody history, and the priest jokes that when Saint Lawrence was being grilled on a brazier, he asked to be turned over because "he was done on that side."

The congregation is small at this early hour, and the procession to the altar moves swiftly. In line for communion, I keep my eyes fixed on the golden crucifix and ask Christ to give me strength for the trials that are always waiting up ahead. I arrive at the altar, and the priest says, "The Body of Christ." Replying "Amen," I receive the host in my hand, eat it, and make the sign of the cross as I walk away. Immediately, a sensation of lightness pours into my chest, the same feeling of transmogrification I had as a boy when I received my first Holy Communion from Father Dolan at Saint Monica's Church. Kerouac believed mightily in the Eucharist and in being saved by Christ; he saw his redemption as intricately connected to his identity as a writer and noted in his journal, "someday I'll wear white robes flowing and write with a Golden Pen of Fire."

After the dismissal, I light a candle for my parents and remain in the sanctuary until the church grows empty and silent. The priest, having exited out the main door, comes back through on his way to the rectory and we meet in the center aisle. "That was wonderful, Father," I tell him. "A very good sermon." He shakes my hand

and says thank you in a distracted way, ruminating over the martyrs and their single-minded odysseys of faith. They have set a daunting example, and every man who hears their stories must peer into the recesses of his own heart to discover what he's willing to give.

5

In the bright, warm sunshine of mid-morning I stop at the Bourgeoisie Pig Café on Fullerton Street and order breakfast outside on a small stone patio fringed with ivy. As I'm waiting, the half-dozen other tables become occupied; everyone here is talking about going to Europe, to Dublin, to Israel, while I'm happy to be in Chicago with a newly washed soul and the prospect of heading west with Surfer. No agendas, no timetable, and maybe even a historic summit meeting between my old pals Surfer and Bongo, who've never met. These pleasant reveries fill my thoughts, but then my mood darkens when I realize that with the time difference, Dash is in France by now.

After breakfast, Surfer calls to announce that he's been in Chicago for over an hour, but his access to the neighborhood where the hostel is located has been blocked by the city's annual gay pride parade. I know this to be true because half the parade walked by the Bourgeoisie Pig en route to the rally point: seven-foot black trans-vestites in glittering spandex and high heels; party boys in feather masks and bikini briefs jumping around on floats; and armies of short, crew-cutted lesbians marching behind rainbow banners stretched the width of Fullerton Street.

On my way back to the hostel, the sky darkens and it begins to rain; not much at first, but then there's a loud cannonade of thun-der, and it begins to roar down like something out of the Old Testament. As the front passes through, I head up to my room for an hour, where I lie on the bed musing on death and other incon-veniences. After awhile the sun breaks through, and I go downstairs and occupy my old spot on the wall outside the hostel. Surfer finally comes strolling up at 3 p.m., carrying a bag in each hand and smiling like a lottery winner. It reminds me of what Bill Porter said about Stonehouse: "The hermits always like to see someone come up the trail." Surfer and I haven't seen each other in a year, and shake hands.

"I got nothing against gay people, but they really know how to fuck up the traffic pattern," Surfer says.

Surfer has left the rental car a few blocks away, and after we stow his bags in the room, he's able to wrangle a parking space just down the street from the hostel. Toting our daypacks filled with exercise gear, John and I head onto Clark Street, where we catch the tail end of the parade and then pay fifteen dollars apiece to work out at a local gym. Their lap pool is on the seventh floor, and I dunk my head, put on my goggles, and swim a mile in the chilly, bleach-smelling water. When I emerge, Surfer has finished his half-mile swim and a two-mile run on the treadmill, and we head into the crowded sauna to sweat out the toxins. Within half an hour, we've reoriented ourselves to what's been happening in each other's lives through the dot-dash-dot Morse code of a tried-and-true friendship.

After a quick dinner, John and I head over to Kingston Mines, a storied old blues club on North Halsted. Inside, there's a double-chambered beer hall with crumbling ceilings, a definite slope to the floor, and walls chocked with framed photographs of old blues masters who've graced the two modest stages. Christmas lights are draped along the railings and up and over the second stage, which is hung with a sign that reads "Charlie Love: The Silky Smooth Band."

Surfer orders a bucket of beers from the waitress, and the long skinny tables fill up on either side of us, while the band, consisting of a drummer, lead guitar player, and the gigantic bassist wearing a Foreign Legion–style cap (with an empty microphone center stage), starts with a running blues number, a long wordless introductory riff that beats against the walls and in the hollow of my chest. Who is Charlie Love? Where is he? What growling bitter truth will he deliver to us in the humid Chicago night?

Out of the corner of my eye, I see a stocky middle-aged black man leaning against the wall, chewing on a toothpick. Wearing a dazzling white zoot suit with baggy pants, a silk coat that hangs to his knees, and a stylish white hat with a rounded brim, he pushes off the wall, passing through the crowd in a hail of friendly greetings and back-pats. Acknowledging his sidemen like he hasn't seen them in weeks, the band leader straps on his shiny Fendercaster and picks out a quick four-part riff, hanging on the final note, shaking the last bit of tremolo from the body of the guitar before saying, "I'm Charlie Love, and we're *silky* smooth."

The band is tight, a trio of skilled session men who follow behind their leader's showy licks and brash stagemanship with the rhythm and percussion sections meshed perfectly underneath. Love works the room like a bored old pro, asking who the lovers are among the beer bottles and glasses of gin, bragging about his prowess in various endeavors, and urging his listeners to "wave your hands in the air—wave 'em like you just don't care."

He's really just goofing on this Sunday night, winking at the crowd as he interrupts a Ray Charles song with a spoken monologue about his wife and how if she wasn't waiting at home, he'd take this big brunette from the dance floor and "shake, shake, shake" all night long. Standing nearby is a young Japanese girl who has a guitar slung over her back in a case that's practically as tall as she is. After a half-dozen songs, Charlie Love spots the girl and asks, "Can you play that thing? Can you play the blues on that guitar?"

The girl shyly nods her head, and Charlie Love makes a grand gesture with his zoot-suited arm. "Well, come on up here and play the blues, then," he says.

The Japanese girl unzips her guitar from its case with shaking hands. When the guitar player, who's slightly built, moves away from the little alcove where she's been standing, her absence reveals an even smaller Japanese girl, about five feet tall and a hundred pounds, with a saxophone by her side. Both girls are in their early twenties, bespectacled, thin as sticks, with prominent faces and the large, soulful eyes of anime characters.

"Can you play the blues on that thing?" asks Charlie Love.

The girl nods her head, and Charlie Love waves her onto the stage beside her friend. In the midst of the hulking bluesmen, the Japanese girls look like elves. Charlie Love signals his band to play a standard backbeat and invites the guitarist to launch into a solo. Bowing to the other musicians, the girl slings her ax over her shoulder and plugs into Charlie Love's amp, then fiddles with the knobs on her guitar and plucks once or twice at the strings.

"She's warming up," says Charlie Love with a smile.

Then, dramatically, the tiny Japanese girl plays two notes low on the register, slides her upper hand over the frets of the guitar, and drops through a snaking chord progression as she picks and twists her way along a greasy-bottomed blues and then a series of wailing riffs straight from the wretched heartbreak of her soul. The crowd cheers; Charlie Love smiles approvingly; the sidemen pivot and grimace and follow the Japanese girl's story, deferring to her, encouraging her with nods and little points of their fingers and head wagging. The drummer beats his foot against the floor and pounds away, sweating over his tom-tom.

Finally, the girl steps aside, joining the others in formulating a steady, bass-influenced platform, and the saxophone player emerges onto center stage. Her first dozen notes are tentative and soft, like the tootlings of a child on a penny whistle. Beside me, John stiffens up, the bottle in his hand poised like a baton. "C'mon, baby," he says. "You can do it."

Onstage, the tiny horn player spreads her feet, flexes her elbows outward, and *really* starts to play: confident spurts of breath that rise into a majestic constellation of short and long phrases, repeated notes, anticipated three- and four-beat architectures blended with surprise improvisational passages, and then a long, ascending climactic outpouring and cascade of previously unheard sounds, but immediately understood and accepted as the honest and true meaning of the little Japanese horn player's life on this earth.

"Dat—" says Charlie Love, sweating in rivulets as the audience explodes with joy, laughter, and applause. "Dat, ladies and gentlemens, is da *blues*."

6

Early the next morning, I'm sitting on the front steps of Ernest Hemingway's birthplace at 339 Oak Park Drive in Oak Park, Illinois, where John and I have stopped before heading out of town. It's a three-story Victorian structure with a broad, curving front porch, tall storm windows, and a widow's walk on the uppermost floor where the young Ernest no doubt stood musing on what awaited him beyond this quiet upper-class neighborhood.

This is the perfect spot to consider Ernest Hemingway and Jack Kerouac, each an American writer of the twentieth century and both now enshrined in the literary canon. Although "Papa" Hemingway has long been considered a member of American literature's varsity team, "Ti Jean" Kerouac is fresh off the bench, an eager young newcomer to the roster of legends that includes William Faulkner, John Steinbeck, Flannery O'Connor, and Walt Whitman, to name just a few. On reflection, it's clear that Hemingway and Kerouac are like teammates in several respects. Both men wrote in torrents, especially in the springtime of their lives. Famed Viking editor Malcolm Cowley, though not enamored of Kerouac's prose style, played a key role in each of their careers. Both writers also suffered from drink and died prematurely: Hemingway of a self-inflicted shotgun wound in Idaho at age sixty-one, and the forty-seven-year-old Kerouac of an esophageal hemorrhage in Florida. And both men had public and private selves that were markedly at odds with each other.

The Hemingway-Kerouac football analogy is appropriate because both men played the sport, the former, mostly on the "lightweight" team, here in Oak Park just before World War I, and the latter, starring first at Lowell High School in the late 1930s and then at the Horace Mann School in New York. Kerouac, who was good enough to earn Coach Lou Little's invitation to play for Columbia University, was an explosive and mercurial scat back who caught passes and returned kicks for touchdowns but was undersized even for that era and considered undisciplined in his practice habits.

Of further interest in the comparison is the evidence, via letters, interviews, and other people's reminiscences, that Hemingway, the macho avatar of the "Lost Generation," was a self-serving bully—vain, misogynistic, and dismissive of other artists, even impotent. Yet he consciously projected and cultivated an image of a virile, compassionate stoic who would leave behind far more than he took from this world.

The *idea* of Jack Kerouac also differs radically from his true self, but in the opposite manner. Because of the buzz that accompanied *On the Road*, much of it generated by camp followers who hadn't bothered to read the book, Kerouac was perceived as a hip, free-loving iconoclast with an outlaw's disdain for authority. In fact, by the time *On the Road* was published, ten years after it was conceived, its author was a grumpy middle-aged man, a devout Roman Catholic who lived with his mother, Gabrielle, and his third wife, Stella, the older sister of his cherished boyhood friend Sebastian Sampas, who died at Anzio during World War II. (In a 1959 letter to the poet Gary Snyder, Kerouac wrote, "I'm fat, dejected, ashamed, bored, pestered & shot.") After being anointed "King of the Beats" and saddled with the useless freight of widespread bohemianism in the 1960s, Kerouac would expend nearly all of his remaining energy trying to convince critics, interviewers, and seekers that he was "actually not 'beat' but strange solitary crazy Catholic mystic." But no one listened; the irony that his work commanded such a large audience, yet was misread, turned the optimistic, energetic kid from Lowell into a sullen and sodden crank. Being misunderstood is what killed him.

People are listening now. In *On the Road* and the works that followed it, readers are able to experience the trembling virtuosity of Kerouac's style and explore the social and spiritual consciousness that shines through the apparent banality of his subject matter—including the holiness of the poor, interracial love affairs and friendships, and an authentic concern for the natural environment—while grasping the Proustian breadth of Kerouac's mournful self-examination. Forty years after his death, Kerouac can rest assured that he belongs on the same playing field with Ernest Hemingway, Jack London, F. Scott Fitzgerald and the other stalwarts of American letters.

On the Hemingways' stoop, I picture the teenage Ernest looking out, then his school chums calling on a beautiful June morning like today; the husky young athlete thundering down the stairs onto the porch and then along the wooden sidewalk dressed in his knickerbockers, letter sweater, and a newspaper boy's cap. Ernest carries his textbooks on a leather strap as he bounds along, hallooing to young Dick Atkinson and his other football pals who loiter in the shade of one of the massive oak trees that crowd the block. And then together they rush off in the slanted morning light, playing grab-ass and hollering, excited about the possibilities that life has to offer them, with no hint of the dark bloody future that lies ahead.

While writing this, with the breeze stirring the trees and the houses on either side darkened and quiet, it occurs to me that the one thing I inherited from my mother that Hemingway cherished is the "built-in, shockproof bullshit detector" that has landed me on his front porch, on this day and in this particular quality of light, with a good part of the road still waiting up ahead.

• • •

Soon we're driving out of town on Route 83, listening to Dexter Gordon blow his horn on the local jazz station. In Joliet, a few miles east of the infamous prison, we jump onto Route 6, the bumpy two-lane that Kerouac envisioned crossing America on when he left Ozone Park in 1947. We ride for miles between acres of waist-deep corn, broken only by small plots of land occupied by neat farmhouses and cylindrical aluminum silos, and then stop for a late breakfast at the Seneca Family Restaurant in Seneca, IL, where Surfer digs into his omelet, hash browns, and Texas toast like he's on a last-ditch gastronomical tour of the Great Plains.

Outside town, the two-lane undulates through massive soybean fields interrupted by lines of trees that stretch across central Illinois. The asphalt, whitened by the sun, is flanked by power lines on one side and the occasional slow-moving piece of farm equipment rolling along on the shoulder. With Loretta Lynn singing "Van Lear Rose" over the radio, we pass a sign that says, "Welcome to Atkinson, IL, pop. 1,100," which consists of a few small brick stores, some wooden ranch houses, and a couple of bars. "I could be king here," I say.

We cross the Mississippi River at the border of Illinois and Iowa, its swollen breadth spilling onto the fields and dales on either side and its surface whipped into froth. A Pearl Jam song is playing on the radio, and I start laughing, and Surfer asks me what's up. Eddie Vedder is singing, "I changed by not changing at all." In traditional narrative, the protagonist emerges from his odyssey a different person: enlarged and enlightened, somehow transformed by his experiences. I tell Surfer that someone recently asked me if I'd been "changed" by following Kerouac's treasure map across America.

"Talk about missing the point," I say. "I'm writing this book so I can stay the way I am."

Reading Kerouac as a young man ignited something in me, what I would call a professional restlessness, an insistent yearning for new things; really just "kicks," to use Neal Cassady's term for it. It's difficult, though not impossible, to get your kicks in a small town; to live up to your responsibilities as a parent, teacher, and coach while accepting a parallel duty to take chances in life. Embracing this project was the best way I could think of to keep that particular fire burning.

"It ain't about change," says Surfer, grinning from behind the wheel. "It's just the road, man."

7

Iowa is flatter and greener than Illinois and stinks sweetly of manure. The sky is vast and open, with cottony clouds riding overhead in a heavenly field of blue. Located just off the tiny business district in Wilton, Iowa, the Wilton Candy Kitchen, which is known as the "Oldest Ongoing Ice Cream Parlor in the World," features an old-fashioned soda fountain with a marble counter and red leatherette swivel stools. The menu, written in soap on a large, gilt-edged mirror, includes such long-lost items as the pink lady, lime coke, odd ball, dipsy doodle, hadacol, and the green river, as well as a list of hand-turned ice cream flavors like butter brickle, cherry-pecan, and banana-pineapple.

The eighty-eight-year-old proprietor, George Nopoulos, is a short, white-haired fellow in gray trousers, a white shirt with thin black stripes, and a pair of gold-rimmed spectacles. He explains that hadacol is a fountain drink comprised of "a little bit of everything, but not too much of anything." I order that and a turkey sandwich, and within two minutes, George places my lunch on the counter. "Here it is," he says, "I hope you like it."

"I'll tell you momentarily."

The white-haired Nopoulos looks over at Surfer, who's about to launch into his root beer and chicken salad sandwich. "Wait," says George, motioning toward me. "Hold your breath."

George's father was a Greek immigrant named Gus Chimpanis, who claimed to have invented the banana split and changed his name to Nopoulos. In 1910, he bought the candy store from its original owners, the McIntire family, who opened for business in 1860. George has been working at this very same counter since 1926, when, as a young lad, he was required to wind up the store's record player.

I take a bite of the turkey sandwich and a sip of the tall, sweating fountain drink. "Excellent," I tell him.

Standing beside a display case filled with gleaming slabs of fudge and neat rows of peanut butter cups and almond bark, George places a hand on his chest. "*Whew.* That's a relief," he says.

In answer to the question if he runs the place, George winks and says, "Only when my wife isn't around," referring to the former Thelma Soteros, whom he married in 1949. Mrs. Nopoulos is dressed in a striped gray skirt and bonnet, scooping ice cream at the far end of the counter, and smiles pleasantly at us.

George has personally owned and operated the store, which is listed on the National Register of Historic Places, since the early forties. "I'm on the hit list," he says, referring to his age. "It's like when you're running out of toilet paper—the roll spins faster."

The long narrow main room contains a half-dozen small walnut booths, checked white-and-red floor tiles, and a candy counter stacked with homemade malted milk balls, chocolate turtles, black and red licorice, and various other confections. Photographs dot the far wall, depicting George and Thelma with such visiting luminaries as Richard Nixon, Gregory Peck, Bob Dole, and the actress Brooke Shields.

It's a lazy summer afternoon in Wilton, nobody passing in the street, and just a couple of pickups in front of the wood-paneled Odd Fellows building across the way. "Do you make the licorice?" I ask.

"No. I just eat it," says George. "Quality control, you understand."

John waves at him from his stool, where he sits perusing the menu. "Is a 'suicide' a bunch of everything?" he asks.

"It's murder," George replies, drying a glass with a small white towel. In answer to our groans, he says, "Hey, it's a 'corny' state."

Adding up our bill with pencil and paper, George makes a mistake and crosses a number out. "See, this is my first day here," he says.

Dessert is a single scoop of that creamy vanilla ice cream of Iowa that Kerouac raved about. The quiet of the afternoon is shattered when five youngsters lean their bicycles outside and pile in the door, gabbling in a chorus of voices.

"See you boys in church," says George, as we head out the door. "I'll drive by."

In a 1950 letter to Stella Sampas, his future wife, Kerouac wrote, "I want to revisit the mysteries of my past, which is my job." Back at the car, I choose a pencil out of the well between the front seats to write all this down—an old-fashioned wooden pencil, orange in color, with a smooth, rounded eraser on the end. When I was a young boy, growing up on Sunset Avenue, an old ragman would arrive every so often in a wooden cart, his single, blinkered horse clip-clopping up the steep hill, occasionally splashing the pavement with manure. The ragman seemed ancient to me, a wrinkled, humorless fellow whose wardrobe appeared to have come from the shuttered bay of the wagon with its large, spoked wheels. Along with the fruit peddler who drove up in an old diesel truck with bins of pleasant-smelling apples and grapes and cherries arranged in a single, crowded row, the rag man's visit was one of the unusual and noteworthy occurrences of my youth.

I'm not sure how his transactions were conducted—who paid whom, and for what—and I don't recall my mother doing business with him very often, but the sound of hooves on stone always roused me from the house, because I realized even then that one of the last vestiges of the old world was passing by.

8

Route 6 is flooded in various spots across the county, forcing us to detour onto Highway 22 West. After a sign advertising "Lutheran Homes," we drive past entire neighborhoods standing in water up to their first-floor windows. In Riverside, Iowa, the tiny defunct business district is a collection of whitewashed shops and empty brick buildings. Among this grim array of failures is a single bustling storefront.

"You'd think the last thing anyone would need out here is a tanning salon," says John, squinting at the small bright sun above the town square. On the other side of the road, a weathered-looking Mennonite farmer with his white beard, battered straw hat, and work shirt passes by in a horse-drawn cart.

"Look what a bronzing has done for that fella," I say.

North and South English roll up next, vast farms, panoramic sky, then a dead hound dog on the side of the road and a tow-headed boy on a bicycle who peddles along waving at us. I resist the temptation to look back, since what has happened to the boy's dog is about to intersect with his innocent, corn-fed mind, and as a dad myself, I don't want to see it.

In the midst of a massive corn field outside Thornsburg is a processing plant made up of stark-looking elevators and silos, eliminating the middleman with pure Iowa efficiency. Next door is a large stone farmhouse beneath a quartet of shade trees and surrounded by rolls of hay ten feet high. In that farmhouse, there's a man who has figured life out and sleeps soundly.

We enter Grinnell at high noon, a bucolic college town with golden-haired children rolling past on old-fashioned bicycles and well-shaded, two-story homes set back from the clean, empty roadway. A little girl waves to us from her lemonade stand, and a mailman tips his cap.

"Everyone's so friendly, it's unnerving," I say. John laughs and I continue in this vein. "If they tried that back home in Dorchester or Charlestown, you'd go, 'Do I fucking know you? How do I know you? Are you following me?'"

At the only bike shop in town, we make the acquaintance of Craig Cooper, a large, cheerful man with a shaved head and close-cropped goatee. A former wrestler at Central Iowa and local rugby player, Coop says that he usually closes his shop at 5 p.m. and rides out to his home on a lake ten miles out of town. His young son meets him halfway, and they take a swim and have a nice chat pedaling along the shoreline.

But Coop's wife and children are away visiting presidential libraries this week, and he's reduced to bachelor circumstances. Before long, we're following him up the back stairs of Lonnski's Pub and Deli, which consists of two large open rooms paneled in light hardwoods and decorated with Iowa Wrestling posters. It's the last day before the statewide smoking ban takes effect, and five grungy college kids are puffing on Kools and Newports at the bar.

Leaning over the colorful display of the jukebox, I select an old Neil Diamond song and order a bowl of Lonnski's corn-and-potato chowder and a long-necked bottle of the local IPA and then settle in at the table with Surfer and Coop. My best friend at Acadia was a laid-back dude from Valois Bay on the West Island in Montreal named Drew Cooper, a first-rate rugby and football player, and one of the funniest guys I know. Drew is Craig's son's name, and immediately the three of us are talking like we've known one another for years.

Just like in Iowa, you had to make your own fun back in Nova Scotia. One night in late October, when snow had not yet fallen but the threat was in the air, Drew and I were sitting around the Anvil tavern when we decided to go for a swim. We paid for our beers and walked back to Coop's place and dug his Norton 850 out of the shed, and he kick-started it with a roar. Then we blasted off down Main Street.

Lumsden's Dam is just a few miles outside of Wolfville on the old Evangeline Trail. A desired bathing and picnicking spot in summer, it was dark and empty when Coop and I arrived just before 10 p.m. on that bitter cold night. Leaving the motorcycle on a little cutoff, we descended through the trees to the edge of the river, which was fast and black, running for the dam a half-mile off. A birch tree hung over the water, and about thirty feet up the thick, slanted trunk someone had nailed up a little diving platform.

Shivering in the wind, Coop and I took off our clothes and started up the rough hide of the birch tree. "What if the water's only two feet deep?" I asked.

"Nobody would be dumb enough to build a diving board over shallow water," Coop said, scaling the tree behind me. "Not even the townies."

On the platform, I took one look down at the water running swiftly in the moonlight, glanced over toward the dam, and launched myself into the air. Plunging in knocked the wind out of me, and I started kicking and flailing like a man possessed. The water was so cold it felt like it was burning my skin, and when I came up, gasping and choking, I was already thirty or forty yards downstream.

Coop let out a "Geronimo!" and jumped in straight after. Howling like idiots, we pulled hard for shore and flopped onto the embankment, tingling from head to foot and breathing in forced sobs like we'd been sprinting up a mountain. The roar of the dam, which remained invisible through the screen of trees, sounded like a jet taking off.

We dried off as best we could using our shirts and jackets and got dressed and ran up through the trees to the bike. Adrenaline shot through me like heavenly blue fire, and crouched on the back of the Norton, screaming down the two-lane in the dark, I felt like we'd traveled the entire world in one night and were going home to tell everyone what we'd seen.

9

After an early morning workout in the vast, empty Grinnell College weight room, John and I are served breakfast at the Carriage House promptly at 8 a.m. The Victorian dining room is set with polished silver and crystal, and a holiday centerpiece made of tiny American flags clustered in a bouquet and festooned with red, white, and blue ribbons. "This place is a little too swank for us," Surfer whispers, as we take our seats among the other guests who have spent the night.

What the genial Irish proprietress calls a "stuffed peach" adorns each of the place settings, a halved and candied peach dressed with vanilla yogurt and sweetened raw oats. A carved wooden fireplace and three oak china cabinets line the room, which is dark green and trimmed at the upper edge with a band of pink-and-blue-flowered wallpaper. A cuckoo clock in the vestibule announces the half hour, and the mostly retired folks sharing the bed and breakfast are busy dining on Irish oatmeal with cranberries and walnuts, homemade soda bread, fresh cantaloupe, watermelon and grapes, and deep-dish egg casserole. As Surfer continues his food safari, and I write in my notebook, a piano concerto is background to the hushed, sibilant tones of the breakfasting folks who share the table.

In 1895, a Grinnell lumber baron named Carney had the Carriage House built at 1133 Broad Street. A large Queen Anne–style Victorian, it's situated on a shady lot in a well-tended neighborhood of spacious homes, deep green lawns, and ratcheting sprinklers. The pace is idyllic here, with early morning strollers occasionally passing by and a slender, freckle-faced boy slinging a copy of the *Des Moines Register* onto the porch with an easy flick of his wrist.

Inside, the main sitting room is decorated in dark reds and burgundy and dominated by a large pillared fireplace carved from oak, and a high ceiling squared off by oaken beams. A wide staircase leads up seven steps to a platform meant to contain a quartet of musicians, who were hired to entertain at dinner parties and provided with their own exit into the side yard so as not to disturb the guests. Listening to the Bach concerto, I wonder what kind of sophisticated turn-of-the-century cats used to visit this house with their violins and flutes and cellos.

While I'm scribbling, a tall, lean-faced man across the table is studying me. Passing through Grinnell with his wife, he's a fine art photographer named Lawrence Oliverson. When the room empties out, Mr. Oliverson and I sit among the cantaloupe rinds and wilted pats of butter and have a conversation about Edward Hopper and Vermeer van Delft and their use of natural light. Oliverson has had a long and distinguished career as a photographer, selling pieces on commission and displaying his work in the top museums and galleries. After zeroing in on my notebook, Mr. Oliverson has surmised that I'm writing a book, and wants to know about my "process." After noting that I use a computer to make revisions, I tell Oliverson that I really enjoy writing with a pencil on paper most of all.

Oliverson also prefers to work traditionally, using only the light of the world to display his subjects, eschewing any postproduction effects, and spending hours in his darkroom to produce a small number of images. And I know exactly what Mr. Oliverson is talking about when he relates a conversation he had recently with a young photographer who said, "Oh, I get it. You're not digital—you're analog."

10

Rolling through central Iowa with Stevie Ray Vaughn and Albert King playing "Pride and Joy," Surfer jumps on the interstate to avoid the clogged arteries of lunchtime in Des Moines. Near the South Skunk River, we pass the "Adult Superstore," a nondescript concrete warehouse that aspires to be the Wal-Mart of pornography.

Just outside Des Moines there's a squat prison building encircled by barbed-wire fences and marked with the obligatory sign that says, "Do Not Pick Up Hitchhikers." Kerouac was introduced to Cassady and became intrigued by his energy and optimism through letters the "young jailkid" wrote to mutual friend Hal Chase while in a Colorado reform school. Among Cassady's most famous writings is the so-called Joan Anderson/Cherry Mary letter, surviving now only in fragments, which helped inspire Kerouac to develop his method of "spontaneous prose." The voluminous correspondence between the two pals went zinging back and forth for well over a decade, forming an epistolary novel for the ages; in 1950, Cassady wrote, "Stop the presses, hold that headline; Insert this: Keroassady to fuse. . . ." In one of the last letters Neal Cassady ever wrote to Jack Kerouac, composed on October 27, 1959, while the "Holy Goof" was serving a two-year sentence for marijuana possession (for pot!) in San Quentin state prison, Cassady asked his old road buddy to visit him in jail. Addressing Kerouac as "Herr Beat Brendan Behan Balzac," Cassady noted that Allen Ginsberg and Gary Snyder had come to read their poetry to the class in comparative religion he was taking in prison and that he, Cassady, would be the toast of the "Big Yard" if Kerouac would deign to appear. For reasons of his own, Kerouac never did.

Along this stretch, I-80 is teeming with cement mixers and their rotating tanks; giant flatbeds hauling incredible tractors with wheels ten feet tall; propane trucks warning us to "stay back"; double-trailer rigs lashed with electric generators, large shining roto-tiller blades, and all manner of brand-new farm implements. Des Moines is the Great Plains city of the workingman.

In the little crossroads town of Stuart, Iowa, the police station is located in an old bank building on the corner of Second Street and Division, with a plaque that says, "First National Bank 1882–1944. Site of Bonnie Parker and Clyde Barrow Robbery. Apr. 16, 1934."

Across the street is the small white clapboard Cyclone Drive-in, a homely little diner with a trio of smiling, bovine ladies behind the counter and a handful of denture-wearing customers. Surfer chats with the help and orders a cake batter shake and a giant hamburger with all the fix-ins. Kerouac got stuck in this town a couple of times back in the late 1940s. I can understand why the twenty-five-year-old writer would've been bored here, with all his friends waiting in Denver and San Francisco, but I'm content to sit at one of the tables writing in my notebook.

A few feet away, a bespectacled middle-aged man in a softball jersey has spread the local newspaper over the remains of his hamburger plate and is perusing the sports page, while flies drone at the windows and a ceiling fan whirs overhead. He has an aloof, small-town air about him, and it's obvious that we'll cease to exist as soon as we pay our bill and leave.

After lunch, we enter Route 148 South near Anita, IA, heading through sloping, tree-filled country on a sun-whitened and cracked two-lane road. Downtown Anita consists of an American Legion post, a concrete band shell, the First National Bank, a corn silo and processing plant, and local workmen in wide-brimmed hats resting in the shade cast down by the awnings. Right outside town, we regain Route 6 West, where there are enormous plots of corn and an occasional Iowa horse farm; from the radio, Charlie Parker is blowing his bop fertilizer all over the corn, corn, corn, which is stunted by the flooding of late but reaching past the curve of the earth, enough corn to feed the starving hordes of Outer Mongolia and Mesopotamia.

On a stretch of undulating road ten miles from the Nebraska border, Surfer guns the car past a farmer on his tractor, crossing the solid white line. Just before we clear the front bumper of the trac-tor, an approaching pickup rises from the water mirage on the road ahead and Surfer jerks the wheel to the right, avoiding a horrible wreck.

"*Whoa*," he says. "That was a bigger dip in the road than I thought."

"So are you," I reply.

11

We're on 59 West, barreling toward Omaha and Lincoln beyond, where via a prearranged call from a Montana pay phone we're scheduled to meet Bongo just off Exit 399 precisely at 5 p.m. local time. Now it's 3 p.m., and we're a hundred miles away with little margin for error; Keith's a restless soul and will push on for Ohio and Michigan if we're more than ten minutes late.

Onto 39 West, where the land has grown hilly and some of the farms are arranged in cascading steppes, with berms keeping the various crops from sliding into one another. The bridge over to Nebraska on Highway 39 is out, and we're forced to go north toward Council Bluffs looking for another place to cross.

"The Missouri flood plain is, well, flooded," John says, gazing out at the ruined fields and trees half obscured by the risen water.

We cross the chocolate brown Missouri River into Nebraska at 3:49 p.m. There's a little white toll booth at the far end of the bridge, with some kind of neat, one-room operator's apartment stacked above it and a sign that says, "Welcome to Belleville, Ed Babbitt, Mayor." Ed ain't home today.

Heading south on 34 until it doglegs west, it's another seventy miles to Lincoln, past the No-Frills Plaza, aptly named, and a couple of rundown strip clubs alongside a sign for the nearby air force base. Past Weeping Water, NE, with soybeans and corn and many large fields ruined by the wet weather or lying fallow, out of this season's rotation. Over the Little Nebraska River, which is tucked down in a hollow and obscured by shade trees. With Dizzy Gillespie on the radio, we enter Milden, NE, "home of the milking machine," white farmhouses framed by American flags and giant shade trees with the gray ribbon of 34 stretching ahead to dusty prairie horizons.

Entering downtown Lincoln, I spot a guy on the side of the road wearing a sandwich board that says, "Honk if U.S. Bank Sucks."

"Obviously, he got screwed out of something," Surfer says. I tell him not to honk, since Piercey was able to cash my personal check at a U.S. Bank in California. "I have to go with what I see," I tell John.

Keith is waiting just off Exit 399 right at five o'clock as promised, despite the fact that he's driven 380 miles from Montana today and we've come nearly the same distance from the opposite direction, like two arrows hitting each other in mid-air.

In baggy pants and a gray, short-sleeved shirt, Bongo is walking along the side of the road with his hands in his pockets like an old-time Nebraska hobo. When Surfer parks the car on the dusty shoulder, we amble over to Keith, who squints at the glittering coin of the sun. "Sure is a hot day," he says.

It sure is, and we retreat into the dark, musty stench of a nearby sports bar, order a rack of beers, and get acquainted and reacquainted while puzzling over a huge map of Nebraska that belongs to Keith.

"I feel like I know you because of all the stories Jay told me, and you were easy to remember because of your nickname," Bongo says to John. "How'd you get it?"

Surfer explains, quite accurately, that he was pretty much the first real surfer I had ever seen, and that I hung the moniker on him in a punk rock bar in Gainesville called "Friday Night Live" after playing rugby together on the day we met. For the next hour, ensconced in the mold-smelling gloom of the bar, I connect Surfer's half of stories I've told to Keith's half, since what I'm doing, as my writing teacher Harry Crews always said, is very similar to shipbuilding or masonry, and the real craft of storytelling itself is weaving a giant tapestry of interesting people and sights and events for all to marvel at; then you walk away, hands-a-pockets, like any old Western road tramp, which is what I've been doing my whole life.

After sitting on our asses all day, we're pretty restless, so Keith pays for the beer and we emerge from the saloon and go walking up the street. Its early evening and the dropping sun throws a sideways light over the waving furze of the prairie, reddening the grasses and turning the Lincoln skyline black across the river.

Bongo stops at his car and unloads a dozen cans of Tecate beer from his cooler, stowing them in Surfer's daypack. The gigantic rail yard lies half a mile to the east, the trains entering with long plaintive wails and clouds of dust, and Keith just naturally heads for it.

We reach the yard through an industrial park comprised of low cinder-block buildings and then down a dirt road overgrown with weeds on either side. A Union Pacific sign printed only in Spanish warns us that entrance to the freight yard is prohibited. Bongo and Surfer are walking just ahead, talking and gesturing, and I follow them past a giant Terex crane into the construction site beside the tracks. I haven't told anyone, but I'm feeling pretty sick and just want to sit down and rest. Those guys are jumping around and drinking beer and I'm about to keel over.

A train half a mile long blows air from its brakes and then rattles by, as dusk settles over the lights of the city. The yard is more than a dozen tracks wide at this point, trains moving or sitting, coming in from the west loaded with coal and from the east with empty coal cars, or cylindrical tankers and boxcars.

Slowly and quietly, we pick our way toward the eastern fringes of the yard, looking for an open platform car where it's harder for the railroad detectives to spot you if you want to sit or take a ride. Bongo rode the rails extensively in the 1970s and '80s, across the U.S. and western Canada, into Mexico and down to Central America; he routinely hopped freighters from where we went to college in Nova Scotia home to Texas.

Near one of the little concrete signal houses, Bongo spots a deer lingering in the swale, which reminds me of something I want to ask him about. Back at Acadia, I played soccer with a guy named

Paul Tubbe, an athletic six-footer with a maniacal grin and wild curly hair. On the field he moved with the joyful bounding glee of a young buck, and in Wolfville's only tavern, the Anvil, dressed in his woolen overcoat and soft hat, he filled the beer-smelling room with the manic hell-blown fire of his soul.

But Tubbe also has a willful, self-destructive side, and in 1983, he was paralyzed from the waist down in a horrible crash on his motorcycle. Still, being Tubbe, he wasn't going to let something as insignificant as a wheelchair hinder his frenzied enjoyment of life. In earlier times he had accompanied Keith on numerous train rides, and then in 1994 he convinced Bongo to emerge from his "retirement" to hop a freight train from White Fish, Montana, 265 miles through the Glacier National Park to Havre, Montana.

The trick was getting Paul and his wheelchair onto the train. When a Burlington Northern freighter rolled into the yard, slowing for a crew change, Bongo went charging from the tree line, pushing the chair down a gentle slope to the tracks. Coming alongside the train, Bongo maneuvered so Tubbe was able to grab the edge of the moving boxcar, using his considerable strength to kip over the edge like a gymnast, while Keith picked up the wheelchair and threw it in after him. Then he ran back up the slope for the cooler.

Running hard after the car as the train began to speed up again, at the last possible instant Bongo heaved the cooler through the yawning doorway and flung himself into the boxcar alongside Tubbe and his wheelchair.

They rode for three days out of White Fish, until the train split in Shelby. "It's hard with two walkees, but with a gimp, forget it," says Bongo. When they heard the train blowing air in Shelby, he jumped down from the train and approached one of the yardmen and explained what he was doing and asked which half of the train was going to Havre. After that, the crew looked after him and Tubbe until they reached their destination.

It's after dark now and Keith, Surfer, and I are sitting on an empty caboose in the middle of the Lincoln yard, sipping our cans of beer. "When we got to Havre, we were the toast of the hobo jungle," Bongo says. "They were all asking how we did it, and trying to help us."

Bongo goes on to say that hobo jungles are still prevalent outside rail yards across the country, but that they can be nasty, violent places. Most of the men riding the rails are alcoholics or mentally ill and very unpredictable. He once saw two tramps in a casual disagreement over whether each or the other had ever ridden a particular train; after the argument had simmered down, one of the hoboes got up, crossed in front of the fire, and stabbed the other man in the belly. "You ain't never rid the Santa Fe," he said.

Near midnight, 8262 BNSE comes into the yard with its horn renting the summer air. Over a hundred fully loaded coal cars go rolling past, heading east. Keith says that he always preferred to ride the Burlington Northern because the attitude of its original owners was, "If the bums built it, let the bums ride it."

When the train slows to obtain yard clearance, Bongo gets up, swats his dirty hands against the side of his pants, and demonstrates how to ride one of the coal cars. Taking a few smooth, easy strides alongside the moving train, he grabs for the highest rung he can reach on the vertical steel ladder attached to the side of the car. The force of the train sweeps him into the air, and he pulls hard with both hands, bringing his feet under him, and then finds a soft purchase for his shoes on the bottom rung. He rides along for a ways and then drops off, trotting back to us.

"You gotta get those feet up," Keith says, "or you'll lose both your legs from the knee down."

At midnight, we saunter out of the yard with the last can of beer hanging from its distorted plastic holder. The underbrush is teeming with fireflies, and the abrupt sound of air brakes and then a clanging bell rip into the stillness.

"We're pseudo-tramps," says Surfer. "Trustafarians."

12

The next morning we meet Bongo fifteen miles outside of Lincoln at the Café on the Square in the little, manicured town of Seward, Nebraska. It's Keith's birthday, and I'm buying his lunch before he heads east toward Ohio and we push on for Wyoming. So there we sit, annotating and remonstrating over Kerouac and his book like three German philosophers deconstructing Friedrich Nietzsche at the Hofbräu.

Digging into his meatloaf, John relates to Keith his disdain for Neal Cassady and how he treated his friends. Then Bongo says, "I was going to tell you this anyway, Jay, but in this book don't trash Cassady. Let Surfer trash him. Because the readers of this book are going to be Cassady worshippers, and they'll tell everyone not to read it."

Keith never gives anybody advice and I'm touched by this, along with the revelation that he has taken to eating organic oatmeal and live-culture yogurt since I stayed with him in Laredo and left some in his fridge.

"Don't worry," I croak, digging into my oatmeal. By now, I've developed a fever and nasty laryngitis from the germ I picked up, and can hardly talk. "I made my peace with Cassady back in San Miguel de Allende. And believe me, I'm more than willing to use both of you to express the most unpopular ideas in my book."

On the lawn in front of the courthouse, Surfer takes a picture of Keith standing beside me in the tacky new shirt I bought him at a convenience store back in Methuen, then we all shake hands at the foot of the memorial to Seward's Union dead. It strikes me that Keith shares at least one personality trait with Neal Cassady; in *On the Road* Sal Paradise mentions that although his old buddy no longer cared about anything in particular, "he cared about everything in principle."

"Nice to meet you, man," says Surfer.

"Same here," says the laconic Texan, his eyes already scanning the horizon.

I smile ruefully. "Let's hop a train sometime," I tell Keith.

"Bangor, Maine, is a good place," he says with a last, stiff wave of his hand.

Soon we're flying out of town on the newly paved section of Route 34, into the flat green vastness of the prairie, while Keith heads back east into his past. Giant silo cities appear in the far distance like the weird grain repositories of Oz. "'Let's go fuck three women at once and drive across the country,'" says John, stuck on his Cassady rant. "All right—I still want to do that myself, if I could get away with it. But I'd never steal from my friends, or leave anybody hanging."

A sign announces that we're on the Henry Fonda Memorial Highway. Large flatbeds loaded with enormous whorls of hay go zipping by in the other direction. Pickup trucks wait at lonely crossroads for us to pass so they can drive the other half of their cornfields, which reach the horizon. "Maybe it's just the ghost of Tom Joad," says Surfer.

A guy in a dusty flatbed, straw cowboy hat, blue shirt with the sleeves rolled up, and a toothpick looks over and gives me "the nod" at the only light in Kearney, Nebraska. On a little wheeled marquee in front of a nameless Mexican joint it says, "Our sign is Gone but We're still Here/So Stop by and Have a Beer."

At the 100th meridian, we're on Route 30 parallel to the railroad tracks where mile-long trains filled with coal are heading east, the sameness of the landscape underscored every ten miles or so by enormous grain elevators connected to their outbuildings by trestles fifty feet in the air.

In North Platte, Nebraska, with the Allman Brothers playing "Blue Sky," we detour a few miles off the county road to visit Buffalo Bill Cody's ranch, Scout's Rest. It's an hour before sunset, the sky deepening to azure and very few clouds overhead, and the ranch and corrals and fields that surround it are deserted. A plaque beside the house reads, "William Frederick Cody (1846–1917) His Second Empire Home, with Italianate and Eastlake features, cost $3,900 in 1886."

A white picket fence runs along the front and up the side yard of the two-story house, white shingles trimmed with green shutters and topped with a widow's peak. The grounds are lush and well maintained, bisected by a small creek and dotted with opulent shade trees. Daring and charismatic, the young Cody was a crack shot, hunting guide, and army scout for the Fifth Cavalry located at nearby Fort McPherson. Soon steeped in his own lore, he was performing onstage by 1872 and founded his "Wild West Show" in 1883 at the age of thirty-seven.

We're here after closing time, which is when I like to visit such historic places, and picture the white-haired hero crossing the prairie grass with a willow switch in his hand, gazing up at the broad Nebraska sky and whistling an old dance hall tune. The prairie wind is subdued here, tamed by the old Wild West showman, and standing in thigh-high grass just down the road from the ranch house, I hear Cody's soft laughter in the gurgle of the creek, high up in the bordering trees, and in the feathery tips of the sage. Laughing, as any one of us would, at his great, good fortune and the deeds of the men he knew.

13

After spending the night in a rustic cabin near Lake McConaughy outside Ogallala, Nebraska, we drive out toward the dam that created the twenty-two-mile lake.

The prairie grass is low and brown here, ruined by the floods that wracked the area in springtime.

"The open road don't get much more open than this," says John.

We're riding the escarpment along the North Platte River, with Robert Plant howling "Immigrant Song" from the dashboard radio.

Kingsley Dam is advertised as the second largest "hydraulic fill" dam in the world, 162 feet high, stretching over three miles and separating Lake McConaughy from its smaller eastern counterpart, Lake Ogallala. Down in the State Park below the dam on the Ogallala side is a forty-foot-wide spillway and an aerator, which shoots a thick, powerful spray of water into the lake. A middle-aged fellow from Colorado with a braided gray ponytail is fishing beside his fifteen-year-old son on top of the spillway.

"You never catch 'em when the water's runnin,'" the man says over the roar. "But we're getting thirty-, forty-pound catfish when it ain't." After cutting off the tails, they put the catfish on a long stringer back into the water for the rest of the afternoon. The catfish remain alive but will "bleed out," the fisherman says, making them taste better when the fish are filleted. In his journals and reminiscences, Kerouac always portrayed himself as a workingman, in an "old moth-eaten sweater," scrambling among the wreckage, bitching, sweating, and "hustling to catch the fresh dream . . . a fisherman of the deep."

At the Ogallala Post Office, a whitewashed building just off the main drag, Surfer decides to lighten his backpack and mail some of his gear back home. In the queue ahead of him is a lumpy, sunburned fellow wearing, of all things, a pillbox-style cap with a fake Chinese ponytail attached to it. The man is attempting to mail a shotgun in a cardboard tube to his brother in the next county, which creates a stir in the tiny post office.

"That ain't happenin'," Surfer says to me.

Finally, the manager comes from out back with his shirtsleeves rolled up. "You know you need a special per-mit to do that, Lyle," he says.

But Lyle insists the shotgun isn't going far, that it's being mailed to a relative, and that his brother really needs it. After a moment's deliberation, which I'd bet my left nut will result in a federal warning of some kind, the manager stuns everyone, including the clerk who fielded the request in the first place and perhaps even Lyle himself. With his arms folded over his chest, the harried-looking manager says, "All right, Lyle. I'll let you do it."

Coming out of the post office, John says, "That's gotta be the only place in the world they're gonna let you mail somebody a fuckin' shotgun."

"The only place besides the Gaza Strip," I say.

Just west of Ogallala we turn onto Route 138, which dips into Colorado. Beneath a row of shade trees we pass through the town of Big Springs and into the golden flatlands. There are plenty of cattle fences now, and spotted horses grazing over gently swelling pastures. Azure skies, puffy clouds. Farmers on tractors loaded with rounds of hay twenty feet in diameter. A mountain plover hops from fence post to fence post outside the Hi-Vu cattle ranch on the outskirts of Sedgwick, Colorado, as Jim Morrison sings to us about Texas Radio and the Big Beat. Morrison loves America and he is its wild-hearted poet of the grasslands, a psychedelic Whitman of various styles, genres, and artistic habits, with a multitude of contradictions in his soul.

There's a story that Jim Morrison and the Doors were playing at the old Commodore Ballroom in Lowell in 1968, when Kerouac was running out of gas but back living on Sanders Avenue in his hometown. Morrison found the address and knocked on the door, but Memere saw the Lizard King as just another hippie and chased him off; her hard-drinking son had been haunted by so many Beat acolytes and ass-grabbers that she trusted none of them. Ironically, twenty years later, Doors keyboardist Ray Manzarek visited Lowell for the dedication of the Kerouac Commemorative and played music and read poems with Michael McClure, Allen Ginsberg, Lawrence Ferlinghetti, and Robert Creeley, among others. During a private tour of the commemorative, McClure remarked with satisfaction that the memorial was "really subversive," since the work that Kerouac produced was not the type usually carved into stone in this country, or anywhere else for that matter.

Right now, I'm eating barbecued sunflower seeds and spitting the shells out the window. There's a giant wall of hay bales outside a ranch called the Calichee, and then "Ventura Highway" comes over the radio and Surfer laughs. The only eight-track tape his best friend at Spruce Creek High, Michael Peranio, owned was *America's Greatest Hits*, and they listened to it over and over whenever they were out cruising Daytona Beach.

"He bought a used car and it came with an eight-track player, right when they were phasing them out," says Surfer. "Hell, it might've even come with that tape in it when he bought it."

In Sterling, Colorado, there's a huge rail yard and a Sears outlet and a little adobe restaurant called Baja Tacos. The sky is so vast here we've been talking about the Big Bang theory, etc., and Surfer gives me his engineer's take on the Watchmaker's Argument and the intelligent design theory. Gassing on about the ever-expanding universe, I'm pestered by my ever-expanding bladder and get Surfer to pull onto a dirt road that forks off the highway. We climb out to take a piss and the only other car on the horizon is barreling toward us, throwing great clouds of dust and forcing us to wait until it passes.

"That guy probably leaves his house once a week," says John, sending out a stream like the aerator at Lake McConaughy.

"He's on his way to the post office to get that shotgun," I say.

Entering the 193,000-acre Pawnee National Grassland, we encounter a slightly rolling and dun-colored landscape with incredible vistas on either side. There are no buildings here, no trees or underbrush, just county roads like 85, 86, and 115, nothing but dirt two-lanes running out in hoops over the hills to nowhere. The Pawnee Indians, who called themselves Chahiksichahiks, "men of men," rode these hills on their ponies and built lodges in the hollows and paid nobody any mind.

Just beyond a trio of oil wells, we turn onto county road 390, mount the berm, and then drive past a sign that says, "Open Range." A half mile along, a small herd of perhaps eighty or ninety cattle walk in a cloud of dust, as in days of old. Ahead, the white dirt of the road cuts for miles across the short, tufted grass.

Surfer knows me as well as anyone, and in the midst of a long silence crossing the grassland, I go to the well for his advice on Dash: push hard for her, or just let it ride?

The old Daytona Beach Zen master looks out at the parched expanse of the horizon and shapes a koan out of some lines from Dylan: "'I helped her out of a jam I guess, but I used a little too much force.'" Then it's quiet again except for the dry grass rustling on either side of the road.

After driving for an hour, we encounter a water tower, some abandoned buildings, and half-ruined adobe walls. Outside of this ghost town, there's a small, fenced-in cemetery with nothing else around for miles and miles.

"This is literally the definition of BFE, right here," says Surfer, referring to the mythical outpost of Butt Fuck, Egypt.

14

After a stop at Grover, Colorado's one little store, we head north and regain the paved road. Yellow wildflowers line the side of the highway heading into Wyoming, and a weird-shaped cloud forms what looks like a giant cactus in the sky, the celestial signature of the West.

On the outskirts of Cheyenne, huge new homes are packed close together in the abundant subdivisions. "'Move to the great open spaces of Wyoming, and live six feet away from your next-door neighbor,'" Surfer says. "That makes no sense."

On the radio, Dylan is singing about his girl's brand-new leopard skin pillbox hat as we boom onward for Laramie. We get off at Happy Jack Road and head straight for the Old Western town's "Jubilee Days." I haven't been feeling right all week, and in the hot baking sun of S. 3rd Street, I start to feel dizzy and nauseous. In the window of a Laramie chophouse, a large, jowly Western gent in dress boots and Stetson is lifting his pinkie at the menu. He sends the waitress scurrying after his second martini, king crab legs, a pint of lager, then a huge bloody steak with roasted potatoes and a wedge of pie, which he eats daintily, keeping that pinkie aloft.

"Yo," I say, calling to Surfer, who's strolling along gazing at rodeo posters. "I gotta lie down."

15

In Laramie, the noxious bug that's been dogging my footsteps since Cleveland overtakes me, and I drop into a sweaty, fretful malaise. Near the end of *On the Road*, when Sal fell seriously ill in Mexico City and Dean Moriarty, after pushing through his divorce, abandoned him, Sal finally "realized what a rat he was." Confined to our rat hole of a motel room, in the pique of my fever, I start to feel like I'm really sick, like something awful is happening to me. As soon as we arrived, Surfer took off to attend some kind of Laramie music festival and hasn't returned. Finally, I sleep for about ten or twelve hours, and when I wake up, it appears that John still hasn't come back. On the small, balky television, I start watching an old *Twilight Zone* episode where Lee Marvin plays "Steel" Kelly, a punchy ex-boxer relegated to managing an outmoded robot in the automated fight game of the future. When the unit, known as "Battling Maxo," conks out right before a match with a more sophisticated robot, Steel Kelly is compelled by financial pressures and pride to enter the ring, made up to resemble Battling Maxo.

Of course, pitted against a machine, Kelly absorbs a terrible beating but survives on a combination of guts and guile. Instructed once again by Lee Marvin, that lean, authentic character of the West,

I escape from the sweaty tangle of the bedclothes and, after a quick shower, go staggering into the streets of Laramie. Surfer is just coming back from a five-mile run at altitude, dripping with sweat and smiling broadly at the specter of his old buddy, gaunt, lightheaded, and rickety on his pinned-together ankle.

"I found a place right around the corner with ginger and wheat grass and shit like that," he says, leading the way. "They'll fix you right up." My attempt at a wisecrack explodes in a fit of coughing, but truth be told, I'd take Surfer John over Neal Cassady any day.

16

Soon we're traveling down Route 287 into Colorado with dense pine forests skirting the highway and the shrouded, snowy peaks of the Rockies appearing in the blue hazes to the west.

Driving through valleys crisscrossed by fast-moving rivers that wind off through the hills, and rail fences marked every few miles by tall ranch gates decorated with elk horns. We pass a small lumberyard by a running stream, planks and four-by-sixes in neat little piles among the grass. Another yard is stacked with trestles for skinning and notching pine logs to make barns and cabins. Watering holes located a mile away on grazing land are surrounded by aspens and marked off with wire fencing.

By lunchtime, Surfer and I are girl watching from an outdoor restaurant on the upper end of Pearl Street in Boulder: lean, muscled brunettes in cycling clothes; skate chicks with short, filthy dreadlocks and tribal tattoos; high-heeled babes in gauzy summer dresses; cheerful, sunburned lesbians holding hands; Amerasian hotties in tight white pants; and dynamite cowgirls in cut-off jeans and tank tops.

Two nicely proportioned forty-year-old blondes come swinging along the sidewalk with their tennis rackets, and John says, "There's two playing in our league. The Senior League."

But every five minutes, a Rocky Mountain version of Dash goes by, long-limbed and fresh, her shiny blonde hair streaming behind and that enigmatic smile on her lips. Accompanied in every instance by what appears to be a smirking French dude, Dash is more remote than she has ever been, which rents my heart in two. It makes me want to leap over the Continental Divide like a stag, getting farther and farther away from her as we head west.

17

Low on cash, John and I head for one of Boulder's historic downtown hotels to jump on their free Internet and search for a cheaper place. The lobby is paneled in old mahogany and upholstered in leather, hung with elk antlers, black-and-white portraits of its owners dating back to 1909, and staffed by young men and women with shiny shoes and excellent manners.

Surfer and I waltz in like a pair of software moguls, diverging by the concierge desk as I pause at the gift shop, and John follows his nose upstairs to the "Business Center."

The door is locked, but a maid is dusting off the computers and allows Surfer access when he taps on the glass. When I arrive, he's zipping through various local listings and finds a bargain at the Boulder International Hostel for $50, while a room sale in Denver buys us another discount crash pad for tomorrow night.

Keeping with our guerrilla reconnaissance, while on a piss call in their well-appointed gentleman's room I write a message on the chalkboard above the urinals: "Read Jay Atkinson's *City in Amber*. I did."

Late in the afternoon, Surfer and I go west of the city on Canyon Boulevard into the foothills. Dozens of college kids and local fun seekers are bombing down Boulder Creek on inner tubes or splashing in pools on the side of the road. Ten miles out, we stop on a gravel crescent and bushwhack down to the creek. Rock hopping into the center of the rushing snowmelt, I dangle my feet in the water and let the roar of the creek pound in my lungs and rip through my soul.

There's a cluster of waterborne flowers growing in the lee of the rock: tiny purple and white bells on a slender green frond. I reach into the pool and cup the flowers gently in my hand as the dropping bulb of the sun makes Indian designs on the canyon wall above me. From high up on Boulder Creek, I scan my track across the heartland and the prairies onto the shelf of the Great Divide, understanding once and for all that my reward for these labors is seeing this little purple-and-white flower bent by the current.

18

Our room in Boulder is a sparsely furnished garret under the eaves of an old sorority house. At 10 p.m., Surfer and I walk down to the corner of 12th and College to watch the fireworks emanating from the stadium across town. They explode over the rooftops like an array of fiery sea anemones in various colors, the dry booms of their apotheoses cracking against the mountains behind us.

Afterward, from my vantage point in our room I see across the way to a boarding house that resembles a Kitty Genovese tenement from the 1960s; a half-dozen windows face the alley, each of them a portal into the lives of their inhabitants. Top left, a man and a woman silhouetted at a kitchen table with booming hip-hop music playing from within; center, a large television containing the image of a man wearing a bright red shirt (a window into another window); top right, two sinuous young women in tight dresses moving to a Latin beat; bottom right, a dozen college boys drinking beer and laughing; center, a woman, head in hands, sobbing into the telephone; and bottom left, the shaded and darkened window of an empty apartment, which is the least mysterious of them all.

The *snap-snap-snap* of firecrackers underscored by loud music and the raucous cries of passing drunks go on for hours, making it difficult to sleep. At 3 a.m., a guy traveling through the alley belts out, "*Oh* when the saints, oh when the saints, oh when the saints go marching in, I want to *be-e-ee* in that number, when the saints go marching in" about twenty times, until his voice thins out and then disintegrates into the night air.

Close to dawn, I hear a couple of people talking beneath a streetlight on the corner and roll up onto my elbow for a better view. I reach for my notebook on the bedside table, recalling Kerouac's advice to "stop thinking, just look." It's a slender, dark-skinned young man with a yellow bandanna on his head; he looks like Cochise. Leaning against the utility pole is a girl in blue jeans with feathery mounds of light brown hair. They speak cordially for another minute or so, and then part without a kiss or even a handshake. Fifteen or twenty feet along the sidewalk, the young man turns and calls softly to the girl.

"Have a nice journey—a nice life," he says.

19

Outside of Boulder, we're heading for the Rockies on Route 93. Green-golden fields stretch to the west for a mile or two, then there's the rumpled hills and the snow-dusted crags beyond. Denver is just fifteen miles to the east, its great towers wavering in the plumes of rising heat. But soon we're back on Kerouac's old Route 6 going west and then north on 119 toward Central City.

Steep walled canyons line Clear Creek, and long straight highway tunnels have been blasted right through solid rock. After passing an old defunct mine with a propped-up double-wide trailer and junk cars, we enter Black Hawk, CO, and right after it, Central City, phony casino towns filled with monstrous, green-roofed brick buildings and fake-looking Western shops and saloons.

Gold was discovered here on May 6, 1859, and within a few months, it was known as "The Richest Square Mile on Earth." Today, the upper end of Central City, where Kerouac and his friends threw that famous beer blast in 1947, is a collection of ramshackle homes, empty Wells Fargo storefronts, dilapidated barns, and the Central City Opera House, erected by the citizenry in 1878.

The great gray bulk of the opera house, with its twin stone columns and mansard roof, was the pride and joy of the Cornish and Welsh miners who built it. Buffalo Bill Cody trod the boards here

in the early years, and actress Lillian Gish opened the summer
series with an appearance in 1932. Assisted by Neal Cassady's
dubious mentor, Justin W. Brierly, referred to as Denver D. Doll
in *On the Road*, Kerouac attended a performance of *Fidelio* during
his visit in 1947, and poached the shaving things and towels of
the young opera singers to freshen up before getting drunk that
night.

A wooden sign advertises this summer's offerings, which include
West Side Story, composed by Lawrence, Mass., native Leonard
Bernstein, proving that the artists of the Merrimack Valley are still
bleaching their creative bones among the defunct gold mines of
Central City.

Down the street, the shack where Kerouac stayed is now a little
multihued gingerbread house with flowerpots astride the walkway. Wrecked piles of timber mark an abandoned gold mine on
the edge of town. And the "ghost" of a totally restored classic 1967
blue metal-flake Pontiac GTO is parked outside the closed-down
Baldwin General Store & Trading Post opposite the old mine.

At one of the local museums, a dejected curator says that the thousands of gamblers who come up from Denver rarely leave the air-
conditioned casinos to explore the rest of the town. I glance around
the sad little museum and give Surfer a look that says *Let's get the
hell out of here*. In Central City, scheming politicians with their moneyed interests and lobbyists have managed to take the actual history
of America's frontier and turn it into what Kerouac would've called
"hullabaloo boom-boom horseshit."

20

Late in the afternoon, I head into Denver for the first time in
twenty-eight years, past the rundown Mexican joints and storefront art galleries along Santa Fe. On Colfax, we pass Denver High,
where Neal Cassady went hot-rodding for girls, and where I used to
roam on foot and on city buses back and forth to the law school and
to rugby practice at various city parks.

After graduating from Acadia University in 1979 and working at a camp on Lake Winnipesaukee that summer, I was offered a scholarship to the University of Denver Law School. Arriving in town with one decent pair of pants and a couple of oxford shirts, I played for the Mile High Rugby Club, ate huge T-bones in Lyle Alzado's Steak House, and was bored out of my mind at school.

Listening to the Allman Brothers' "Rambling Man," we drive past Smiley's, "the World's Largest Discount Laundromat," and the Fillmore Auditorium, and Dulcinea's 100th Monkey Adult Books and Videos, right down the street from the ornate golden doors of the Immaculate Conception Cathedral.

On South Adams Street, I rented a bedroom in a high-rise apartment from a beautiful dark-haired legal secretary named Priscilla, or Percy for short. Recording artist Todd Rungren's sister was right across the hall and would have dinner with us sometimes. I lived on the eighth floor from September to December and spent too many lonely hours in my room puzzling out tort cases and reading over hundreds of dull contracts for Professor Littlefield, who was a tall, stern fellow from Maine. It was here on South Adams Street that I heard the far-off call to go back across the continent and take up the pencil and paper I have in my hand right now. Jack Kerouac was a big part of that, and as the cars zoom past on Ellsworth, I say a Hail Mary for the old Memory Babe and thank him for his example, which along with his life's blood is really what he gave to the world.

21

The Denver neighborhood where Jack and Neal searched for Cassady's alcoholic father has been updated and gentrified by juice bars and outdoor restaurants and brick-fronted lawyers' and Realtors' offices. A junkie-thin guy in his thirties walking along Market Street is carrying a beat-up paper bag and yakking on his cell phone: "I came out of my room and it was goin' on right at the kitchen table and they said, 'Mark, go back to bed,' and I turned around and went straight into my room."

A few blocks away, Coors Field rises from a jumble of low brick buildings like a steel-girded baseball paradise. A few years ago, I went digging through the old newspapers in the basement of the Pollard Library in Lowell, trying to find out just how good an athlete Jack Kerouac really was. As a child, he invented his own miniature backyard version of baseball. He wrote a novel at the age of eleven, and "published" his own newspapers covering the baseball and football leagues of his imagination. But Kerouac was more than just an avatar; he was the real deal. In the spring of 1939, his name appears in the *Lowell Sun* and *Evening Leader* box scores for the varsity baseball team, outdoor track, and American Legion baseball—all in the same week. That year, he finished first in five indoor track races and placed in several more, leading the team with 40¼ points. I even talked to Jack's old friend and teammate John Lang about Kerouac's foot speed. Mr. Lang's old, yellowed program shows that Kerouac scored the only points for Lowell High in the 1939 statewide Class A Annual Indoor Meet at Boston Garden, with a third place in the forty-five-yard hurdles.

For $39 apiece, Surfer and I buy seats a few rows up from the first base dugout for a National League game between the Rockies and the Florida Marlins. On a mild, pleasant evening, we drink beer and eat roasted peanuts, and the home team pounds the visitors, 11–6.

After the game, Surfer and I walk down to a place called Ted's Montana Grill at the far end of Larimer Street. There's an intricate design on the tessellated floor, and hung on the wall above the dark wainscoting are oil paintings of buffalo hunters and Indians on horseback. John orders a glass of porter, and I get a pint of the local wheat beer as warped, phantasmagoric shapes pass by on the other side of the frosted windows.

"You'd be hard pressed to find a wino around here," says Surfer, surveying the chi-chi boutiques and cafes with Bongo-like disgust.

"Unless you bring your own," I say.

We order another round from the bartender. "This book is gonna put me over the top, so I can get into some heavy drinking and marry a girl who reminds me of my mother," I say.

John snickers into his pint. "You've set a lofty goal for yourself there, Oedipus," he says, pushing off for the men's room.

I've traveled nearly two thousand rail and road miles in the past week and more than ten thousand in the past year. Sitting alone at the bar, I'm reminded of a couplet from Yeats.

I must lie down where all the ladders start
In the foul rag and bone shop of the heart

It's no surprise, really, that the Larimer Street that Kerouac and Cassady knew has disappeared, but then, it's not the same Denver, the same New Orleans or Chicago, or the same North America, for that matter. I was never looking for Kerouac, anyway; just as he and Cassady were not really searching for Neal Sr. in the pool halls and beer joints that once occupied this block. It was just time to go, and all I wanted was joy, kicks, darkness, and music, which are the only reasons to take such a trip.

I stare down the large furry buffalo head at the conclusion of the bar and raise my glass to its mute indifference. Way back at Peekskill Hollow Farm, David Amram provided just the right note to launch my journey, and I picked up the tune and had a funkitissimo time of my own. Besides, my mother didn't raise a fool. I have long known and frequently understood that the road has always been in the going, and the story resides in the telling.

ACKNOWLEDGMENTS

I have said in print and elsewhere that it was Harry Crews, the blood-soaked novelist and beloved son of the violent South, who steered me away from becoming just another Kerouac imitator and thereby helped launch my career. But that's too easy. Down at the University of Florida when I was there studying with Harry, he broke my addiction to the old Memory Babe's cadences as surely and resolutely as you'd help break any nasty habit. Saving me from that led, after many years, to this book, which is written in my own voice. For that, and many other things, I am forever grateful to Harry, one of the best writers and best writing teachers to ever come walking down the American road.

In a more immediate and practical way, this book would never have been written if it wasn't for my old Acadia friend, Keith "Bongo" Bowden, who called me from Texas with the idea of reproducing Kerouac's journey, though he could've tackled the project himself and done a fine job. But Keith has always been generous to a fault, which you'll see here in the story. I also want to thank "Surfer John" Hearin and Chris Pierce for doing all the driving, handling most of the logistics, and providing colorful commentary over the thousands of road miles that passed beneath our feet in the course of tracing Kerouac's route. These guys are the salt of the earth, and I am lucky to call them my friends, and brothers.

My agent, Peter McGuigan of Foundry, did an expert job on the proposal and has contributed to the book at every stage (I crashed at his place while researching Kerouac's New York years), which is becoming increasingly rare in the profession. My favorite editor, Pete Fornatale, called from the bullpen by publisher Kitt Allan at the pivotal moment like a fire-balling right-hander, saved the project in the bottom of the ninth inning. Wiley's executive editor Tom Miller acquired the book, and his assistant, Dan Crissman, contributed a raft of suggestions. Dick and Jesse Haley of Haley Booksellers in Boston have done a ton of work promoting the book and my career, demonstrating an enormous loyalty in an industry not known for that trait.

Several friends of Jack Kerouac as well as scholars and aficionados have been extremely helpful and accommodating. Chief among these are "Uncle Dave" Amram, who collaborated with Jack on spoken word performances in New York in the fifties; my dear friend Paul "Dalton Jones" Marion, poet, publisher, essayist, community organizer extraordinaire, and the true Bard of Lowell; the novelist, critic, and teacher David Daniel, who bought most of my pints at the Old Court; Reverend Steve Edington, president of the non-profit Lowell Celebrates Kerouac!; immediate past presidents Larry Carradini and Meg Smith; Dr. Melissa Pennell of the University of Massachusetts Lowell English Department; and my rugby pal Frank Baker of the Associated Press in Los Angeles and his wife, Brandee, and son, Jackson.

Kerouac got by with a little help from his friends, and so did I. "Stormin' Norman" Litwack and his wife, Dana, of the Atlanta Renegades Rugby Football Club, my old teammate from Florida, helped me out of a jam more than once (and true to form, used a little too much force). Attorney Linda Harvey dispensed lots of good advice over two years, neglecting to send a bill. Dr. Joe Costagliola, Dr. Brian Mangano, Dr. Marc Klein, and my old travelin' companion, Dr. Karen Koffler, treated me for an array of road-induced mishaps, taking only gratitude for their payment. Dr. Jay Phillips sawed through my left foot while I watched (very good drugs), and then put it back together with five titanium screws while admitting, "I'm the only surgeon in this town [Boston] who would've done this procedure. But you're a 'max' kind of guy, so I gave you a 'max' correction." Thanks to Dr. Phillips, I could walk around Chicago and Denver and New Orleans and San Francisco.

My car insurance expired when I was away, twice, and Fred Malcolm of Malcolm Insurance paid it for me out of his own pocket. (I paid him back.) The reference librarians at Nevins Memorial Library in my hometown of Methuen, Massachusetts—Kirsten Underwood, Tatjana Saccio, Sue Jefferson, Maureen Tulley, Beth Safford, and Sharon Morley—routinely dug up details and facts that no one else could find. The scholars Jay McHale and Peter Quinn shared their Kerouac materials and ideas with genuine enthusiasm for the project. My spiritual advisers for this book, and life in general, Father Paul O'Brien, Father Paul McManus, and Father John Farren, helped keep this weak-willed Catholic (mostly) out of dutch with the Man upstairs.

Traveling so hard and so fast across such varied terrain would've been much more difficult if not for my many friends in public safety. The Westchester County Police Department was extremely professional and helpful when I bogged down hitchhiking in New York. Revere, Mass., police lieutenant John Goodwin; Lynn, Mass., police detective Bob Hogan; Methuen, Mass., fire lieutenant Glenn Gallant; Salem, NH, police detective Mark Donahue; Salem, NH, police captain (retired) Bill Teuber; Somerville, Mass., police sergeant Joe McCain Jr.; Arizona sheriff's deputy and my old Acadia wrestling teammate, Jay Buckler; Manchester, NH, firefighter Dan "Original Sully" Sullivan of Amoskeag Rugby; FBI Special Agent John "Woody" Woudenberg; Mass. state police lieutenant (retired) Gene Kee and his wife, Ellen; Mass. state police trooper Mario Millett; Mass. state police sergeant Rick Ball; Lowell, Mass., police detective Dave Lally; Revere, Mass., police chief Terry Reardon; Mass. state police sergeant Bob Beckwith; Mass. state police trooper Dennis Febles; Methuen, Mass., firefighter Steve Battles; Mass. state police trooper Damian Halfkenny; FBI Special Agent (retired) Bill Chase; FBI Special Agent Darwin Suelen; Mass. state trooper Russ Phippen and family; Chelsea, Mass., police detectives Scott Conley and Dan Delaney; Winchester, Mass., police lieutenant Jimmy Pierce; Methuen, Mass., police detective (retired) Gus

Flanagan; and U.S. Secret Service agent (retired) Stew Henry provided insight into human behavior and the human condition that you don't find in psychology textbooks. Besides, they work nights, giving me someone to talk to while driving across the Great Plains.

Special thanks to my colleagues in the Boston University journalism department, Lou Ureneck, Mitchell Zuckoff, and Tom Fiedler, for keeping me gainfully employed during and after the writing of this book. Novelist, essayist, and teacher Peggy Rambach provided homegrown vegetables and a writer's eye and ear. Maeghan Ouimet, Joe Ippolito, Rachel Wolf, Bill Marx, Dr. Richard Elia, Dr. Charles Warren, writer Dave Robinson, Estrella Kuilan, literary agent Jake Elwell, Pete Olson, Jason Massa, Lisa Rosenberg, Chris Sideri, John Harrison, Sara "Tiny G" Cann, Bill Coyle, Bob and Carol Needham, Kerri Landry, Professor Rob Brown, Jon Anderson, Kerri Pearson, Jovanni Geha, Alyssa Gendron, J. Juniper Friedman, Keira Lyons, Brian McGrory, Anne Nelson, Patricia Brooks, Kayla Brown, Yumi Araki, Tom Samph, Mayor Bill Manzi of Methuen, Mass., and his family, Dr. Paul Jude Beauvais and his wife, poet Diane Kendig, Sophie Hoeller, Hannah Gordon Brown, Fred Roedel and Butch McCarthy of Amoskeag Rugby, Sarah Correia, Ron and Julie Martin, Drew and Sheila Cooper, Bob and Linda Sheehan, Tim and Denise Croteau, Billy and Dawn Giarusso, Bill and Kathy Fitzgerald, the Yourtee family, attorney Randy Reis, "Super Dave" LaFlamme, John Solomon, Bubba McIntosh, Hollywood impressario Julian Bristow, Marc Sullivan, Marc Murray, Bill Bishop, Tom Turner, Rich Ashfield, Lyle Jones, Freshy, Daniel Carter, Tom Rege and the entire Vandals Rugby Club, Helen and Maureen McCain, Leslie Crook, Chris and Michelle Penta, Steve Fisichelli, Geoff Pitcher, Chuck Hogan, Dutch Kurmaskie, Joe Taylor of Livingston Press, Dag and Judy Fullerton, Jim and Maryanne Connolly, and Virginia Elenor Maple of Caribou, Maine, all contributed something to this book, and if dedicated scholars of the distant future look carefully, they will find these fingerprints on the pages of *Paradise Road*.

Jack Kerouac always found a safe harbor with his mother, and although my parents, Lois and Jim, are long vanished from this earth, their legacy of family, faith, and togetherness endures. I couldn't sustain myself as a writer if it wasn't for John and Jackie Atkinson; Barbara Leonhart; Scott and Mary Leonhart; Paul and Shirley Crane and all my cousins; Arthur and Natalie Wermers; Lawrence Berry and Peg Burr; James Atkinson Jr.; Jill, Jay, Nick, and Michaela Sparks; Jodie, John, Matthew, and Katelyn Berry; Patrick, Deanna, Owen, Reese, and Shane Bower; and my beloved son, Liam. You guys are the best.

INDEX

245

CREDITS